"This is a necessary book. Our representations of climate change aren't adequate, our modes of interpretation are evasive, and the actions and policies based on those representations and interpretations take us further toward an uninhabitable planet. Most perversely, as Zimmerman emphasizes, even our most apparently sincere engagements with the climate crisis turn out to be new forms of denial. We *say* we recognize the problem; then *act* as if we do not. In canny readings of uncanny texts, Zimmerman shows the missing parts and points to where our thinking needs to go."

James Berger, Yale University, USA; author of *After the End: Representations of Post-Apocalypse*

"In *Trauma and the Discourse of Climate Change*, Lee Zimmerman offers a brilliant, unforgiving, and much-needed analysis of what we talk about when we talk about climate change, and what we don't talk about, and why. The book persuasively argues that the dominant discourses of global warming that enabled denialism are a reaction to the trauma of the knowledge of that crisis, of the threats it poses not only to the planet but to our ways of knowing our world and ourselves. As the earth burns, Zimmerman's is a call to recognize our grief for what is being lost and to work to save what still stands."

Samuel Cohen, University of Missouri, USA; author of *After the End of History: American Fiction in the 1990s*

"Lee Zimmerman's closely reasoned book is committed to telling 'the truth, the *whole* truth, and nothing but' about climate change—even as it explores how the 'whole truth' will necessarily exceed our grasp. Zimmerman points out the major omissions in what many leading authors on this topic have said. Unlike Al Gore skipping over the inconvenient truths that were inconvenient to his ideological premises or other authors who felt, like Jack Nicholson's character in 'A Few Good Men,' that the public can't handle the truth, this book holds nothing back. The stakes are too high, the implications too significant, to do less."

Michael D. Moore, Ph.D.; founder, *Core Narrative* and former Senior Vice-President, Communications at Thomson Reuters

Trauma and the Discourse of Climate Change

The more the global north has learned about the existential threat of climate change, the faster it has emitted greenhouse gases into the atmosphere. In *Trauma and the Discourse of Climate Change*, Lee Zimmerman thinks about why this is by examining how "climate change" has been discursively constructed, tracing how the ways we talk and write about climate change have worked to normalize a generalized, bipartisan denialism more profound than that of the overt "denialists."

Suggesting that we understand that normalized denial as a form of cultural trauma, the book explores how the dominant ways of figuring knowledge about global warming disarticulate that knowledge from the trauma those figurations both represent and reproduce, and by which they remain inhabited and haunted. Its early chapters consider that process in representations of climate change across a range of disciplines and throughout the public sphere, including Al Gore's *An Inconvenient Truth*, Barack Obama's speeches and climate plans, and the 2015 Paris Agreement. Later chapters focus on how literary representations especially, for the most part, participate in such disarticulations, and to how, in grappling with the representational difficulties at the climate crisis's heart, some works of fiction—among them Cormac McCarthy's *The Road* and Russell Hoban's *Riddley Walker*—work against that normalized rhetorical violence. The book closes with a meditation centered on the dream of the burning child Freud sketches in *The Interpretation of Dreams*.

Highlighting the existential stakes of the ways we think and write about the climate, *Trauma and the Discourse of Climate Change* aims to offer an unfamiliar place from which to engage the astonishing quiescence of our ecocidal present. This book will be essential reading for academics and students of psychoanalysis, environmental humanities, trauma studies, literature, and environmental studies, as well as activists and others drawn to thinking about the climate crisis.

Lee Zimmerman is Professor of English at Hofstra University, USA, and editor of the journal *Twentieth-Century Literature*.

Trauma and the Discourse of Climate Change

Literature, Psychoanalysis, and Denial

Lee Zimmerman

LONDON AND NEW YORK

First published 2020
by Routledge
2 Park Square, Milton Park, Abingdon, Oxon OX14 4RN

and by Routledge
52 Vanderbilt Avenue, New York, NY 10017

Routledge is an imprint of the Taylor & Francis Group, an informa business

© 2020 Lee Zimmerman

The right of Lee Zimmerman to be identified as author of this work has been asserted by him in accordance with sections 77 and 78 of the Copyright, Designs and Patents Act 1988.

All rights reserved. No part of this book may be reprinted or reproduced or utilised in any form or by any electronic, mechanical, or other means, now known or hereafter invented, including photocopying and recording, or in any information storage or retrieval system, without permission in writing from the publishers.

Trademark notice: Product or corporate names may be trademarks or registered trademarks, and are used only for identification and explanation without intent to infringe.

British Library Cataloguing-in-Publication Data
A catalogue record for this book is available from the British Library

Library of Congress Cataloging-in-Publication Data
Names: Zimmerman, Lee, 1953- author.
Title: Trauma and the discourse of climate change : psychoanalysis, literature and denial / Lee Zimmerman.
Description: Abingdon, Oxon ; New York, NY : Routledge, 2020. | Includes bibliographical references and index.
Identifiers: LCCN 2019057370 (print) | LCCN 2019057371 (ebook) | ISBN 9780367355562 (hardback) | ISBN 9780367355579 (paperback) | ISBN 9780429340222 (ebook)
Subjects: LCSH: Climatic changes–Psychological aspects. | Climatic changes–Political aspects.
Classification: LCC BF353.5.C55 Z56 2020 (print) | LCC BF353.5.C55 (ebook) | DDC 155.9/15–dc23
LC record available at https://lccn.loc.gov/2019057370
LC ebook record available at https://lccn.loc.gov/2019057371

ISBN: 978-0-367-35556-2 (hbk)
ISBN: 978-0-367-35557-9 (pbk)
ISBN: 978-0-429-34022-2 (ebk)

Typeset in Times New Roman
by Swales & Willis, Exeter, Devon, UK

In memory of Hilda Zimmerman

Contents

	Acknowledgments	x
	Introduction	1
1	Pavel's lament: Climate and trauma	12
2	What we don't talk about when we talk about global warming	27
3	Butcheries	40
4	Climate change and fiction I: Disarticulations and the Great Derangement	70
5	Climate change and fiction II: On not eating the baby	88
	Coda: "Don't you see?" The burning child's reproach	125
	Index	138

Acknowledgments

This book begins and ends with a question—"Don't you see I'm burning?"—and attempting to give that question anything like adequate expression in the present moment of climate catastrophe could not have been possible without the help of a number of people who were willing to read parts of the manuscript in its various stages of composition. In ways too various to recount, the book has depended on the careful attentions of Alison Bahr, John Bryant, Ray Budelman, Megan Cherry, Tom Couser, John Engle, Donna Gregory, Katherine Hazzard, Eunju Hwang, Debora Lidov, Michael D. Moore, Michele Pacheco, Ann Porter, Tom Ross, Adam Sills, and Carolyn Weaver. James Berger and Melissa Connolly took special pains to provide detailed, invaluable readings of the manuscript as a whole. Cordelia Sand has remained, from the start, an essential interlocutor, her acute questionings a source of energy, endurance, and widened insight. Ultimately, the book couldn't have survived its animating question without the feeling that the question is shared with others in emergent and defamiliarizing ways. These secret sharers include Wolf Pappenheim, Paul Zimmerman, and Zoey Zimmerman.

I'm grateful to Hofstra University, especially Craig Rustici, Chair of the English Department, for a Special Scholarly Leave and other institutional support.

Quotations from Russell Hoban's *Riddley Walker* have been reprinted by permission of Harold Ober Associates, Copyright 1980 by Russell Hoban, and also used with permissions from "The Trustees of the Russell Hoban Trust."

The lines from *The Book of Ephraim* are quoted with the permission of James Merrill's literary executor and Merrill's Literary Estate at Washington University, St. Louis.

CREDIT LINE: "The Burning Child" from *The Collected Poems of Amy Clampitt* by Amy Clampitt, copyright © 1997 by the Estate of Amy Clampitt. Used by permission of Alfred A. Knopf, an imprint of the Knopf Doubleday Publishing Group, a division of Penguin Random House LLC. All rights reserved.

Introduction

In this book, I argue that the dominant discourses of global warming contribute to a form of denial, beyond the overt form associated with the officially designated "denialists" or "skeptics," and that we might understand that more fundamental, pervasive, and largely unrecognized species of denial by thinking of global warming as a kind of trauma. In arguing this, I take as a premise that anthropogenic global warming represents an existential threat—not, as it is often carelessly put, to the "planet" or to "Earth," which, it is thought, will presumably exist in some form for another five billion years or so, but, rather, to the current climate system, a condition of possibility for the countless life forms by which the planet is now (or, in countless cases, was until recently) inhabited, including many of the iterations of itself the human species purports to value.[1]

Of course, global warming names much more than simply a "threat," having already contributed to massive loss of life, just as—because carbon stays in the atmosphere for a long time—it has already guaranteed massive loss of life in the future. Calling it an existential "threat," however, reflects a second premise: there might still be some theoretical chance to prevent our reaching a tipping point, a degree of warming that will trigger a much more extreme, rapid, and violent collapse, our current climate system undergoing not merely a linear, gradual, reversible "change" but a relatively swift, irreversible, radical transformation into a different system altogether.[2] Timothy Morton's suggestion that discovering global warming "is like realizing for some time you had been conducting your business in the expanding sphere of a slow-motion nuclear bomb" (103) pointedly expresses the extremity of our present dilemma, but the conceit would be more telling if there were some way to arrest that expanding sphere before the full force of the bomb was unleashed. To the extent we can align the threat of global warming with that of nuclear war, Jonathan Schell's warning that "every generation that holds the earth hostage to nuclear destruction holds a gun to the head of its own children" (157–58) seems closer to the mark. Closer to the mark still, Eugene Linden asks about global warming, "will we continue to squeeze the trigger on the gun we have put to our own head?" (263)—though even that figuration itself obscures that we're squeezing the trigger harder and harder, that, astonishingly, the more we "know" about the crisis, and the more dire it gets, the faster greenhouse gas emissions rise.[3] But even in the process of pulling the trigger—of pulling it faster and faster—we might yet be able to stop before the tipping point, before the bullet is discharged.[4] Pressed for an answer to the question raised by the title of his 2012 paper delivered to the American Geophysical Union—"Is Earth F**ked? Dynamical Futility of Global Environmental Management and Possibilities for Sustainability via Direct Action Activism"—Brad Werner replied, "More or less" (qtd. in Klein, 450). That uncertainty informs my starting point: it might be possible to prevent global warming from reaching a tipping point where less fucked turns into more fucked.

Because the window for doing this, if it still exists, is rapidly closing, sufficient action would mean a radical disruption in cultural and economic business as usual—a third premise. Drawing on research into the likely consequences of various greenhouse gas emission scenarios going forward,[5] in 2013 the Tyndall Centre for Climate Change Research observed that "we either continue with rising emissions and reap the radical repercussions of severe climate change, or we acknowledge that we have a choice and pursue radical emissions reductions," and thus it concluded, "*no longer is there a non-radical option*" (my emphasis). I try in this book to elaborate on how our discursive constructions of global warming inform our failure to recognize the present moment as necessarily "radical," the failure to grapple with the existential threat with which it confronts us. But I introduce that sense of urgency itself briefly here less to engage in debate about that premise than to try to address, at the outset, two critiques articulations of that urgent threat often provoke: alarmism and cynicism.[6] In doing this, I'll try also to introduce how framing the necessarily radical present as a kind of trauma might help locate a space beyond cynicism—a space where what we know, encountering what we don't or can't, might be constituted as a demand for sufficient action that cannot be refused.

Beyond the obviously denialistic charges of alarmism trumpeted by so-called "climate skeptics," such charges emerge, perhaps more disturbingly, also from within the climate change academic community itself. Mike Hulme, the founding Director of the Tyndall Centre for Climate Change, prefaces his *Why We Disagree about Climate Change*, for example, by announcing "I feel uncomfortable that climate change is widely reported through the language of catastrophe and imminent peril, as 'the greatest problem facing humanity'" (xxxiii), and elsewhere he dismisses "climate change campaigners" with their "thirst for environmental drama and exaggerated rhetoric," the "catastrophists" who "sex-up" the science, in his account, and thus "exacerbate the very risks we are trying to ward off" ("Chaotic World"). In Chapter 3, I'll elaborate on James Risbey's careful rejoinder to Hulme's dismissal, but the core problem, as with charges of "alarmism" in general, is simply that Hulme offers no argument, failing especially to reckon with the evidence that global warming is likely to trigger feedback loops, accelerating that warming to a catastrophic tipping point. The first of his "Five Lessons of Climate Change" is thus that "Climate change is a relative risk, not an absolute one."

Just as Hulme sees "alarmism" as "exacerbat[ing] the ... risks," in *Hyperobjects*, prominent ecocritic Timothy Morton suggests that "the strongly held belief that the world is about to end 'unless we act now' is paradoxically one of the powerful factors that inhibit a full engagement with our ecological coexistence here on earth," and thus he intends to "awaken us from the dream that the world is about to end, because action on Earth (the real Earth) depends on it" (7). For him, "all those apocalyptic narratives of doom about the 'end of the world'" are "part of the problem, not part of the solution" (103), since "by postponing doom into some hypothetical future" they "inoculate us against the very real object that has intruded into ecological, social, and psychic space," obscuring the fact that global warming "spells doom now, not at some future date" (103–04). It is certainly true that we have largely failed to register those "real" and pervasive "intrusions," largely failed to see, for example, how, as Bill McKibben observes, "we've changed the planet ... in large and fundamental ways" so that "climate change is already wrecking thousands of lives daily" (xiii).[7] At the same time, though, we have at least equally failed to register, or act to forestall, the future threat posed by business as usual, especially the likelihood of tipping points—precisely the threat articulated by "all those apocalyptic narratives." And even if some of the "apocalyptic narratives" Morton decries do minimize the way global warming intrudes on the present, it is hard to see these still largely economically and politically powerless narratives as a "part of the problem," especially in relation to dominant narratives that work so powerfully to normalize global warming most frequently as primarily a political "issue," masking that, as Kevin Anderson and Alice Bows show, a commitment to maintaining business as usual is itself a radical choice. More crucially, to claim that global warming "spells doom now and not at some future date" seems to elide the distinction between the disasters we've already produced and guaranteed, on the one hand, and, on the other, the significantly more catastrophic consequences of our surpassing the tipping points, between an altered version of the climate system that has characterized the Holocene and some radically new system, much less viable for the human species—between being less fucked and more fucked.[8]

If Hulme and Morton represent very different understandings of how global warming inhabits the present—as a "relative risk" to be managed vs. as what somehow "spells doom now"—their dismissals of alarmism are both grounded in that elision of the distinction between being less fucked and more fucked. Responding to such dismissals is, again, finally a relatively simple matter of pointing to the science for which such dismissals fail to account. But such warnings about alarmism themselves underlie accusations of "cynicism" not themselves addressable by a recourse to science. Moreover, such accusations of cynicism are also provoked by framings of the climate crisis as rooted in economic, political, and cultural business as usual and thus addressable only by some rapid and extreme reworking of that status quo. Morton, for example, targets the "cynicism … enabled by the left" (157)—by "Marxists" who "argue that huge corporations are responsible for ecological damage and [that] it is self-destructive to claim that we are all responsible" (154)—which is structured, as he sees it, by the following logic: "'Since no one person's action will solve global warming, better to do nothing, or at most await the revolution'" (157). Such "logic," he argues, moreover amounts to a discounting of incrementalism, a "laugh[ing] at the poor fools who are trying to recycle as much as possible or drive a Prius," and involves "postponing ethical and political decisions into an idealized future," thus "leav[ing] the world just as it is, while maintaining a smug distance toward it" (156)—a withdrawal, he suggests, that "maps perfectly both onto U.S. Republican do-nothing-ism and Gaian defeatism ('Gaia will replace us, like a defective component'). Nothing happens … Global warming continues" (157).

It's not surprising that Morton adduces no instances of this "logic," for, far from quietist, those who understand the climate crisis as rooted in the nature and actions of "huge corporations"—or who critique the efficacy of "one person's action" like buying a Prius—in fact frequently insist that questions about global warming cannot be disarticulated from those of climate justice and are thus usually formulated in relation to calls to (political, not primarily consumerist) action.[9] Insofar as he values incrementalism, mocking those he sees as mocking it, Morton's own logic, moreover, fails on his own terms It's hard to see, that is, how incrementalism could matter in the face of a global warming Morton himself so frequently describes as a global or ecological "emergency" (13, 21, 48, 154), at least if, following the science, we recognize that "emergency" as the increasingly rapid closing of the temporal window for meaningful action.

Indeed, if the time left for possibly forestalling tipping points is rapidly dwindling, then recognizing that, by themselves, incremental steps and individual actions are simply insufficient—that they are comfortably accommodated by the catastrophic "radical option" of declining to "pursue radical emissions reductions"—may define the very opposite of cynicism. Donna Haraway warns that framings (like mine, in Chapter 2) of the ecological emergency in terms of the Anthropocene or the Capitalocene "lend themselves too readily to cynicism, defeatism, and self-certain and self-fulfilling predictions, like the 'game over, too late' discourse I hear all around me these days" (59). But in observing the difference between being more fucked and less fucked, I hope that the discourse of trauma I take up may indeed work *against* such a defeatist discourse—that, rather than "postponing ethical and political decisions into an idealized future," taking seriously that "no longer is there a non-radical option" prompts recognition that such postponement is itself a disastrous ethical and political decision, in Schell's terms a continued pulling of the trigger of a gun pointed at the future. Incrementalism is often justified with a logic conveniently abstracted from any historical, scientific, or social context: we must not let the perfect be the enemy of the good. What the particular context of the climate crisis presents us with is a logic of a less convenient sort: we must not let what is comfortably called the "good"—or what is deemed politically "realistic"—be the enemy of the sufficient.

Whether or not it is "realistic" to suppose that achieving the sufficient is likely—that is another matter. Certainly, it is hard to argue with Clive Hamilton's 2010 conclusion that, due to the nature of our political institutions, "we simply are not going to act with anything like the urgency required" (xiii). But there is a fundamental difference between political "reality," always subject to further negotiation, and the unnegotiable realities presented by geophysics. Even as regards the latter, moreover, there is a limit to what we can know for sure—not only about the extent, the precise timing, and the specific forms of the disasters we do know are inevitable, but, especially, about how humans will act in anticipation of them, and thus about whether we act with the required urgency. Climate "skepticism" that insists that knowledge about global warming is not yet sufficient to take action certainly constitutes a prominent danger, as does the more normalized denialism that congratulates itself for calling for obviously insufficient action—but calls for real sufficiency must themselves also negotiate the danger of too much certainty, of crossing what Donna Haraway calls the "brink of becoming much Too Big" (53–54), of "sap[ping] our capacity for imagining and caring for other worlds, both those that exist precariously now ... as well as those we need to bring into being in alliance with other critters" (53). In attempting to think and nourish such "other worlds" outside of the structures of global capitalism in which the climate crisis is arguably rooted (see Chapter 2 below), J. K. Gibson-Graham also resist Too Big analyses, identifying themselves as doing what Eve Sedgwick calls "weak theory," the practice of which "requires acting as a beginner"—requires, that is, not only a "refus[al] to know too much," but also a "refus[al] to extend diagnoses too widely or deeply" (8), to extend a "hypervigilant gaze over the entire world, marshaling every site and event into the same fearful order" narrated as "global capitalism's consolidating regulatory regime" of "neoliberalism" (4).

In Chapter 3, I'll try to attend more closely to the vexing relationship between the dangers of knowing too little and the dangers of presuming to know too much. But in confronting us with the challenge of navigating that relationship, global warming necessarily locates us at what in another context Cathy Caruth calls "the specific point at which knowing and not knowing intersect"—which, if it might nourish "our capacity of imagining and caring for other worlds," is also, crucially, where "the language of literature and the psychoanalytic theory of traumatic experience precisely meet" (3). In this sense, the climate crisis locates us where our fundamental structures and representations of knowledge are necessarily enmeshed with a not-knowing that threatens to dissolve both the knowledge and the knowers such systems produce (threatens to reveal what is called [politically] "realistic" as precisely unreal)—an existential threat one name for which, as in Caruth, is trauma. Timothy Clark thus poses global warming as a "happening whose trauma is to enact or entail the deconstruction of multiple frames of reference in multiple fields and modes of thought at the same time (e.g. politics, economics, ethics, cultural history)" (132). While such deconstruction might open a space for necessary new imaginings, the climate crisis is constituted precisely by the pervasive cultural failure to recognize and reckon with that deconstruction, by the pervasive denial—and thus the continued production—of the trauma that crisis necessarily presents; even as climate change undoes our central "modes of thought," we persist in them, just as Einstein famously observed, about what was then another recently emerged anthropogenic existential threat, that "the unleashed power of the atom has changed everything save our mode of thinking, and thus we drift toward unparalleled catastrophe" (376). Our dominant ways of figuring knowledge about global warming, that is, discursively disarticulate our knowing from the not-knowing by which they nonetheless remain inhabited and haunted.

In what follows, I'll explore these discursive disarticulations. Chapter 1 considers how such disarticulations might be illuminated by framing them in relation to "trauma." In Chapter 2, I'll consider what sort of not-knowing it is that they disarticulate—the degree to which the prospective catastrophes traumatically exceed representation, but, perhaps more crucially, also the epistemological uncertainty, and disruptiveness, inherent in understandings of the climate crisis as rooted in the logics of modernity, at least those iterations of modernity that have, from their inception, been fundamentally entwined with industrial capitalism.[10] Chapter 3 examines in some detail how such trauma is disarticulated across the range of ways we construct and know what global warming is and what it means—how we maintain a mode of thinking, that is, by which we drift, or race, to unparalleled catastrophe. And Chapters 4 and 5, pursuing Caruth's suggestion that literary discourse, like psychoanalysis, might work at the ground where knowing and not knowing can productively inform each other, explores both how literary representations of global warming for the most part still contribute to the foreclosures of the discursive culture at large (Chapter 4), and how it is to imaginative discourses we might nonetheless look for attempts to rearticulate the trauma of global warming (Chapter 5) and thus—however "unrealistic" it might be to say so—to help produce a less fucked, still partly viable future. The book closes with a short meditation centered on the dream of the burning child that Freud discusses in *The Interpretation of Dreams*, suggesting that in the dreamchild's cry, "Father, don't you see I'm burning," we might hear the future crying back a burning ethical appeal to the present—not only to see and grieve what is already traumatically burnt and lost, but also to attend to what is in the very process of burning now and not yet lost: to what we might yet stop from burning.

Notes

1 Referring to "global warming" in my first paragraph isn't meant to privilege that term over terms like "climate change," "the climate crisis," "anthropogenic climate disruption," "climate collapse," "climate emergency," and others, which, though their denotations aren't identical, I'll use more or less interchangeably, as is common in many public discussions of the happening to which they are meant to refer. Of course, in some contexts observing distinctions among those terms remains important (as does attending to their discursive histories). But since my argument is largely that we don't yet have an adequate language for that happening, for the most part rigorously minding the distinctions among the available terms has seemed to risk missing the forest for the trees.
2 Earth's climate history reveals that the climate "does not do gradual change," Fred Pearce writes:

> Under pressure, whether from sunspots or orbital wobbling or the depredations of humans, it lurches—virtually overnight. We humans have spent 400 generations building our current civilization in an era of climatic stability—a long, generally balmy spring that has endured since the last ice age.

Now we are "triggering its imminent and violent collapse" (xxviii). His book examines mechanics of several possible tipping points, as they were understood in 2007. In 2002, Richard Alley et al. had already detailed "surprising new findings that abrupt climate change can occur when gradual causes push the earth system across a threshold," which thus "may 'switch' the climate to a new state" (v). More recently, in establishing his premise that Earth is "now on the threshold of what earth systems scientists call a 'state shift'" (1), Jason Moore cites Barnosky et al.'s 2012 study in *Nature*, in which they write that in our moment lies the "potential to transform Earth rapidly and irreversibly into a state unknown in human experience" (52). And in 2018, in *Proceedings of the National Academy of Sciences*, Will Steffen et al. conclude that "self-reinforcing feedbacks could push the Earth System" beyond a "planetary threshold," a state which could

> prevent stabilization of the climate at intermediate temperature rises and cause continued warming on a "Hothouse Earth" pathway even as human emissions are reduced. Crossing the threshold would lead to a much higher global average temperature than any interglacial in the past 1.2 million years.

In the face of the urgency defined by the presence of such a "threshold," however, a 2014 report by the American Association for the Advancement of Science found that, still, "most projections of climate change presume that future changes ... will happen incrementally" (qtd. in Klein, 1). "Policymakers, in their magical thinking, imagine a mitigation path of gradual change to be constructed over many decades in a growing, prosperous world," David Spratt and Ian Dunlop write in their study of what their subtitle somewhat dryly calls "The Underestimation of Existential Climate Risk," focusing especially on the failures of the Intergovernmental Panel on Climate Change (IPCC) to account for the tipping points that define the worst-case possibilities. The most recent IPCC report, released October 8, 2018, does, quite belatedly, sound a somewhat more urgent note, calling for "drastic action" over the next dozen years, but even that report betrays a failure to register the extremity of the existential risk defined by those tipping points (see Jon Queally's "What's Not in the Latest Terrifying IPCC Report? The 'Much, Much, Much More Terrifying' New Research on Climate Tipping Points" and Scott Waldman's "New Climate Report Was Too Cautious, Some Scientists Say").

3 In 2016, Andreas Malm noted that during the 1990s, the

> annual increase in global CO_2 emissions stood at an average of 1 percent; since 2000 the figure has been 3.1 percent—a tripled growth rate, exceeding the worst-case scenarios develop by the IPCC ... : the more knowledge there is of the consequences, the more fossil fuels are burnt.
>
> (3)

4 When, for conciseness, I sometimes refer to what "we" understand or know, or how "we" speak, or what actions "we" might take or change, the stylistic expediency of the pronoun can obscure a crucial (geo)political dynamic: the power both to determine the dominating representations of the challenge posed by climate change and to initiate an adequate response is concentrated in the hands of those most fully invested in business as usual—elites within the rich, industrialized nations most responsible for the crisis in the first place, but also those nations as a whole in relation to poorer ones, who have suffered, and in the short term will suffer, the most disastrous consequences. Focusing especially on formulations that attribute the development of the crisis to "humanity" in general, as opposed to the tiny minority who drive what he calls the fossil economy, Malm observes that "the trope of the undifferentiated *we* does violence to the historical record" (392). According to that record, as Richard Heede reports in the science journal *Climatic Change*, almost two-thirds of the increase in atmospheric greenhouse gas over preindustrial levels has been produced by ninety (private and state-owned, mostly energy) companies. A crucial implication is that, as Pope Francis, Naomi Klein, and others increasingly insist, the challenge presented by the climate crisis is fundamentally entwined with the imperatives of social justice, an insight structuring the recently emerged Green New Deal.

5 Kevin Anderson and Alice Bows's "Beyond 'Dangerous' Climate Change: Emission Scenarios for a New World," in *Philosophical Transactions of the Royal Society A*, and their "A New Paradigm for Climate Change," in *Nature Climate Change*.

6 One good summary of the science underlying formulations of global warming as an "existential threat" appears in the first chapter of Clive Hamilton's *Requiem for a Species* (2010), "No Escaping the Science." He articulates there

why, in the absence of our taking almost unthinkably extreme measures, greenhouse gas emissions will rise "well above a number of critical tipping points that will spark uncontrollable climate change. The Earth's climate would enter a chaotic era lasting thousands of years" (22). Since this 2010 summary, of course, as we speed toward the threshold, the necessary preventative measures have grown correspondingly more extreme. Jem Bendell's "Deep Adaptation" (2018) offers a more recent overview of the science, and David Spratt and Ian Dunlop, in their section entitled "Existential Risk to Civilization," bring together some recent research on the consequences of our maintaining a non-radical response to the crisis (13–15), as does David Wallace-Wells.

7   In 2011, Christian Parenti elaborated on some of the ways climate change has significantly exacerbated social conflict, especially in the global south, the "tropic of chaos." More recently, extreme drought in Syria, during the first decade of this century, has been understood as significantly contributing to the ongoing appalling violence there (see Colin P. Kelley et al.). And, of course, the climate crisis has driven migration from the global south to the north, and the attendant violence, both in Europe and the Americas. See, for instance, Jonathan Blitzer's "How Climate Change is Fueling the U.S. Border Crisis."

8   In a culture so committed to remaining unalarmed, accusations of "alarmism" remain powerful. Commenting on David Wallace-Wells's 2017 "The Uninhabitable Earth"—"a portrait of our best understanding of where the planet is heading absent aggressive action," which, the annotated version notes, in less than a week became "the most-read article in *New York Magazine*'s history"—Susan Matthews details a number of responses expressing "horror": "Not horror at the future, though that would be understandable. Instead, they are horrified by the rhetorical strategy of using alarmism to make a point about climate change." In the flurry of media responses provoked by "The Uninhabitable Earth," that is, concern about that prospective uninhabitability itself, and about why the business as usual that produced and escalates the threat continues unabated, has been largely displaced by the concern that such a prospect might *sound* too frightening. Jem Bendell makes a similar point about responses to Wallace-Wells.

9   See, for example, part three of Klein's *This Changes Everything*, "Starting Anyway," or Chapter 15 of Malm's *Fossil Capital*, "A Return to the Flow? Obstacles to the Transition."

10   Observing that, conventionally, "modernity is identified with capitalism," Ellen Meiksins Wood argues that such identification is "a fundamental mistake," that "the so-called project of modernity may have little to do with capitalism" (540).

References

Alley, Richard B., et al. *Abrupt Climate Change: Inevitable Surprises.* National Academy P., January 2002, www.researchgate.net/publication/200043984_Abrupt_Climate_Change_Inevitable_Surprises.

Anderson, Kevin, and Alice Bows. "Beyond 'Dangerous' Climate Change: Emission Scenarios for a New World." *Philosophical Transactions of the Royal Society A*, vol. 369, 2011, pp. 20–44.

Barnosky, Anthony, et al. "Approaching a State Shift in Earth's Biosphere." *Nature*, vol. 486, 7 June 2012, pp. 52–58.

Bendell, Jem. "Deep Adaptation: A Map for Negotiating Climate Tragedy." *IFLAS Occasional Paper* 2, 27 July 2018, www.lifeworth.com/deepadaptation.pdf.
Blitzer, Jonathan. "How Climate Change Is Fueling the U.S. Border Crisis." *The New Yorker*, 3 April 2019, www.newyorker.com/news/dispatch/how-climate-change-is-fuelling-the-us-border-crisis.
Caruth, Cathy. *Unclaimed Experience: Trauma, Narrative, and History.* Johns Hopkins UP, 1996.
Clark, Timothy. "Some Climate Change Ironies: Deconstruction, Environmental Politics and the Closure of Ecocriticism." *Oxford Literary Review*, vol. 32, no. 1, 2010, pp. 131–49.
Einstein, Albert. *Einstein on Peace.* Edited by Otto Nathan and Heinz Norden, Simon & Schuster, 1960.
Freud, Sigmund. *The Interpretation of Dreams, in the Standard Edition of the Complete Psychological Works of Sigmund Freud.* 24 vols., vol. 5. Hogarth, 1953–74.
Ghosh, Amitav. *The Great Derangement: Climate Change and the Unthinkable.* U of Chicago P, 2016.
Gibson-Graham, Julie Katherine. *A Postcapitalist Politics.* U of Minnesota P, 2006.
Hamilton, Clive. *Requiem for a Species.* Earthscan, 2010.
Haraway, Donna. "Staying with the Trouble: Anthropocene, Capitalocene, Chtulucene." *Anthropocene or Capitalocene?* edited by Jason Moore. PM Press, 2016, pp. 34–76.
Hulme, Mike. "Chaotic World of Climate Truth." *BBC News*, 4 November 2006, http://news.bbc.co.uk/2/hi/science/nature/6115644.stm.
———. "Five Lessons of Climate Change." www.mikehulme.org/wp-content/uploads/the-five-lessons-of-climate-change.pdf.
———. *Why We Disagree about Climate Change.* Cambridge UP, 2009.
Kelley, Colin P., et al. "Climate Change in the Fertile Crescent and Implications of the Recent Syrian Drought." *Proceedings of the National Academy of Sciences of the United States of America*, vol. 112, no. 11, 2015, pp. 3241–46.
Klein, Naomi. *This Changes Everything: Capitalism vs. The Climate.* Simon & Schuster, 2014.
Linden, Eugene. *The Winds of Change: Climate, Weather, and the Destruction of Civilization.* Simon & Schuster, 2006.
Malm, Andreas. *Fossil Capital: The Rise of Steam Power and the Roots of Global Warming.* Verso, 2016.
Matthews, Susan. "Alarmism is the Argument We Need to Fight Climate Change." *Slate*, 10 July 2017, www.slate.com/technology/2017/07/we-are-not-alarmed-enough-about-climate-change.html.
McKibben, Bill. *Eaarth: Making a Life on a Tough New Planet.* Henry Holt, 2010.
Moore, Jason. "Introduction." *Anthropocene or Capitalocene? Nature, History, and the Crisis of Capitalism*, edited by Jason Moore. PM Press, 2016, pp. 1–11.
Morton, Timothy. *Hyperobjects: Philosophy and Ecology after the End of the World.* U of Minnesota P, 2013.
Parenti, Christian. *Tropic of Chaos: Climate Change and the New Geography of Violence.* Nation Books, 2011.

Pearce, Fred. *With Speed and Violence: Why Scientists Fear Tipping Points in Climate Change*. Beacon Press, 2007.

Queally, Jon. "What's Not in the Latest Terrifying IPCC Report? The 'Much, Much, Much More Terrifying' New Research on Climate Tipping Points." *Common Dreams*, 9 October 2018, www.commondreams.org/news/2018/10/09/whats-not-latest-terrifying-ipcc-report-much-much-much-more-terrifying-new-research.

Schell, Jonathan. *The Fate of the Earth*. Avon, 1982.

Spratt, David, and Ian Dunlop. "What Lies Beneath: The Underestimation of Existential Climate Risk." *Breakthrough—National Centre for Climate Restoration*, revised and updated 2018, https://52a87f3e-7945-4bb1-abbf-9aa66cd4e93e.filesusr.com/ugd/148cb0_a0d7c18a1bf64e698a9c8c8f18a42889.pdf.

Steffen, Will, et al. "Trajectories of the Earth System in the Anthropocene." *Proceedings of the National Academy of Sciences*, vol. 115, no. 33, 14 August 2018, pp. 8252–59. www.pnas.org/content/early/2018/08/07/1810141115.

Tyndall Centre for Climate Change Research. "The Radical Emission Reduction Conference." 2013, https://tyndall.ac.uk/sites/default/files/radicalplanabstracts_0.pdf.

Waldman, Scott. "New Climate Report Was Too Cautious, Some Scientists Say." *Scientific American*, 11 October 2008, www.scientificamerican.com/article/new-climate-report-was-too-cautious-some-scientists-say/.

Wallace-Wells, David. "The Uninhabitable Earth." *New York Magazine*, 9 July 2017, www.nymag.com/intelligencer/2017/07/climate-change-earth-too-hot-for-humans.html.

Wood, Ellen Meiksins. "Modernity, Postmodernity or Capitalism?" *Review of International Political Economy*, vol. 4, no. 3, Autumn 1997, pp. 539–60.

Chapter 1

Pavel's lament
Climate and trauma

Listening to the forest, Robert Frost hears an oven bird singing out a melancholic question: "What to make of a diminished thing"? A century later, in attending to that forest, we might hear that formulation seeping beyond its past tense: what to make not only of what is diminished but also of the prospect of diminishment to come, not only of the leaves and flowers the falling of which, as Frost has it, prompts the oven bird's question, but of the planetary climate system that, to the bird or Frost, might seem simply there, as taken-for-granted as the ground to stand on or the air to fly through. And not only diminishment, but collapse—both of that complex system itself and of the ways our dominant systems of knowledge have understood it.

One name for the existential collapse inherent in a fundamental epistemological disruption is trauma, and I hope that approaching the climate crisis in relation to that term might help us think about why it is that—given that the more we know about global warming, the faster we emit greenhouse gases—our knowledge of that crisis hasn't yet seemed to sufficiently matter. This is the case, anyway, to the extent that, as opposed to "catastrophe" or "disaster," "trauma" not only refers to violent happenings but also raises questions about how these happenings are or aren't known and experienced, how knowing or experiencing those happenings is felt to dissolve the knower itself—its "frames of reference" and "modes of thought," as Timothy Clark puts it (132)—and thus cannot be processed into meaning or intelligibility, remaining, in Caruth's still telling phrase, an "unclaimed experience," or, in other psychoanalytic contexts, provoking what D. W. Winnicott terms "unthinkable anxiety" (*Playing* 97) or W. R. Bion calls "nameless dread" (16).

Though in grappling with what is "nameless" there is a limit to what attending to questions of terminological precision might tell us, it is true that in this context trauma might seem like a notably imprecise term.[1] Where, though constituted partly by catastrophes in the present, the climate crisis is largely oriented toward the future, for instance, understandings of trauma have mainly concerned not what's to come but (the persistence of) what's already happened. In seeming to focus on the present in relation to the catastrophes of the past, moreover, the discourse of trauma might seem by definition to deflect attention from how the present is implicated in the production of catastrophes in the future. Indeed, Tom Cohen implies just this critique, classifying trauma theory among the "critical agendas coming out of the twentieth century" that, with their "nostalgic agendas," have "unwittingly maintained" an "unseen collaboration" with the "accelerated trajectories" of "*eco* disaster" (15). Though for Cohen Bruno Latour's formulation of this disaster still remains "inscribe[d]" (26) in that collaboration—evident, he argues, in Latour's resorting to what Cohen dismisses as the "tired ... trope" of Benjamin's Angel of History—Latour's reading of Walter Benjamin's Angel might nonetheless seem to indict trauma on the same terms:

> The ecological crisis is nothing but the sudden turning around of someone who had actually never before looked into the future, so busy was He extricating Himself from a horrible past. ... [T]his hero [is] fleeing His past so fiercely that He cannot realize—except too late—that it is precisely his flight that has created the destruction he was trying to avoid in the first place.[2]
>
> (qtd. in Cohen 27)

Cohen's own formulations themselves, however, seem to raise questions about whether, in attempting to grapple with the climate crisis, "twentieth-century critical idioms" (29) like trauma qualify as merely nostalgic. If trauma by definition involves not merely the belated effects of past events that, in Winnicott's terms, "cannot get into the past tense" (*Psychoanalytic* 91), but also, as Clark's nonce use of the term suggests, the inadequacy of "frames of reference" and "modes of thought" themselves, then it is precisely trauma that Cohen himself rehearses in his claim that "the referent—as climate change discloses—is ... always exceeding our calculative and referential captures" (23). If, in Caruth's terms, trauma describes not only an "overwhelming experience of ... catastrophic events" (11) but also an event that "is not experienced as it occurs" (17), then climate change emerges precisely as such an event in Cohen's observation that

> the perceptual and cognitive regimes we have at our disposal are increasingly incapable of *experiencing* the mutations and changes that mark our climate. ... [W]e have sped by and failed to witness the cataclysmic geology that is rupturing (or ought to be rupturing) the present.
>
> (23)

Because much of the carbon dioxide humans directly or indirectly impel into the atmosphere stays there for hundreds (and some persists for thousands) of years, and because present warming (from carbon and other greenhouse gases) itself initiates chains of long-term consequences, most of the disastrous effects produced by greenhouse gas emitted in the present will occur in the future,[3] just as the disastrous effects of climate change in the present have been produced mostly by emissions in the past. Climate change, that is, is defined by the same "inherent latency" by which Caruth defines the experience of trauma. Likewise, if, as a global phenomenon, the very existence of anthropocentric global warming can't be perceived by any one person directly but—like the causal connections between global warming and disasters in both the present and future—must be interpretively derived from complex calculations based upon masses of abstract data, then, as with Caruth's account of traumatic history, anthropogenic climate change necessarily "is not fully perceived as it occurs" (18), becoming "fully evident only in connection with another place and in another time" (17).

One approach to bringing the question of trauma to questions of climate has been offered by E. Ann Kaplan's *Climate Trauma* (2016). Suggesting that while trauma is usually defined in relation to the effects of something in the past, as in PTSD, she poses it as a matter not only of "post" but also of "pre," as in her concept of "pretrauma" or "Pretraumatic Stress Syndrome" (1), which, in her account "offers a new lens for an expanded trauma theory" (4), by "exploring the trauma of the future" (28).[4] She develops this notion largely by defining and describing examples of a subgenre of "pretrauma cinema" (4), the "pretraumatic disaster film" (5). Sharing her impulse to bring notions of trauma to the climate crisis, and to attend to catastrophes not only of the past and the present but to those the present is in the act of producing for itself and for the future, I nonetheless pursue that impulse in very different directions and reach very different conclusions. Where Kaplan's focus is on examining a cinematic subgenre, examples of which she hopes might serve as an "invitation … to viewers" to start "dealing with the crisis" (150), I consider (in Chapter 4) how prevailing discourses, including genres like the disaster film, might help serve the opposite function—how they may help contribute to the normalization of the "crisis," obscuring the urgency of its traumatic threat. Stressing how "genres shape how we think about our lived worlds by establishing certain kinds of story, certain repeated narratives and situations, that lead to well-defined expectations" (28), she sees the pretrauma dystopian genre emerging "as European cultures become newly aware of the uncertainty of human futurity"; I register a fundamental disjunction between such ostensible "awareness of uncertainty" and the "well-defined expectations" constructed by the sort of genres she describes. Commensurately, where she sees hopeful growing awareness in, for example, the fact that "President Obama finally found the courage not only to veto the Keystone Pipeline … but also to make a deal with China to cut greenhouse gas pollution" (144), I see such perhaps ecocidally belated events as minor sops, virtually irrelevant to the imperative to limit warming to 2 degrees C above preindustrial levels—farcically inadequate steps taken by a president who, in 2012, boasted "under my administration, America is producing more oil today than at any time in the last eight years" (Obama). Where she points to an article in the *New York Times* as "exemplifying the new public awareness," my Chapter 3 focuses partly on the *Times* as an important organ of normalized denial (and of mock "neutrality" in the face of an ostensibly controversial "issue," as in its 2017 hiring of Brett Stephens as a columnist, giving a major public platform to a self-described "climate agnostic" [Calderone and Baumann] who sees climate change as an "imaginary enemy" producing a "hysteria").

In distinguishing hers from other works in the environmental humanities, Kaplan suggests that where they "eschew psychoanalytic perspectives," she "make[s] such perspectives central" (6). And here again, where my argument is also rooted partly in psychoanalytic premises, it grows in a rather different direction. Kaplan turns mainly to "the always reliable Sigmund Freud" and his "theories about anxiety and the death drive as a way to understand why humans seem unable to move forward to mitigate their drastic negative impact on the planet." "Trauma haunts us because of its connection with death," and, in her account, "this led Freud in 1920 to conceptualize a death drive, related to pretrauma phenomenon" (6), though she also sees in his work "the concept of group repression of ideas too uncomfortable to confront," including "ethnic genocide and other historical events in which a population is complicit" (25).[5] Going largely against the grain of much cultural trauma theory, which has operated largely within a discourse established by Freud and inflected by Jacques Lacan, my own engagement with trauma draws mainly on work in the British object-relational vein, especially that of D. W. Winnicott and W. R. Bion. In this it joins works like Donna Orange's *Climate Crisis, Psychoanalysis, and Radical Ethics* (2017) and, in some ways, Sally Weintrobe's edited collection, *Engaging with Climate Change: Psychoanalytic and Disciplinary Perspectives* (2013) (which draws heavily also on Melanie Klein).

Examining how the urgency of the climate crisis (framed partly as a matter of "justice") has, in the U.S., left unperturbed what she calls the "business as usual" that produces it, Orange asks, "What's wrong with this picture?" (1). I think her answer is indispensable. "Unconscious and silent about the U.S. history of settler colonialism, ignorant and mute about our crimes of chattel slavery and racial domination, neither government nor citizens can seriously tackle climate injustice until we confront this 400-year history" (37). She focuses especially on "colonialism and slavery, because," as she sees it, the "habits of keeping these crimes—genocides before the term came to usage after World War II—hidden from ourselves may also be keeping us unaware of the impacts of climate change on people who live out of our daily sight" (40), those in "the Global South," and, I'd add, those who will suffer the increasing violence of a collapsing climate system in the future, distant from the source of most greenhouse gas production not only in space but in time (see the discussion of "slow violence" below). Crucially, she thus locates "our" failure to respond to the radical urgency of the moment in the fact that "we are so embedded in the cultures that have created the climate problem" in the first place (64). Sharing her fundamental premises, where Orange elaborates her argument largely in in terms both of psychoanalytic theory and practice and of philosophies of radical ethics, I attend closely to particular iterations of climate discourse itself (including literary ones), grounding a vision of the "wrongness" of the "big picture" in detailed looks at how those "habits of keeping [things] hidden from ourselves" are partly shaped precisely by the ways "climate change" is ostensibly brought out of hiding—how denial is normalized not only by neglecting (or "denying") "climate change" but by the very ways it is discursively constructed, by how its traumatic challenge to business as usual is disarticulated precisely by the ways we *do* talk about it. Thus, for example, where Orange can lament that "even when Al Gore worked so hard ... to convince us of the 'inconvenient truth,' his message didn't really penetrate or change the lives of many of us who spend our lives working with the unconscious" (1), I attend closely to how *An Inconvenient Truth* introduced "global warming" into the public sphere *precisely* in terms of the triumphalist national amnesia that elsewhere she sees as the core problem. And where Orange (like Gore) tends to frame the crisis in terms of "our carbon-and-methane spewing lifestyles" (45), I explore how discourses of consumer "lifestyles" themselves obscure the larger economic structures, of industrial capitalism, defining our ecocidal common sense.

In trying to rouse a psychoanalytic community out of what she sees as its "analytic slumbers" (64) in relation to the climate crisis, Orange does note that "a few psychoanalysts have begun to speak" (60). With two exceptions, however, even in those works she still "miss[es] ... an adequate sense of urgency" (62). One of those exceptions is Sally Weintrobe's (edited) *Engaging with Climate Change*. Again, though, where in that volume Orange hears a "clarion voice" (60) I see it as in some ways enacting the very "disavowal" it takes as its main subject of analysis—muting, not trumpeting, a "sense of urgency." For Weintrobe, the main danger of disavowing the "anxiety" prompted by the climate crisis is that "this can lead us rapidly to lose a sense of proportion," and, indeed, "the first casualty of the environmental crisis we are in" for her isn't the horrific environmental damage per se (or any of the consequent losses of species and of human lives) but, rather, "proportional thinking" itself ("Anxiety" 46). While no one would argue against the value of keeping things "in proportion" in some decontextualized sense, it is hard to see how that phrase, with all its connotations of moderation, could function to compel urgent attention to the unregistered *extremity* of the existential threat that ought to disrupt our "slumbers." This apparent commitment to moderation reflects also in Weintrobe's concern that an insufficient facing of climate anxieties produced the "unwitting projection" that "may have been part of some of the early 'catastrophizing,' stridently doom-laden communication about climate change" (45)—as if the dilemma has been that "communication" has somehow been *too* extreme, or, we could say, too stridently "disproportionate."⁶

Although Weintrobe does glance at "cultures of denial" (40), and in places attends to the "side of human nature" that "is strongly ingrained in current Western societies" (43), for the most part her focus remains on a universalized individual psyche operating in a depoliticized, universal, external "reality." Drawing on Melanie Klein's model of the structure of the psyche, her premise is that "the biggest conflict we face in life is between the concerned part of us that loves reality and the more narcissistic, vain part of us that hates reality when reality thwarts our wishes or deflates our view of ourselves," which, in this account, where "reality" is a fixed term, cannot not happen (33); informed by a more relational psychoanalytic model, focused on the degree of responsiveness characterizing any particular "reality" (an early caretaker, the ideological structures defining the very terms of belong), I explore more fully how the prevailing "culture of denial" works not only to "thwart" but also to wage, even as it normalizes, a violent attack on those conditions that make wishing, or loving or hating, possible in the first place.

Where, sketching the "part of us that loves reality," Weintrobe writes that it "recognizes its right size and where it fits within the scheme of things" (33), my focus on trauma raises questions about what it might mean to "fit" within a cultural "scheme of things" the dominant logic of which cannot recognize attempts to articulate its ecocidal premises. Where for her the "part that loves reality" finds that "it is struggling with reality that ultimately provides meaning and self-worth" (33–34), I thus attend to how such "meaningful" struggle is challenged not only by the "vain part of us" but by a particular cultural "reality" whose dominant terms seem to disallow any such dialogic struggle. As one result, perhaps, where Weintrobe focuses in large part on how individuals can negotiate the challenge of facing the direness of our straits, and her discussion of "policy implications" ("Introduction" 13) points to policies "which support people in making environmentally friendly changes in real and more lasting ways" (14), I explore how such attention to the individual-behavior trees risks obscuring the traumatic threat to the ideological-economic forest itself. And where for her "in current Western cultures we all bear some small individual responsibility for climate change and environmental degradation, and we are also, realistically, largely not individually responsible" ("Anxiety" 46), I stress how discussions of "responsibility," for the most part, as here, presuming a relatively undifferentiated "we," often beg questions about vast differentials in economic, political, and cultural power (see note 5 to the Introduction).[7]

In this regard, I think of trauma in relation to global warming less in light of Kaplan's pretrauma or Weintrobe's concern with individual response and responsibility than in relation to what Rob Nixon so compellingly identifies as environmental "slow violence." In *Slow Violence and the Environmentalism of the Poor* (2011), he delineates a "violence decoupled from its original causes by the workings of time" (11), a "pervasive but elusive violence of delayed effects" (3) the "fatal repercussions [of which] are dispersed across space and time" (10) and thus remain largely invisible, especially in the industrialized North, where such violence—suffered disproportionately in the global South—is mainly initiated.[8] Crucial here is that the causal relation between anthropogenic global warming and any particular consequence—like the causal relation between atmospheric greenhouse gasses and such warming itself—cannot be seen directly but, rather, must be inferred from data collected over a period of years. "In an age when media venerate the spectacular," Nixon stresses that

> a central question is strategic and representational: how can we convert into image and narrative the disasters that are slow moving and long in the making, disasters that are anonymous and star nobody, disasters that are ... of indifferent interest to the sensation-driven technologies of our image-world?
>
> (3)

His book thus focuses on writers who, "through testimonial protest, rhetorical inventiveness, and counterhistories in the face of formidable odds ... pit their energies against what Edward Said called 'the normalized quiet of unseen power'" (6).[9] These writers must grapple with "the representational bias against slow violence" in general, but also, Nixon suggests, with the particular fact that "efforts to make forms of slow violence more urgently visible suffered a setback in the United States in the aftermath of 9/11, which reinforced a spectacular, immediately sensational, and instantly hyper-visible image of what constitutes a violent threat" (13).[10] Indeed, he proposes that "the fiery spectacle of the collapsing towers was burned into the national psyche as *the* definitive image of violence, setting back by years attempts to rally public sentiment against climate change"—a dynamic, I suggest, very much at play in the weeks before the December 2015 climate summit in Paris, when public attention was utterly absorbed not by the existential stakes of that gathering but by the spectacular terrorist violence that had been recently inflicted on the city (when the media did attend to the summit, the focus fell largely on security challenges posed by the expected demonstrations, not on the drastic urgency that prompted them; similarly, though widely hailed as "historic," the Paris Agreement itself quickly disappeared from a mediasphere absorbed for a few weeks with a series of spectacular weather events, individual "weather" dots for the most part left unconnected to each other or to larger questions of climate[11]).

While the representational challenge posed by slow violence "can seem overwhelming" (38), Nixon focuses mostly on how "writer-activists can help us apprehend threats imaginatively that remain imperceptible to the senses" (15), how they can "bring emotionally to life ... threats that take time to wreak their havoc" (14). If we consider, though, how what can "seem" overwhelming might in some ways *be* overwhelming, this representational challenge points to questions not only about "how to devise arresting stories, images and symbols adequate to" slow violence (3), but also about what "adequate" might mean in this context—points, that is, to questions about how to represent that challenge itself: how to represent a knowledge of "havoc" as necessarily inhabited by a not-knowing that threatens to dissolve knowledge and knower both. In this regard, Malm's observation is telling: Nixon

> finds and reads stories and essays on the slow violence of the Bhopal disaster, oil exploitation in the Arabian Gulf and the Niger Delta, mega-dams in India, natural parks in South Africa, depleted uranium in Iraq *but none on climate change as such.*[12]
>
> (*Fossil* 9)

Again, recent attempts to grapple with this kind of representational challenge often pose it in terms of cultural trauma, especially as it emerged in what Roger Luckhurst observes as "the boom in cultural trauma theory in the early 1990s" (4). In his account, a key text there was Cathy Caruth's *Unclaimed Experience*, in which, he suggests, "the lines feeding notions of cultural trauma converge," especially "the diverse models of trauma developed by, and in the wake of, Freud" and "the problem of aesthetics 'after Auschwitz'" (13).[13] If, as Marianne Hirsch and Irene Kacandes observe, "even before they return from the camp" Jorge Semprun and others liberated from Buchenwald "heatedly debate the most effective genre for their narration" (1–2), four decades later, in Art Spiegelman's *Maus*, survivor Pavel laments, "Look at how many books have already been written about the Holocaust. What's the point? People haven't changed. ... Maybe they need a newer, bigger Holocaust" (*II* 45). Similarly, when climate scientist James Hansen realizes the extremity of what global warming means, he first wonders "how in the world can a situation like this be communicated credibly" (89), and after repeatedly trying to "explain the science as well as [he] could" (98) in many futile meetings with government officials, he can only wonder again "how to portray the horror of that devastation in a way beyond graphs and numbers and phrases we have heard before, like 'climate disaster'?" (260). Where Pavel responds to the discursive limits of "books about the Holocaust" by wondering if a "newer, bigger Holocaust" might disrupt the normalization of large-scale violence, Hansen's final response to his blunt encounter with the discursive limits of science is to sketch a "science-fiction scenario"[14]—as if popular genres like science fiction didn't by definition constitute precisely the kind of discourse "we have heard before" (a matter I'll return to in Chapter 4). Pavel's lament, of course, is itself an element of Spiegelman's attempt to grapple with the representational challenge posed by traumatic history and experience. But where, again, that challenge has been taken up by "books about the Holocaust," the ways we talk, write, and know about climate change have functioned mostly to disavow its traumatic meanings.

The following chapters will elaborate both on how these traumatic meanings derive from understandings of the climate crisis as inherent in the ideological premises of capitalist modernity and on how the dominant discourses of the crisis disarticulate those understandings. But I want to close this one by considering how such particular disarticulations reflect the more generalized existential dilemma they pose to modernity's fundamental modes of (self-)knowing.

In butchery, as James Berger reminds us, "disarticulation" refers to the "amputation of limbs at the joint" (*Disarticulate* 2). If the disarticulations performed by dominant discourses of capitalist modernity obscure the traumatic violence inherent in what Eileen Crist calls the "industrial-consumer complex" (55), such butchery also forestalls the traumatic self-shattering of what it would mean for the industrial-consumer self—"so embedded in the cultures that have created the climate problem," as Donna Orange suggests (64)—to see and know that violence. "Shredding the ideology" with which you are identified, in Naomi Klein's terms, or disrupting "the core values and principles underpinning capitalist consumer democracies," in Ingolfur Bluhdorn's (1), or disavowing the "raw material from which we increasingly construct our sense of who we are" (65) in Clive Hamilton's—these involve the collapse of the very ground on which, it might be felt, the modern subject could stand in order to undertake such shredding, disrupting, disavowing. Though for the most part their own formulations don't account for it, such challenges to the dominant discourses of climate change themselves thus constitute a traumatic threat. If, as Klein writes, it is "blindingly obvious" that the climate crisis is "rooted" in "contemporary capitalism's quest for perpetual growth," then the modern subject, rooted in that same ideological ground, must be careful not to look, lest looking rupture vision itself. Into a public sphere constructed to normalize that modern subject, recognitions like Klein's, that global warming "changes everything," or the Tyndall Centre's, that "no longer is there a non-radical option"—recognitions that would undo the prevailing ways of making sense—thus help make legible the discursive butchery by which they remain disarticulated.

Attempts to locate the roots of the climate crisis in the logics of capitalist modernity are thus confronted with the same rhetorical quandary as attempts to convey its catastrophic consequences. Describing a meeting where climate activists urged the board of the San Francisco Employees Retirement System to divest from fossil fuel stocks, Rebecca Solnit writes that "it was as though the people in that room were having different conversations in different languages in different worlds. And versions of that schizophrenic conversation are being had all over this continent and in Europe." In Solnit's terms, these "different worlds" are grounded in different logics of "rationality"; the Retirement board "talked interminably about how wild and reckless it would be to divest" while, identified with the activists, she suggests that "inaction and caution may seem so much more rational than action, unless you're in a burning building or on a sinking ship." But we might consider also how what seems rational is conditioned not only by *where* you are but also by *who* you are, or who you imagine yourself to be. Divesting from fossil fuel stocks might not compute to those whose subjectivity—like the fiduciary responsibility that signals their authority and "success"—is constructed around the "core values" of modernity. If you feel yourself to *be* the ship, what can abandoning it mean? To the extent it remains identified with a knowing sequestered from the not-knowing to which that question gestures, the Board can neither see the ship is sinking nor take the urgent action such an emergency would prompt.

Notes

1 If trauma might by definition be understood to vex the process of definition itself, this is also reflected in attempts to define "trauma studies" as a field of study. In 2000, one critic had already observed what she called "trauma saturation," as, for literary and cultural critics, "trauma as an object of inquiry ... [had] become a preoccupation, if not a fetish" (Ball 1), and, as a "fetish," we might read trauma studies as enacting a sort of trauma of its own. Its attempts to give shape and meaning to catastrophe, that is, necessarily fall short and thus provoke a redoubled attempt, which must also in some sense fail. "In spite of the rapid growth in the treatment and study of PTSD," Ruth Leys noted, again in 2000, "researchers ... acknowledge the existence of confusion, even 'chaos,' a situation that leads to further appeals for order" (6n12). In any case, my own engagement here with "trauma" isn't meant to try to bring "order" to the field. Rather, I'm drawing on a particular conception of trauma as a way of trying to think about why it is that, in the face of all we "know," ecocidal business as usual persists and escalates.

2   It's also certainly true that the prevailing critical "agendas"—like the disciplinary constructions of knowledge they often critique—have (until relatively recently) often evaded explicit engagement with the prospect of ecocatastrophe, an evasion epitomized perhaps by what Cohen observes as "Derrida's omission of ecocatastrophic logics from his otherwise compendious agenda," logics "for instance nowhere to be found in *Specters*' 'ten plagues' of the new world order" (28) (though, David Wood reports, Derrida subsequently "willingly assented to naming our global environmental crisis as the eleventh plague" [287]). Similarly, Andreas Malm has suggested that critical theoretical discourses of many stripes have, in one way or another, obfuscated the reality of an ongoing global "biocide" (*Progress* 15).

Subjecting such discourses to scrutiny from a very different angle, in "Why Has Critique Run Out of Steam? From Matters of Fact to Matters of Concern," Latour worries that global warming "skepticism" may have been aided and comforted by the debunking spirit of critical theory, which emphasizes how "facts" themselves aren't self-evidently natural but, rather, are social constructions, and so subject to endless doubt (226). I think this would be a more troubling prospect if the centrist acceptance of the "fact" of climate change were, as I argue, itself not a more normalized species of denialism. The problem may be not that critique has delegitimized real "facts" but, rather, that the "facts" presumed by the dominant structures of knowledge have themselves seemed *beyond* effective critique. Critique, that is, can be understood as a drive not only to throw out the bathwater of so much of what passes for "common sense" but also as a matter of "concern," in Latour's terms, for the baby who appears to be drowning in it.

3   In *Nature Climate Change*, Peter Clark et al. argue that the general failure to respond anything like adequately to global warming has been contributed to by

> the focus of the scientific community on near-term climate changes and their uncertainties. In particular, the scientific emphasis on the expected climate changes by 2100, which was originally driven by past computational capabilities, has created a misleading impression in the public arena.
>
> (1)

This minimizes the more disastrous consequences of business as usual by framing out those likely in the next century. Clark et al. argue that "many key features of future climate change are relatively certain in the long term, even if the precise timing of their occurrence is uncertain."

4   Along these lines, see Daniel Oberhaus's "Climate Change Is Giving Us 'Pre-Traumatic Stress.'" Such "pre-trauma" is sometimes located especially in climate scientists, as in David Corn's "It's the End of the World as They Know It: The Distinct Burden of Being a Climate Scientist," though, at this late date, it's hard to see why a community whose reticence on the subject has been routinely critiqued would be more sensitive than others to the traumatic meanings of its findings—hard to see its burden as "distinct."

5   James Berger offers a more refined view of trauma in Freud's work, tracing there an "ambivalence regarding the significance of historical events" themselves. Indeed, we might wonder, "do events in history have consequences—as Freud argues in the first movements of each of his theoretical ventures—or, as he concludes in each of his second movements, are events secondary to desire, instinct, or a form of genetic history?" (*After* 23).

6   Here Weintrobe echoes the psychoanalytically framed critique of climate "alarmism," mounted by Paul Hoggett, that I examine below, in Chapter 3.

7 The other instance where Orange find psychoanalysts addressing climate change with adequate "urgency" is the website of the Climate Psychology Alliance. "Challenging the consumerist paradigm" that sees humans as "separate from Nature," that finds "all the problems we create can be solved by technology," and that critiques the "dangerous delusion that economics is of a higher order than ecology," the CPA announces itself as dedicated to promoting the process of "Facing Difficult Truths" that follow from that challenge ("What We Do").

8 In environmental humanities, another current figuration for what is dispersed across space and time, exceeding our frames of reference, is Timothy Morton's "hyperobject." In contrast to Nixon's "slow violence," though, the capaciousness of Morton's category seems to moot its meaning. "'In a strange way, every object is a hyperobject (201),'" Ursula Heise quotes Morton as concluding, and she thus wonders: "If scale makes no difference, and global warming is not as a matter of principle different from 'pencils, penguins, and plastic explosive' (176), what useful work does the concept of the hyperobject do?" (460).

9 Nixon situates the concept slow violence in relation to Johan Galtung's notion of "structural violence," the sort, as Nixon defines it, "embodied by a neoliberal order of austerity measures, structural adjustment, rampant deregulation, corporate megamergers, and widening gulf between the rich and poor" (10). Analogously, Slavoj Žižek addresses the distinction between spectacular, acknowledged violence and the more pervasive, normalized sort in terms of "subjective" and "objective" violence:

> Subjective and objective violence cannot be perceived from the same standpoint: subjective violence is experienced as such against the background of a nonviolent zero level. It is seen as a perturbation of the "normal," peaceful state of things. However, objective violence is precisely the violence inherent in this "normal" state of things. Objective violence is invisible since it sustains the very zero-level standard against which we perceive something as subjectively violent.
>
> (2)

10 As Nixon's formulation here suggests, a violence that is in some sense "slow" might nonetheless demand an "urgent" response.

11 Since 2015, as extreme weather has predictably intensified, the major media's failure to frame it in relation to climate change has doggedly persisted. According to a July 2018 Media Matters report, for example, "major broadcast TV networks mentioned climate change just once during two weeks of heat-wave coverage" (Media Matters). See also, for example, Emily Atkin.

12 We might see in this absence a reflection of Amitav Ghosh's assessment that "climate change casts a much smaller shadow within the landscape of literary fiction than it does even in the public arena" (7), a notion pursued in Chapter 4.

13 For Luckhurst, a third "line" converging in Caruth's work is "the aporia of representation in poststructuralism" (13). Samuel Cohen offers a similar account of the rise of trauma studies more generally. Tracing how "Freud's focus on the mechanism of how the psyche deals with the extreme or limit event" prompted the "birth" of trauma studies in the late 1980s, or early 1990s, he suggests that also prominent at the scene of this "birth" were "Holocaust studies; the medical institutionalization of post-traumatic stress disorder …; and the catastrophe-heavy 20th century, which saw genocides, ethnic cleansing, world wars, and the use of the atom bomb" (389–90).

14 Beyond his book, Hansen has also responded to this blunt encounter by participating in political protest, including civil disobedience, getting arrested, for example, at the August 2012 White House protest against the Keystone pipeline.

References

Atkin, Emily. "The Media's Failure to Connect the Dots on Climate Change." *The New Republic*, 25 July 2018, www.newrepublic.com/article/150124/medias-failure-connect-dots-climate-change.

Ball, Karyn. "Trauma and Its Institutional Destinies." *Cultural Critique*, no. 46, Autumn 2000, pp. 1–44.

Berger, James. *After the End: Representations of Post-Apocalypse*. U of Minnesota P, 1999.

———. *The Disarticulate: Language, Disability, and the Narratives of Modernity*. NYU P, 2014.

Bion, W. R. *Second Thoughts: Selected Papers on Psycho-Analysis*. Heinemann, 1967.

Bluhdorn, Ingolfur. "Locked into the Politics of Unsustainability." *Eurozine*, 30 October 2009, www.eurozine.com/locked-into-the-politics-of-unsustainability/.

Calderone, Michael, and Nick Baumann. "Hiring Another Anti-Trump Voice Expands Opinions Represented in Paper, *New York Times* Says." *Huffpost*, 14 April 2017, www.huffpost.com/entry/bret-stephens-new-yorktimes_n_58f12c80e4b0b9e9848bed3e.

Caruth, Cathy. *Unclaimed Experience: Trauma, Narrative, and History*. Johns Hopkins UP, 1996.

Clark, Peter U. et al. "Consequences of Twenty-First-Century Policy for Multi-Millennial Climate and Sea-Level Change." *Nature Climate Change*, vol. 6, no. 4, February 2016, pp. 360–69.

Clark, Timothy. "Some Climate Change Ironies: Deconstruction, Environmental Politics and the Closure of Ecocriticism." *Oxford Literary Review*, vol. 32, no. 1, 2010, pp. 131–49.

Cohen, Samuel. "The Novel in a Time of Terror: *Middlesex*, History, and Contemporary American Fiction." *Twentieth-Century Literature*, vol. 53, no. 3, Fall 2007, pp. 371–92.

Cohen, Tom. "Murmurations—'Climate Change' and the Defacement of Theory." *Telemorphosis: Theory in the Era of Climate Change*, vol. 1, edited by Tom Cohen. Open Humanities, 2012, pp. 13–42, http://.quod.lib.umich.edu/o/ohp/10539563.0001.001/1:3/--telemorphosis-theory-in-the-era-of-climate-change-vol-1?rgn=div1;view=fulltext.

Corn, David. "It's the End of the World as they Know It: The Distinct Burden of Being a Climate Scientist." *Mother Jones*, 8 July 2019, www.motherjones.com/environment/2019/07/weight-of-the-world-climate-change-scientist-grief/.

Crist, Eileen. "Beyond the Climate Crisis: A Critique of Climate Change Discourse." *Telos*, vol. 141, Winter 2007, pp. 29–55.

Frost, Robert. *The Poetry of Robert Frost*, edited by Edward Connery Lathem. Henry Holt, 1979.

Ghosh, Amitav. *The Great Derangement: Climate Change and the Unthinkable*. U of Chicago P, 2016.

Hamilton, Clive. *Requiem for a Species.* Earthscan, 2010.
Hansen, James. *Storms of My Grandchildren.* Bloomsbury, 2011.
Heise, Ursula. Review of *Hyperobjects*, by Timothy Morton, *Critical Inquiry*, vol. 41, no. 2, 2015, pp. 460–61.
Hirsch, Marianne, and Irene Kacandes. "Introduction." *Teaching the Representation of the Holocaust*, edited by Marianne Hirsch and Irene Kacandes. MLA, 2004, pp. 1–33.
Kaplan, E. Ann. *Climate Trauma: Foreseeing the Future in Dystopian Film and Fiction.* Rutgers UP, 2016.
Klein, Naomi. "Capitalism vs. The Climate." *The Nation*, 9 November 2011, www.thenation.com/article/capitalism-vs-climate/.
Latour, Bruno. "Why Has Critique Run Out of Steam? From Matters of Fact to Matters of Concern." *Critical Inquiry*, vol. 30, no. 2, Winter 2004, pp. 225–48.
Leys, Ruth. *Trauma: A Genealogy.* U of Chicago P, 2000.
Luckhurst, Roger. *The Trauma Question.* Routledge, 2008.
Malm, Andreas. *Fossil Capital: The Rise of Steam Power and the Roots of Global Warming.* Verso, 2016.
———. *The Progress of This Storm: Nature and Society in a Warming World.* Verso, 2018.
Media Matters. "Major Broadcast TV Networks Mentioned Climate Change Just Once During Two Weeks of Heat-Wave Coverage." *Media Matter for America*, 12 July 2018, www.mediamatters.org/blog/2018/07/12/Major-broadcast-TV-networks-mentioned-climate-change-just-once-during-two-weeks-of-heat-wa/220651.
Morton, Timothy. *Hyperobjects: Philosophy and Ecology after the End of the World.* U of Minnesota P, 2013.
Nixon, Rob. *Slow Violence and the Environmentalism of the Poor.* Harvard UP, 2011.
Obama, Barack. "Remarks by the President on American-Made Energy." The White House, Office of the Press Secretary. https://obamawhitehouse.archives.gov/the-press-office/2012/03/22/remarks-president-american-made-energy.
Oberhaus, Daniel. "Climate Change Is Giving Us 'Pre-Traumatic Stress.'" *Motherboard*, 4 February 2017, www.vice.com/en_us/article/vvzzam/climate-change-is-giving-us-pre-traumatic-stress.
Orange, Donna. *Climate Crisis, Psychoanalysis, and Radical Ethics.* Routledge, 2017.
Solnit, Rebecca. "By the Way, Your Home Is on Fire: The Climate of Change and the Dangers of Stasis." *TomDispatch.com*, 11 March 2014, www.tomdispatch.com/post/175817/tomgram%3A_rebecca_solnit%2C_evacuate_the_economy/.
Spiegelman, Art. *Maus II: And Here My Troubles Began.* Pantheon, 1992.
Stephens, Bret. "Liberalism's Imaginary Enemies." *The Wall Street Journal*, 30 November 2015, www.wsj.com/articles/liberalisms-imaginary-enemies-1448929043.
Tyndall Centre for Climate Change Research. "The Radical Emission Reduction Conference," 2013, https://tyndall.ac.uk/sites/default/files/radicalplanabstracts_0.pdf.
Weintrobe, Sally. "The Difficult Problem of Anxiety in Thinking about Climate Change." *Engaging with Climate Change*, edited by Sally Weintrobe. Routledge, 2013, pp. 33–47.
———. "Introduction." *Engaging with Climate Change*, edited by Sally Weintrobe. Routledge, 2013, pp. 1–15.

"What We Do." *Climate Psychology Alliance*. www.climatepsychologyalliance.org/about/what-we-do.
Winnicott, D. W. *Playing and Reality*. Routledge, 1971.
———. *Psychoanalytic Explorations*. Harvard UP, 1989.
Wood, David. "On Being Haunted by the Future." *Research in Phenomenology*, vol. 36, no. 1, 2006, pp. 274–98.
Žižek, Slavoj. *Violence: Six Sideways Reflections*. Picador, 2008.

Chapter 2

What we don't talk about when we talk about global warming

Eugene Linden writes that when we consider what "droughts that last for more than a century, an advance of arctic zones southward, [and] incessant and epic storms" will mean for a "a world of 6 billion people depending on an exquisitely balanced food system," it "simply overwhelm[s] the imagination" (268–69). And if the imagination's capacity to grapple with such catastrophe might seem more than a "simple" matter, it's certainly the case that even those most attuned to the urgency of the present dilemma often disarticulate their not-knowing from their attempts to address fundamental questions about it. Straining for an orientating fixity in defining an overall tipping point, for example, in 2012 Bill McKibben describes the widely and officially accepted limit of 2 degrees C, confirmed in the 2009 Copenhagen Accord, as "the bottomest of bottom lines" ("New Math")—the degree of planetary heating (above the preindustrial level) that the 167 countries signing the 2009 Copenhagen Accord, agreed should not be crossed. Even as he introduces this bottomest line, however, McKibben observes that "many scientists have come to think … two degrees is far too lenient a target," that James Hansen, for example, has defined that target as a "recipe for disaster," and that some Copenhagen delegates saw two-degrees as "a 'suicide pact' for drought-stricken Africa." Establishing a "bottomest" line, McKibben thus abandons it forthwith—but then abandons that abandonment, proceeding to present "global warming's terrifying new math" as if the ostensibly solid ground of 2 degrees C on which he stands hadn't already given way.[1]

Descriptions of the geophysical consequences of global warming exceeding 2 degrees C also often betray a straining for fixity. "In 2013, researchers with the World Bank took a look at the science on projected effects of 4 degrees C warming," Brad Plummer writes, and while they "were appalled at what they found … what seemed to unnerve them most was all of the stuff we *don't* know," since "impacts may interact with each other in unpredictable ways."[2] But if, as Linden acknowledges, the *meaning* of those geophysical consequences "overwhelms the imagination," it hasn't for the most part seemed to overwhelm the way the stakes of the climate crisis have often been generally represented.³ In McKibben's "New Math," for instance, he refers to an "essentially impossible future" and a threat "to the survival of our planetary civilization"; he warns "the planet will crater," and quotes other warnings of "long-term disaster," of energy companies "wrecking" or "destroying the planet." Such confident and pithy formulations, typical of attempts to rivet attention on the dire stakes of present actions, cannot withstand the scrutiny they seem meant to provoke. An "impossible future" refers to a future that cannot happen—exactly the opposite of what it seems to want to mean; if, to the extent there is a single "planetary civilization," and if it has generated the very self-obliterating forces by which it is so violently threatened, is the value of its "survival" (as opposed to its transformation, or the survival of its people) self-evident? (Similarly, when Kevin Anderson elsewhere describes a 4-degree warmer world as "incompatible with any reasonable characterization of an organized, equitable and civilized global community" [qtd. in Klein, 13], we might reasonably wonder how such a world would differ from our own.) A "long-term disaster" cannot seem a matter of more urgency than any of the many disasters, many of them unfolding over many years and with no end in sight, that constitute our daily news. And, again, since Earth will likely exist in some form or another for, say, another five billion years or so, warnings about destroying or wrecking or cratering the "planet"—as with "civilization"—substitute drastically imprecise terms for ones that might do more adequate justice to even what we do know

As attempts to articulate the stakes of the climate crisis, such representations exemplify the generalized disarticulation of one kind of not-knowing—a not-knowing about the future. But, more crucially, the culturally prevailing climate discourses also disarticulate how the prospects of that future shake the dominant premises by which we know the present.⁴ If the "crisis" concerns the geophysical conditions of the planet, that is, it also thereby constitutes a traumatic challenge to the dominant economic, political, and ideological businesses as usual, and, thus, to the fundamental ways that those whose subjectivities have been shaped by those businesses know who they are. I've suggested this in Chapter 1 but would like now to more fully elaborate the nature of that challenge.

Such an understanding of the crisis derives from an important, though of course severely marginalized, strain of climate discourse, one that locates the crisis in relation to the normalized practices of European modernity. In some accounts, these practices have ushered in what in the academy is increasingly referred to as the Anthropocene—a new geological period, supplanting the Holocene, designating an Earth that has been changed in fundamental ways (recorded in the fossil record) by humans.⁵ But rather than presenting an indictment of the practices that have brought to an end that period of relative climate stability (a condition of possibility for the emergence of "civilization"), that term has increasingly served to valorize those very practices. "There is already an official narrative of the Anthropocene," Christophe Bonneuil and Jean-Baptiste Fressoz observe:

> "We," the human species, unconsciously destroyed nature to the point of hijacking the Earth system into a new geological epoch. In the late 20th century, a handful of Earth system scientists finally opened our eyes. So now we know; now we are aware of the global consequences of human action.
>
> (xii)

In *The Shock of the Anthropocene*, Bonneuil and Fressoz elaborate the ways that "this story of awakening is a fable. The opposition between a blind past and a clear-sighted present, besides being historically false, depoliticizes the long history of the Anthropocene" and, "in its managerial variant, the moral of the official account consists of giving the engineers of the Earth system the keys to 'Spaceship Earth'" (xiii). Their book attempts to "deconstruct ... the official account in its managerial and non-conflictual variants," the sort epitomized in the Breakthrough Institute's Ecomodernist Manifesto, which calls for the using of "humanity's extraordinary powers in service of creating a Good Anthropocene" (John Asafu-Adjaye et al.).[6] Elaborating such critique, Jason Moore writes: "Questions of capitalism, power and class, anthropocentrism, dualist framings of 'nature' and 'society,' and the role of states and empires—all are frequently bracketed by the dominant Anthropocene perspective" (5). In his *Anthropocene or Capitalocene?* Moore curates several challenges to that dominant perspective, each considering alternate namings, but, as that title suggests, perhaps the predominant alternative designation is "Capitalocene." Though the "Capitalocene" names just one of Bonneuil and Fressoz's seven alternative histories of the Anthropocene ("Thermocene," "Thanotocene," etc.), they all reflect the conclusion that "the change in geological regime is the act of the 'age of capital' (Eric Hobsbawn), rather than simply the 'age of man' as the dominant narratives claim" (222).[7]

When, in observing that the climate crisis poses "challenges to existing systems of knowledge," Leigh Glover argues that it reveals itself as "a problem of modernity itself" (3), it's thus most helpful to hear this as referring to "the concept of modernity as commonly used," as Ellen Meiksins Wood puts it, which "takes capitalism for granted as the outcome" (542). As it enshrines a commitment to infinite economic growth as the expression of abstract and purely "rational" knowledge at the center of post-Enlightenment cultural self-understandings (at the center of business as usual in all its permutations), this version of modernity, premised on industrial capitalism, defines (male European) humans as exceptional, as entirely detached from an entirely knowable and masterable "nature," or from "the environment" it can therefore manipulate without unintended consequence.

Such fantastical thinking, insisting on itself as purely "rational," has produced the "existential crisis for the human species" (15) Naomi Klein addresses in her starkly titled *This Changes Everything: Capitalism vs. The Climate*, in which she traces the problem to "core civilizational myths on which post-Enlightenment Western culture is founded—myths about humanity's duty to dominate a natural world that is believed to be at once limitless and entirely controllable" (159), fantasies inflicted on the real world by the industrial development of fossil fuel. Klein stresses the recent extreme enactment of such myths in the neoliberal "fetish[izing] of GDP growth" (87) and of "free" markets dating from 1988, "the exact year," as "bad timing" would have it, that "governments and scientists began talking seriously about radical cuts to greenhouse gas emissions" (18).[8] In this account, the subsequent normalization of neoliberal extremism has produced a present in which there is no non-radical option:

> our economy is at war with many forms of life on earth, including human life. What the climate needs to avoid collapse is a contraction in humanity's use of resources; what our economic model demands to avoid collapse is unfettered expansion. Only one of these sets of rules can be changed, and it's not the laws of nature.[9]
>
> (21)

Offering an important complement to Klein's indictment, Amitav Ghosh acknowledges that "Klein and others are right to identify capitalism as one of the principal drivers of climate change" but adds that "this narrative often overlooks an aspect ... that is of equal importance: empire and imperialism" (87). In this account, a fuller understanding of the nature of the climate crisis involves not only examining the particular economic model that demands the unlimited burning of fossil fuel, but also how that particular model, emerging, as Wood emphasizes, out of the very particular set of historical conditions pertaining in eighteenth-century England, became the dominant model globally.[10] The historically specific formation that was industrial capitalism claimed modernity for itself, Wood contends, a purportedly universalized modernity that in turn "treat[ed] specifically capitalist laws of motion as if they were the universal laws of history" (542), a "conflation of capitalism with modernity [that] has had the effect of disguising the specificity of capitalism, if not conceptualizing it away altogether," even as that conflation "may disguise the specificity of modernity too" (543). Contesting that conflation, Ghosh writes that modernity arose not in Europe only, from where, as the dominant narrative would have it, it spread naturally throughout the world, but "was rather a 'global and conjunctural phenomenon,' with many iterations arising almost simultaneously in different parts of the world" (95). Of course, as Ghosh elaborates, a crucial aspect of the contemporary crisis is indeed the ultimate global dominance of a carbon-intensive, Western modernity. In this account, that dominance reflects not the status of the universal law of history that Western modernity claims for itself but, rather, the "empire and imperialism" Ghosh offers as the necessary complement to arguments (like Klein's) that focus on capitalism per se. "What determined the shape of the global carbon economy," he suggests,

> was that the major European powers had already established a strong (but by no means hegemonic) military and political presence in much of Asia and Africa at the time when steam was in its nascency. ... From that point on, carbon-intensive technologies were to have the effect of continually reinforcing Western power with the result that other variants of modernity came to be suppressed, incorporated, and appropriated into what is now a single, dominant model.
> (108)

Such understandings of the climate crisis are premised on the notion that the economic model of industrial capitalism, conflated with that now globalized "single, dominant model" of modernity, operates by definition as a carbon economy. And the fullest account of how the climate crisis derives from that economic model is offered in Andreas Malm's *Fossil Capital: The Rise of Steam Power and the Roots of Global Warming* (2016). For Malm, it is not merely that that model, industrial capitalism, "demands unfettered expansion," but also that industrial capitalism by its very nature demands that that expansion be powered by fossil fuel. What in the "lexicon of climate politics" is often called "'business-as-usual,'" he suggests, is synonymous with "the fossil economy," defined as "an economy of self-sustaining growth predicated on the growing consumption of fossil fuels, and therefore generating a sustained growth in emissions of carbon dioxide," which is "the main driver of global warming" (11). Because this fossil economy "first appeared in the Industrial Revolution," Malm closely examines how it was that industrial capitalism, as it arose and developed particularly in "the British cotton industry—the fast lane of the industrial revolution, in which self-sustaining growth first appeared" (17)—came to rely primarily on steam power, generated by the burning of coal. Contesting "the storyline that has dominated much of the historiography of the Industrial Revolution and the rise of steam power in particular" (35)—the story, grounded in Ricardo and Malthus, that an ostensibly natural human development toward industrial capitalist production was bottlenecked by an energy scarcity then relieved by the unleashing of the power of fossil fuels enabled by the invention of the steam engine, Marx's formulation of which is "'steam begets capital'" (qtd. on 35)—Malm stresses that "the factory system, from which commodities were churned out in unprecedented quantities, arose" *not on the basis of coal* but "on the basis of water" (47). Nonetheless, by the 1830s, the cotton industry had become committed to steam power, produced by burning coal. And this was *"in spite of water being abundant, cheaper, and at least as powerful, even and efficient"* (93). What "cries out for an explanation," then, isn't only why steam ultimately supplanted water, but *"why steam power was adopted at all"* (56).

Centered on that question, Malm's book argues that coal came to prevail over water because it was a superior source not of mechanical power but of *other kinds of power*, the valuing of which was inherent in the logic of industrial capitalism: power over labor, power over nature, and power over competitors for the production of commodities to be sold in the marketplace.[11] Though the British cotton industry originated in river valleys, for a variety of reasons, including the economic crisis of the 1820s, it developed that locating factories in cities—where labor was plentiful and largely, for that reason, weak—increasingly maximized owners' power over workers, and thus, Malm observes, the steam engine "was a superior medium for extracting surplus wealth from the working class, because, unlike the waterwheel, it could be put up anywhere" (124).[12] It was the mobility of fossil fuel, that is, that enabled the mobility of capital in its original pursuit of cheaper, weaker, and thus more compliant labor (a pursuit today driving neoliberal globalization). As it increased social power (over workers), the coal-fired steam engine also freed industrial production from the seasonal rhythms and daily vicissitudes of the river, augmenting what mill owners understood as another increase in non-mechanical power, their power relative to nature. "The British bourgeoisie could not stand the flow" of the river, Malm writes, because the flow "possessed an *autonomous mechanical power*, conforming to the laws written by her [sic] own sovereign nature, over which the masters could exert no stable control" (213). Indeed, the autonomous power of the flow itself paralleled the power of labor:

> workers might go on strike and water freeze; workers might depart in a restless and migratory spirit and water run faster in faraway hills; workers might refuse orders and water dry out; workers could embezzle materials and water flood premises.

As the mill owners saw it, such autonomy could be overcome by the turn to coal-fired steam power, which freed them not only from the spatial constraints of having to operate near flowing water, thus weakening labor power, but also from the temporal constraints imposed by the vagaries of that flow: just as it could be burnt any place, coal could be burnt any time—or, ideally, all the time.

In exploring why steam represented an enhancement not of mechanical but of non-mechanical power, Malm's arguments about increased power relative to labor and relative to nature are elaborated more fully than his argument about how it augmented an individual mill owner's feeling of autonomy in relation to his competitors. And yet, in an important way, the prospect of that autonomy can be understood as having represented perhaps coal's strongest claim. If water power could be made sufficiently mobile, it would be possible to locate factories in cities, far from rivers but near plentiful labor; and if it could be made more dependable, it could be deployed at any time. If the spatial and temporal constraints were obviated, that is, water power could offer the same increased power over labor and nature as coal (while remaining cheaper). And, indeed, in Malm's account, focused largely on the projects of Robert Thom, this was possible: "With aqueducts meandering through the landscape, coiling around hills and descending almost imperceptibly along plains, mills could be served from a distant source; reservoirs and self-acting sluices abrogated all irregularities" (102). Such projects, however, would have involved collective planning and funding, and also sharing and cooperatively managing a collectivized power source. And although "history is replete with successful management of common water resources, including for mills" (292), such sharing of power fundamentally clashed both with the competitive logic of emergent market capitalism, by which each owner was pitted against each, and with its fetishization of private property. In coal, on the other hand, "the private property of cotton manufacturers found a source of energy congenial to its logic: piecemeal, splintered, amenable to concentration and accumulation, divisible" (119). As a result, "hydraulic engineering for commodity production was nipped in the bud" (114), and thus the "birth of the fossil economy" involved "inverting the 'tragedy of the commons': here the commons were harvested *below* their capacity because of the irrationality of the private-property maximizers who, rather than uniting in promising reservoir schemes, took flight in the isolation of coal" (298). In short, "the anarchy of capital had to become fossil."

If Malm's is the fullest articulation of how the climate crisis is rooted in the nature of business as usual, the most prominent expression of that vision has perhaps been that of Pope Francis, in *Laudato Si'* (2015). Defining the climate crisis as a "crisis in modernity" itself—in the globalizing iteration of modernity, that is, that Wood argues was early on appropriated by the logics of industrial capitalism—Francis locates the urgent threat to our planetary "common home" in "a certain way of understanding human life," the culturally dominant "technocratic paradigm" according to which "reality, goodness and truth automatically flow from technological and economic power as such," a paradigm premised on the irrational fantasy of a self-sufficient, individual "subject who, using logical and rational procedures ... gains control over an external object." Driven by the corresponding fantastical investment in "the idea of infinite or unlimited [economic] growth ... based on the lie that there is an infinite supply of earth's goods," such a cultural paradigm produces the so-called ecological crisis that, comprising a "crisis in modernity," constitutes an existential challenge to business as usual.

As the response to *Laudato Si'* suggests, however, as the prospects have grown increasingly apocalyptic, such understandings of the climate crisis as rooted in the logics of modernity grow increasingly marginalized, the dominant discourses working to render those understandings increasingly illegible, irrelevant, or "unrealistic." Reviewing the Pope's encyclical, McKibben observes that "any serious effort to alter or even critique the largest trends in our civilization is now scorned" by self-appointed spokesmen for the so-called "real world"; he pairs David Brooks's condescending dismissal of "1970s-style doom-mongering about technological civilization" with *n+1* editor Mark Greif's dismissive instruction that "any time your inquiries lead you to say, 'At this moment we must ask and decide *who we fundamentally are* ...' just stop" ("The Pope").

But "scorn" is a relatively minor concern in relation to the much more pervasive forms of denial. When it appeared, for the most part the Pope's encyclical was widely praised, but such lip service hardly meant that its urgent framing of the crisis, or its call for radical and swift cuts in greenhouse gas emissions, informed the agenda of the December 2015 Paris Climate Change Conference a few months later—the outcome of which, as the Paris Agreement, has become the rallying point for those indignantly decrying Trumpist denialism. Indeed, "in the text of the Paris Agreement," Ghosh writes,

> there is not the slightest acknowledgment that something has gone wrong with our dominant paradigms; it contains no clause or article that could be interpreted as a critique of the practices that are known to have created the situation that the Agreement seeks to address. The current paradigm of perpetual growth is enshrined at the core of the text.
>
> (154)

And even if, beggaring the imagination, all the agreement's voluntary national targets for limiting greenhouse gas emissions were met, it would mean storming past the ostensibly acceptable 2-degree C limit, likely guaranteeing (catastrophic) heating of 2.7 to 3.5 C (Adler)—even as the accord schizophrenically notes the importance of *lowering* the 2-degree target to 1.5 degrees.[13]

Rooted in the logics of modernity that Pope Francis defines as the crux of the crisis itself, the world of policy and politics out of which the Paris Agreement emerges can praise his words but in that world their meaning cannot matter. In this, again, the Agreement stands as an especially stark instance of the ways that, as prospects have grown more dire, the dominant discourses have rendered understandings like the Pope's increasingly remote. Al Gore might belatedly let slip that "the climate crisis is posing an unprecedented threat not only to the future livability of the planet but also to our assumptions about the ability of democracy and capitalism to recognize the threat for what it is and respond with appropriate boldness" (309), but he can do so only well after *An Inconvenient Truth*, as I argue in the next chapter, so powerfully helped construct "global warming" in the public sphere as a problem to which economic growth (and the American can-do spirit) was the solution. "The nature of the public debate," as Clive Hamilton described it in 2010, is thus "no longer about the institutions that perpetuate and reinforce environmental degradation; it's about our personal behavior" (80). Elaborating what he calls "late modern society's adamant resolve to sustain what is known to be unsustainable" ("Sustaining" 272), Ingolfur Bluhdorn has argued that the dominant ways of understanding climate change have "keenly avoided touching upon the core values and principles underpinning capitalist consumer democracies" ("Locked"); where an "earlier critique ... of industrial society and consumer capitalism" once prevailed among political ecologists, he observes, "since the mid-1980s, environmental politics has incrementally come to be dominated by a policy paradigm ... of sustainability, ecological modernisation ... [and] 'ecological industrial politics'" whose "aim first and foremost" isn't to drastically reduce global warming but

> to spur technological innovation, increase consumer demand, create new jobs, open up new export markets, enhance the international competitiveness of national economies and so forth. In other words, they reframe global warming and the environmental crisis as an opportunity, a tool, for a new round of innovation and growth.

In short, as Timothy Clark puts it, "'ecological modernization' has sought to normalize and internalize environmental issues into the workings of industrial capitalism" ("Ironies" 133).[14]

In a public sphere constituted largely by its dedication to such normalization, most of the ways global warming is constructed function as a kind of butchery, disarticulating its traumatic meaning. The following chapter closely examines several instances of how such butchery operates.

Notes

1 Indeed, given the unpredictability of the innumerable, complex processes involved, defining any particular degree of increased warming as a tipping point is really only defining what degree of risk is called acceptable; as Klein frames it, the "well-known target" of two degrees, "which supposedly represents a 'safe' limit of climate change ... has more to do with minimizing economic disruption than with

protecting the greatest number of people" (12). Klein lists several examples of "critical scholarship on the history and politics of the 2-degree target" (468n14); see also the commentaries collected at Andrew Revkin's "Dot Earth" *NY Times* blog, October 3, 2014, "Getting Beyond the 2-Degree Threshold on Global Warming" (updated October 6), and Brad Plummer's "Two Degrees." Of course, the 2015 Paris Agreement lowers the goal to 1.5 degrees—even as it incoherently sets voluntary "limits" on greenhouse gas emissions that, in the unlikely event they were observed, would mean a warming of at least twice that amount. And in 2018, the IPCC adopted that 1.5-degree figure.

2 Of course, the discourse of uncertainty can itself obscure the direness of what is in fact actually relatively certain. Critiquing "the focus of the scientific community on near-term climate changes and their uncertainties"—deriving partly from "the scientific emphasis on the expected climate changes by 2100, which was originally driven by past computational capabilities"—Peter Clark et al. find that "many key features of future climate change are relatively certain in the long term, even if the precise timing of their occurrence is uncertain." Similarly, David Wood warns that focusing on "the unpredictable" ought not to displace attention to the failure to "deal with the predictable" or to minimize the importance of "do[ing] the calculations" (275).

3 See Klein 468–69n17 for "general overviews synthesizing research on the likely impacts of a 4 degrees C world." For a recent example of how warnings about the future often fail to account for the unpredictability of the way various impacts will affect each other, see Phil McKenna's "Coastal Real Estate Worth Billions at Risk of Chronic Flooding as Sea Level Rises," where the discussion of how future flooding will impact the coastal real estate market proceeds as if such flooding would be the only effect of a rapidly heating planet.

4 This has been true not only for the most alarmed scientists like Hansen but also for some prominent instances of climate activism, as I suggest in "The Importance of Rescuing the Frog" and "Reflections on the People's Climate March."

5 See Christophe Bonneuil and Jean-Baptiste Fressoz, 3–18, for one account of the science underlying the concept of the Anthropocene and of Paul Crutzen's influential use of the term, in 2000.

6 Similarly, Eileen Crist points out that "in a 2011 special issue on the Anthropocene, *The Economist* ... highlights that what we need in the Age of Man is a 'smart planet'" ("On the Poverty of Our Nomenclature" 19)—a view more widely distributed since then, I'd suggest, in IBM's advertising slogan: "Building a Smarter Planet."

7 In what follows, I focus largely on the emergence of industrial capitalism in the late eighteenth century, though the Capitalocene can be located as becoming dominant earlier than that. Donna Haraway writes that "the infectious industrial revolution of England mattered hugely, but it is only one player in the planet-transforming, historically situated, new enough, worlding relations" (51). Jason Moore argues that "the emphasis on the Industrial Revolution as the origin of modernity" and "Green Thought's love affair with the Industrial Revolution [have] undermined efforts to locate the origins of today's crises in the epoch-making transformations of capital, power, and nature" over "the three centuries after 1450" (7). No matter when the Capitalocene itself is said to begin, however, in the history of global warming the industrial revolution in English remains crucial—the sharp rise in atmospheric carbon from the 270ppm of the Holocene to (as of this writing) the current 415ppm beginning at just this period, with the turn toward burning coal to power factories.

8   As Nixon observes, the escalating eco-catastrophe ushered in by the unleashing of neoliberalism has also been aligned with exploding economic inequality ("The Great Acceleration and the Great Divergence"). He stresses that "since 1751 ... a mere ninety corporations, primarily oil and coal companies, have generated two-thirds of humanity's CO_2 emissions." (This claim is grounded in a study by Richard Heede.)
9   Klein's argument is a recent version of one long familiar in certain discourses even further removed than hers from the mediasphere that increasingly defines what "we" know. In 2007, for example, from a perspective of Deep Ecology, Eileen Crist defined the "*real* problem" as "the industrial-consumer complex that is overhauling the world in an orgy of exploitation, overproduction, and waste" ("Beyond" 55).
10 Bonneuil and Fressoz elaborate how "without the [British] empire, the industrial revolution would have been physically impossible" (234), and how "Great Britain projected fossil capitalism onto the whole world" (238), and thus "overturned the ecologies of the periphery" (234).
11 Again, we can turn to Ghosh's more globalized view to add military and colonial power to this list: "carbon-intensive technologies were to have the effect of continually reinforcing Western power" (108) in Asia and Africa.
12 In Britain, this was true at least to the extent that schemes for the transport of water power over long distances were themselves rejected, for reasons discussed below.
13 As Kevin Anderson explains, the possibility of meeting even the Agreement's own disastrous targets for emissions reductions depends upon the almost immediate development of massive "industrial scale negative emission technologies" that don't exist and, though they go unmentioned in the text, reflect the techno-utopian premises of which the Agreement is a desperate expression ("The Hidden Agenda").
14 As one result, as ecocatastrophic collapse has grown increasingly likely—and as evidence of that likelihood has amassed—even the dominant so-called "environmental" organizations have worked hard to normalize "global warming" as a political "issue" narrowly defined, a development elaborated in Klein's "Fruits, Not Roots: The Disastrous Merger of Big Business and Big Green" (*Changes* Chapter 6).

References

Adler, Ben. "Here's What You Need to Know about the New Paris Climate Agreement." *Grist*, 12 December 2015, https://grist.org/climate-energy/heres-what-you-need-to-know-about-the-new-paris-climate-agreement/.

Anderson, Kevin. "The Hidden Agenda: How Veiled Techno-Utopias Shore up the Paris Agreement." *Kevinanderson.info*, 6 January 2016, www.kevinanderson.info/blog/the-hidden-agenda-how-veiled-techno-utopias-shore-up-the-paris-agreement/.

Asafu-Adjaye, J., et al. "An Ecomodernist Manifesto." April 2015, www.ecomodernism.org/.

Bluhdorn, Ingolfur. "Sustaining the Unsustainable: Symbolic Politics and the Politics of Simulation." *Environmental Politics*, vol. 16, no. 2, 2007, pp. 251–75.

———. "Locked into the Politics of Unsustainability." *Eurozine*, 30 October 2009, www.eurozine.com/locked-into-the-politics-of-unsustainability/.

Bonneuil, Christophe, and Jean-Baptiste Fressoz. *The Shock of the Anthropocene.* Verso, 2015.

Clampitt, Amy. *The Collected Poems of Amy Clampitt.* Knopf, 1997.

Clark, Peter U., et al. "Consequences of Twenty-First-Century Policy for Multi-Millennial Climate and Sea-Level Change." *Nature Climate Change,* vol. 6, no. 4, February 2016, pp. 360–69.

Clark, Timothy. "Some Climate Change Ironies: Deconstruction, Environmental Politics and the Closure of Ecocriticism." *Oxford Literary Review,* vol. 32, no. 1, 2010, pp. 131–49.

Crist, Eileen. "Beyond the Climate Crisis: A Critique of Climate Change Discourse." *Telos,* vol. 141, Winter 2007, pp. 29–55.

———. "On the Poverty of Our Nomenclature." *Anthropocene or Capitalocene? Nature, History, and the Crisis of Capitalism,* edited by Jason Moore. PM Press, 2016, pp. 14–33.

Francis, Pope. *Laudato Si': On Care for Our Common Home.* 2015, http://w2.vatican.va/content/francesco/en/encyclicals/documents/papa-francesco_20150524_enciclica-laudato-si.html.

Ghosh, Amitav. *The Great Derangement: Climate Change and the Unthinkable.* U of Chicago P, 2016.

Glover, Leigh. *Postmodern Climate Change.* Routledge, 2006.

Gore, Al. *Our Choice: A Plan to Solve the Climate Crisis.* Rodale, 2009.

Hamilton, Clive. *Requiem for a Species.* Earthscan, 2010.

Haraway, Donna. "Staying with the Trouble: Anthropocene, Capitalocene, Chtulucene." *Anthropocene or Capitalocene? Nature, History, and the Crisis of Capitalism,* edited by Jason Moore. PM Press, 2016, pp. 34–76.

Heede, Richard. "Tracing Anthropogenic Carbon Dioxide and Methane Emissions to Fossil Fuel and Cement producers, 1854–2010." *Climatic Change,* vol. 122, no. 1–2, January 2014, pp. 229–41, https://link.springer.com/article/10.1007/s10584-013-0986-y.

Klein, Naomi. *This Changes Everything: Capitalism vs. The Climate.* Simon & Schuster, 2014.

Linden, Eugene. *The Winds of Change: Climate, Weather, and the Destruction of Civilization.* Simon & Schuster, 2006.

Malm, Andreas. *Fossil Capital: The Rise of Steam Power and the Roots of Global Warming.* Verso, 2016.

McKenna, Phil. "Coastal Real Estate Worth Billions at Risk of Chronic Flooding as Sea Level Rises." *Inside Climate News,* 18 June 2018, www.insideclimatenews.org/news/18062018/climate-change-coastal-flooding-zillow-real-estate-data-sea-level-rise-homes-businesses-union-concerned-scientists.

McKibben, Bill. "Global Warming's Terrifying New Math." *Rolling Stone,* 19 July 2012, www.rollingstone.com/politics/politics-news/global-warmings-terrifying-new-math-188550/.

———. "The Pope and the Planet." *The New York Review of Books,* 13 August 2015, www.nybooks.com/articles/2015/08/13/pope-and-planet/.

Moore, Jason. "Introduction." *Anthropocene or Capitalocene? Nature, History, and the Crisis of Capitalism,* edited by Jason Moore. PM Press, 2016, pp. 1–11.

Nixon, Rob. "The Great Acceleration and the Great Divergence: Vulnerability in the Anthropocene." *Profession*, March 2014, https://profession.mla.org/the-great-acceleration-and-the-great-divergence-vulnerability-in-the-anthropocene/.
Plummer, Brad. "Two Degrees." *Vox*, 22 April 2014, www.vox.com/2014/4/22/5551004/two-degrees.
Revkin, Andrew. "Getting beyond the 2-Degree Threshold on Global Warming." *New York Times*, 3 October 2014, www.dotearth.blogs.nytimes.com/2014/10/03/getting-over-the-2-degree-limit-on-global-warming/.
Wood, David. "On Being Haunted by the Future." *Research in Phenomenology*, vol. 36, no. 1, 2006, pp. 274–98.
Wood, Ellen Meiksins. "Modernity, Postmodernity or Capitalism?" *Review of International Political Economy*, vol. 4, no. 3, Autumn 1997, pp. 539–60.
Zimmerman, Lee. "Reflections on the People's Climate March." *English@Hofstra*, 1 January 2015, www.hofstraenglish.wordpress.com/2015/01/01/lee-zimmermans-reflections-on-the-peoples-climate-march/.
———. "The Importance of Rescuing the Frog: What We Don't Talk about When We Talk about the Climate Crisis." *Post45*. post45.research.yale.edu/2012/10/the-importance-of-rescuing-the-frog-what-we-don%E2%80%99t-talk-about-when-we-talk-about-the-climate-crisis/.

Chapter 3

Butcheries

If, in disarticulating its traumatic meaning, the dominant discourses of climate change help construct a pervasive denialism—and if we again recall that "disarticulation" refers to the separation of bones at the joint, as in butchery—then one crucial mechanism of this denialistic butchery is their framing of the question of "denial" itself. Overt denialism (or "skepticism") of the sort manufactured by the energy industry, and for years operating at the centers of American political power, has of course helped construct global warming as a "debate," or, more recently a politically motivated "hoax," rather than an emergency.[1] But as importantly, it has functioned as a scapegoat, a diversion from how a more pervasive cultural denial, purporting to accept climate change as "real," has been produced across a broad range of centrist discourses.[2] Calling attention to extremist denialism, that is, is a chief way the "responsible" center pretends to align itself with the rationality of science, even as, in its fetishistic identification with the growth paradigm, it fuels the ecocidal status quo—enacting not a partisan conflict but a fundamental political consensus.[3] Indeed, as Naomi Klein argues, even as those she calls the "deniers" certainly deny climate science itself, they seem more attuned than their "realistic" critics to the way taking the science seriously constitutes a threat to that ideological consensus:

> When it comes to the real-world consequences of those scientific findings, specifically the kind of deep changes required not just to our energy consumption but to the underlying logic of our economic system, the crowd gathered at the [denialist Heartland Institute Conference] may be in considerably less denial than a lot of professional environmentalists, the ones who paint a picture of global warming Armageddon, then assure us that we can avert catastrophe by buying "green" products and creating clever markets in pollution.
>
> ("Capitalism")

Similarly, responding to Pope Francis's *Laudato Si'* and related speeches, Wen Stephenson at the time wrote:

In effect, Francis has called Hillary's (and the rest of the mainstream Democrats') bluff. While Democrats, and others on the left, continue to pat themselves on the back for not being climate-change deniers, they avoid the radical implications of what the science is telling us— including the need to rethink capitalism and redefine economic growth. ... But Francis is saying to them: If you're serious about economic and social justice, as you claim to be, then you need to be serious about our impending climate catastrophe. And to be serious about these things, at this late date, means being as radical as he is. Because the time for anything less has long since passed.

***

Since Trump, the sport of Blaming Skeptics has been more or less the only game in the "Global Warming Is Real" town.[4] But, as Stephenson's remark indicates, such scapegoating operated as a mainstay of ostensibly "green" discourse during the Obama years as well. A paradigmatic case of how centrist denialism, especially that of "thought leaders," structures itself around such scapegoating is the *New York Times*'s 2014 editorial response to reports that year by the IPCC and the American Association for the Advancement of Science. "Perhaps now the deniers will cease their attacks on the science of climate change," it begins, as if the main cause of insufficient action thus far were the rejection of science by "the deniers" ("Climate Signals"). Radiating sober rationality, the editors seem to acknowledge the severity and urgency of the problem, stressing that the reports "declared that the world is already feeling the effects of global warming, that the ultimate consequences could be catastrophic, and that the window of effective action is swiftly closing." But in then turning to "effective action," the editorial starts babbling in the sort of "schizophrenic" discourse described by Solnit, focusing on "President Obama's efforts to use his executive authority to limit greenhouse gases" by means of his "Climate Action Plan." It's not only that that Plan was farcically inadequate in relation to the size or urgency of the problem. It's also that, whatever political cover the Plan might have offered the president, it didn't fundamentally alter the administration's original commitment to an *increase* in fossil fuel production.[5] In what Noam Chomsky—not writing in the *Times*—calls "an eloquent death-knell for the species," in 2012 Obama proudly reported

> under my administration, America is producing more oil today than at any time in the last eight years. That's important to know. Over the last three years, I've directed my administration to open up millions of acres for gas and oil exploration across 23 different states. We're opening up more than 75 percent of our potential oil resources offshore.

> We've quadrupled the number of operating rigs to a record high. We've added enough new oil and gas pipeline to encircle the Earth and then some.[6]
>
> ("American-Made Energy")

The editorial writers of the *Times* must have known this history, but—as for the overt denialists—the facts cannot matter. Identified with the fundamental structures of economic and political business as usual, the editorial poses the problem as "the deniers" who "attack the science of climate change," even as, in doing so, it performs its own, publicly unrecognized, denial—not as a direct "attack" on the science per se but as a violent disarticulation of its most troubling meanings.

The *Times*'s editorial response to Obama's 2015 "Clean Power Plan" repeats this butchering. Once again, the Plan itself simply ignores the (too high but nonetheless formally agreed upon) 2-degree C limit. It keeps us "on track for more like four degrees warming," as Klein notes:

> if we were to stay below two degrees, we would need to be cutting emissions by around 8 to 10 percent a year. ... And [Obama's] plan would lower emissions in the United States by around 6 percent over all ... by 2030. So compare what we should be doing—8 to 10 percent a year—with 6 percent by 2030.
>
> ("Obama Is Beginning")

Nor does the Clean Power Plan compromise what Chomsky highlighted as Obama's dogged commitment to *increased* production of fossil fuel. Even as, in support of his Plan, Obama announced he will "be the first American president to visit the Alaskan Arctic," where he'll "talk about what the world needs to do together to prevent the worst impacts of climate change before it's too late" (qtd. in Klein, "Obama"), Shell Oil had rigs in Arctic waters Obama had opened up for drilling.[7] The fact of the Plan's utter insufficiency—like his administration's proud assertion that "America is producing more oil today than at any time in the last eight years"—could not, however, trouble the *Times* editorial board's enthusiasm for what it calls a "Tough, Achievable Climate Plan" ("President Obama's Tough"). Rather than examining it in relation to what might prevent the worst-case, but likely, eco-catastrophic scenarios, the board summarized the Plan as a way of responding to "the plan's opponents in industry, the states, and Congress," who "are already gathering forces to try to undermine it"— again, establishing its own ostensible reasonableness by positioning itself against the extremists on the right, who think the Plan will "irreparably damage the economy." "The truth" about the Plan, it concluded, "is this: There is nothing radical about it." Offering this accurate assessment as reassuring praise rather than crushing indictment, the *Times* obscures the crisis of the present moment, brandishing centrality as if we could still somehow choose a non-radical future.[8]

In important ways, it has been the journalistic framings of "climate change" or "global warming"—especially by "thought leaders" like the *Times*—that have enabled overt denialism to perform such an important role in normalizing the more pervasive "rational" denialism. Throughout its history in the media "global warming" has been located mostly in relation to a simple binary: is it real, or, more recently, is it caused by humans? In opposing the science-defying denialists who say "no," "moderate" voices like the *Times* align themselves with "yes," begging crucial questions about the radial implications of the science they purport to affirm. Partly, this reflects the rhetorics of "balance," "dramatization," and "personalization" that (along with "authority, order," and "novelty") Maxwell Boykoff sees as the "journalistic norms" that "shape what become 'climate stories'" (100) in the dominant media, such that, in "discussing the spectrum of possible mitigation," these stories remain limited to "dominant market-based and utilitarian approaches" (117)—to inscribing those "stories," that is, into economic business as usual. As one result, Eugene Linden argues, "the story presented to the general public has diverged ever more markedly from the story as it is seen by the scientists studying the phenomenon" (220). More pointedly, Ross Gelbspan writes that "if ... the oil and coal industries are criminals against humanity" by virtue of their massive propaganda campaign, then "the U.S. press has basically played the role of unwitting accomplice" (67).[9]

***

To this indictment of the fossil fuel industry and the media, however, I suggest we might add a range of other culturally dominant institutional discourses. Mike Hulme's *Why We Disagree about Climate Change* articulates something of that range, examining "the idea of climate change from seven different standpoints" or "lenses"—"science, economics, religion, psychology, media, development and governance" (xxxv). Crucially, however, the range of ways such discourses obscure the existential threat represented by climate change is typified by Hulme's work itself. Where what's at stake in such various framings is for Timothy Clark the "trauma" of the way the "happening" of global warming "deconstructs" them, for Hulme each standpoint presents simply an object of knowledge; in place of a "happening" that undoes modes of knowing—or even of "a problem waiting for a solution" (xxviii)—for him climate change is primarily an important *idea* that "possesses a certain plasticity," one that, "uncomfortable" with "the language of catastrophe" (xxxiii), he "resituate[s] ... as the subject of a more creative and less pejorative discourse" (xxxiv). Denial is thus itself denied, "resituated," as Hulme's title stresses, as mere "disagreement."

Hulme's discomfort with languages of catastrophe itself marks a very particular kind of climate change discourse, characteristic of the sort of institutionalized study of "Climate Change" as an academic field of knowledge—a context where authority is bound up with a fantasized detachment from the object of study and thus from its traumatic meanings. Defining the central issue as "why we disagree about climate change," that is, functions to beg the more destabilizing and urgent question: why are we failing to act to prevent being more rather than less fucked?

Such question begging is accomplished largely by Hulme's ostensible detachment from the various discourses he examines, his locating himself above the fray, a position from which any particular standpoint—especially what he calls "alarmist" discourse (232) or the "radical" positions from which "the entire growth paradigm is challenged" (264)—is constituted mainly as an object of academic knowledge that cannot threaten the mastery of the one who purports to know. Establishing this detachment as a condition for the whole volume, in his "Preface" Hulme sketches a little *Bildungsroman*, charting his "evolving relationship with climate change through identifying six stages in [his] encounter" (xxix): "Youthful Idealism," "Quantitative Analysis," "Political Ideology," "Lifestyle Choice," "Scenarios for Policy," and "Cultural Enlightenment" (xxix–xxxiii).[10] Here, one framing of global warming is presented as intellectually and ethically equivalent to the next, important not for how it might help illuminate or respond to an escalating catastrophe, but, rather, for its marking a phase in the personal journey of a self free to float from one perspective to the next. The forty-year period during which, in the face of increasingly urgent warnings, we have guaranteed we are fucked to one degree or another is thus narrated as an ascending journey of Professional Success, culminating with Hulme as Founding Director of the Tyndall Centre for Climate Change Research. In confining the question of "political ideology" to a single stage, moreover, Hulme pretends the subsequent stages, where he is increasingly identified with institutionalized knowledges, operate as somehow outside of ideology. In his "political ideology" stage, he viewed climate change "as a manifestation of a free-market, consumption-driven, capitalist economy" (xxx), a view he traces to his response to "the decade of Thatcherite conservatism" (xxxi). This "ideological" view simply disappears, however, apparently merely a stylistic phase, subsumed into his personal/professional "journey," as he graduates to the next stage, "Lifestyle Choices," exemplified by his buying a hybrid automobile—as if in framing the question in terms of individual consumer behavior he has left ideology behind.[11]

The dismissal of critiques of the "consumption-driven, capitalist economy" in the "Preface" is repeated throughout the book, accomplished not by engaging their arguments but by rendering them as specimens. "There are" such "radical critiques," he observes (259), classifying and describing them but remaining unperturbed by the existential challenge they articulate. He identifies a "neo-Malthusian" critique that sees in the climate system "non-negotiable limits" to resource consumption, beyond which that system will collapse. This is allied to the "eco-anarchist" standpoint (263), from which "the entire growth paradigm is challenged" (264). Because such understandings demand "urgency," demand we "act now before it's too late" (259), Hulme characterizes them as "radical," opposing them to the "reformist" positions ("market environmentalism, ecological modernization," etc.) that operate within "the prevailing neo-liberal capitalist political economy" (258), his ostensibly neutral survey performing its own alignment with ostensibly non-radical positions—its failure to recognize that maintaining the "prevailing" economy itself represents a commitment to a radical future. Arguing simply that "there are" challenges to the growth paradigm, that is, Hulme constructs concerns about "urgency" not as a traumatic threat but merely as one more element in his magisterial survey.

As we've seen, Hulme does, in the "Preface," confess his antipathy to framings of "urgency," writing "I feel uncomfortable that climate change is widely reported through the language of catastrophe and imminent peril, as 'the greatest problem facing humanity'" (xxxiii). Later, however, a critique of such language is presented as merely one position in a debate he stages but doesn't adjudicate. "Alarmism" emerges not as a disruptive challenge but simply as one of "twelve linguistic repertoires" (231) observed by the Institute for Public Policy Research, in a study whose "real value" isn't to illuminate why discourses of climate change have drastically failed to provoke meaningful response but merely the (one would have thought self-evident) "revelation of the diversity of linguistic repertoires of climate change that can co-exist in a society at the same time" (232). When Hulme presents two articles as "an example of the contention about the validity of the language adopted by the 'alarmist' repertoire," he does so not to help determine the crucial matter of that validity but merely to illustrate that opposing repertoires "co-exist"—a position of ostensible detachment both epitomized and belied by Hulme's identifying the author of the article critical of "alarmism" as "Mike Hulme."[12] Contending with "Mike Hulme's" article, as Hulme stages the debate, is James Risbey's, which argues, as Hulme summarizes it, that "those who do not adopt ... urgent language in their descriptions of the science [are] failing in their civic duty to inform the public" (233). But having introduced Risbey's response to "Hulme," Hulme simply leaves the matter there, one more example of his fundamental point: the mere fact of disagreement itself.

That the masquerade of academic detachment here seems especially strained—Hulme remaining schizophrenically split from "Hulme"—perhaps reflects the way Hulme's focus on the mere fact of that disagreement is haunted by the substance it would banish. On his own academic terms, that is, Hulme has staged an obviously unfair fight, "Hulme's" assertions mounting only the frailest of defenses against the urgency emanating from Risbey's call for a more alarming discourse. Hulme represents "Hulme's" position, for example, only by a short, especially slight, opinion piece for BBC News On-line, no match for Risbey's response, a scientific article in a peer reviewed journal, *Global Environmental Change*. Even for an opinion piece, moreover, "Hulme's" text is notably argument-free, proceeding by mere assertion, innuendo, and name-calling. He notes, for example, he has been "chastised by climate change campaigners" when his "public statements ... on climate change have not satisfied their thirst for environmental drama and exaggerated rhetoric," without addressing why he sees the rhetoric they call for as "exaggerated."[13] "Recent examples of the catastrophists include Tony Blair," "Hulme" asserts, for his having recently warned "We have a window of only 10–15 years to take steps we need to avoid crossing a catastrophic tipping point," as if such warnings, in 2006, were self-evidently exaggerated—no need to allude to any evidence one way or another. Because "the language of catastrophe is not the language of science," "Hulme" concludes that "to state that climate change will be 'catastrophic' hides a cascade of value-laden assumptions which do not emerge from empirical or theoretical science"—betraying his own "value-laden assumption," modernity's fantasy that the language of science could ever somehow operate abstracted from some ideological ground. As he sees it, the thirsty catastrophists "sex up" the value-free science and thus "exacerbate ... the very risks we are trying to avoid"—just as "the careless (or conspiratorial?) translation of concern about Saddam Hussein's putative military threat into the case for WMD has had major geopolitical repercussions." The haunting presence of the catastrophe "Hulme" would in the name of "empirical science" deny has here ushered him straight through the looking glass: the "catastrophists"—who ground their alarms in carefully detailed evidence—are equated with a political administration notorious (though not held accountable) precisely for obliterating concerns about evidence in favor of foregone conclusions. Similarly, the traumatic prospect of a "catastrophic tipping point" prompting Blair and others to sound an alarm is bizarrely reformulated by and haunts "Hulme's" worry that "the discourse of catastrophe is in danger of tipping society onto a negative, depressive, and reactionary trajectory." Astonishingly, the problem for him isn't that business as usual propels us on a "negative trajectory" toward a tipping point beyond which the climate system that has enabled human civilization will collapse but, rather, that calling attention to that dilemma will itself "tip" us into a "depressive" state—apparently somehow more "dangerous" than the probably suicidal status quo.[14]

Noting that the *New York Times* called attention to "Hulme's" piece as the most prominent expression of the "middle's" rejection of alarmism, in "The New Climate Discourse: Alarmist or Alarming?" Risbey subjects that rejection to the sort of careful empirical consideration "Hulme" claims to champion but declines to pursue. At stake in "Hulme's" piece, Risbey suggests, are eight questions about climate change or "alarmist" assessments of it—is it catastrophic? is it rapid? is it urgent? is it irreversible? is it worse than we thought? is it chaotic? is it science? is it counterproductive?—and, defining each issue (catastrophe, rapidity, etc.) "in terms that are commonly understood," he "briefly summarize[s] the relevant features of the science" for each and "evaluate[s] the 'fit' of the term to these features" (27). Finally, he concludes that

> this review of the language of the new ["alarming"] discourse has focused on terms selected by a critic of the discourse [Hulme] and finds that the terms used to describe the science are at least arguably reasonable and consistent with it. That is, the view of the discourse as "alarming" is not inconsistent with the science.
>
> (35)

The "amount of warming required to initiate irreversible breakdown of Greenland or the West Antarctic"—increasing sea level by about 12 meters—is, for example,

> thought to be only a moderate couple of degrees above pre-industrial global temperature levels. Because of the inertia of the climate and energy systems, we are fast approaching the point at which our energy-industrial system is committed to reaching that critical level of warming.

Indeed, "the few studies that have looked systematically at this issue have concluded that the available window of action ... to avoid locking in that warming is perhaps as short as a decade or two"—a window, that, as of this writing ten years later, may already be closed.[15]

Revealingly, Hulme's demonization of "alarmism" is echoed even within those disciplines most concerned with the processes of denial itself. Writing in *Psychoanalysis, Culture, and Society*, for example, Paul Hoggett evokes Hulme's "sustained critique of disaster-mongering and alarmism within the climate-change community" and, grounded in a psychoanalytic perspective, mounts his own parallel critique (elements of which are repeated on the website of the Climate Psychology Alliance). Framing "the quandary" as "how to avoid the Scylla of paranoia and the Charybdis of complacency" or "how to sound the alarm without being alarmist" (261), he proceeds as if those were equivalent dangers. But whatever dangers might adhere in alarmism (Hoggett points to some of the disturbingly authoritarian musings of James Lovelock, as if Lovelock's "apocalyptic survivalism" were representative of the "alarmists" targeted by Hulme), can these stand as equivalent to those of the complacency at the heart of ecocidal business as usual?[16] For Hoggett, following Hulme, "climate change is a classic example of a 'post-normal science' where 'facts are uncertain, values in dispute, stakes high and decisions urgent' (Hulme 209)," and so he suggests that "lacking predictive powers, we simply do not know how collectively bad is the situation we are confronting" (263)—as if, as Peter Clark et al. show, though "the precise timing of their occurrence is uncertain," many catastrophic "features of future climate" were not "relatively certain in the long term." "Faced with what seems cultural complacency," Hoggett continues, "activists are tempted to exaggerate, to fall into a politics predicated on the necessity to act and act now in the face of imminent catastrophe. This is a dangerous path." As I've suggested in the introduction to this book, it is hard, in light of the science, to see how sounding the need "to act and to act now in the face of imminent catastrophe" can be understood as an "exaggeration," and Hoggett adduces no instances of such "dangerous" exaggeration, instead framing the climate crisis simply as an iteration of an ahistorical apocalypticism; where "each generation tends to think of its times as unprecedented," he writes, "in fact, we have been here many times before, facing the abyss" (264).[17] But whether or not it has been in the past felt that "we" were facing the abyss, that cannot bear on whether the climate crisis in fact *does* present an imminent existential threat the only sufficient response to which could be that we "act and act now." When Hoggett's article appeared, in 2011, the concentration of carbon in the atmosphere had recently surpassed 390ppm, and, as the title of one article at the time put it, "The Last Time CO_2 Was This High, Humans Didn't Exist" (Freedman).[18]

Histories of catastrophic thinking notwithstanding, we have in fact *not* been here before.

***

If Hulme epitomizes how decrying "alarmism" represents one way institutionalized discourse disarticulates the traumatic prospect of climate change, another way seems to acknowledge the alarming dilemma with one hand while, with the other, obscuring it by turning for an "adequate" response to the very economic and political structures in which the dilemma is rooted. The Paris Agreement offers a prominent case in point, and Amitav Ghosh has examined how "enshrined at the core of [its] text" is "the current paradigm of perpetual growth" (154)—exactly what one would expect from negotiations in which "various billionaires, corporations, and 'climate entrepreneurs' played an important part," drawing on premises "borrowed directly from the free-trade agreements of the neo-liberal era" (156) and thereby banishing even "the slightest acknowledgement that something has gone wrong with our dominant paradigms" (154).[19] But here, as throughout the construction of global warming in the contemporary imaginary, Al Gore's *An Inconvenient Truth* has played an especially important defining role. In 2006, Michael Ziser and Julie Sze observe, "the public perception of climate change" underwent a "sea-change ... largely attributable to the release of ... *An Inconvenient Truth*" (402), a work that, as Ingolfur Bluhdorn sees it, "catapulted ... climate change to the top of political agendas both nationally and internationally."[20] As it emerged onto the public scene, however, how was this "climate change" rhetorically constituted? Revealingly, in the introduction to *An Inconvenient Truth* Al Gore roots his own sense of the urgency of global warming in his own traumatic experience. When his young son was seriously injured in an accident, it "abruptly interrupted the flow of my days and hours," Gore writes, and "I began to rethink everything ... and vowed to make the climate crisis the top priority of my professional life" (8).[21] His own felt understanding of the urgency of the problem, that is, was precipitated not merely by scientific study but also by a fundamental disruption of his personal business as usual, a crisis defined by an existential question: will the child survive?[22]

But if this introductory framing of the issue might suggest that *An Inconvenient Truth* would aim to catapult climate change into wide public awareness as an encounter with trauma, such a prospect is quickly foreclosed. Gore's own traumatic experience is here immediately contained within a comfortably familiar narrative shape, what Ursula Heise describes as the work's "*Bildungsroman* structure" (209). He introduces himself, moreover, simply as conveying "information," which, if a sufficient amount is "compiled," can "change minds" (9) without the fundamental disruption that for Gore himself changed the *meaning* of the scientific information he had already long known. Indeed, as an attempt to "make the whole message easier to follow," the book aims precisely at precluding any such disruption. Purporting to ground the climate crisis in "our fundamental way of thinking" about it (254), *An Inconvenient Truth* in fact remains deeply rooted in ideological and economic business as usual, functioning finally not to raise but to elide threateningly disruptive fundamental questions. Far from locating the crisis in the fetishizing of economic growth, for example, or the cultural identification with industrial capitalism—far from urging that we "rethink everything"—Gore thus concludes his discussion of the relationship of the climate crisis to the economy with a fawning celebration of corporate power:

> Luckily, more and more U.S. business executives are beginning to lead us in the right direction. For example, General Electric recently announced a dramatic new initiative on global warming. Jeffrey Immelt, the CEO of GE, explained how the environment and the economy fit together in his vision:
> > We think green means green. This is a time period where environmental improvement is going to lead toward profitability.
>
> (274)

Gore's economic boosterism here reflects the way his account of the climate crisis is deeply embedded also in narratives of American triumphalism—narratives constituted precisely in the disavowal of traumatic disruption to (prevailing) American self-understandings. He thus contextualizes the climate crisis as the most recent of the sort of national challenges America has always risen to meet, throughout a history characterized by an America with "the capacity to do great things" (290). "We made a moral decision that slavery was wrong," Gore writes in describing one of those great things, "and that we could not be half-free and half-slave" (291), representing the end of slavery as entirely a matter of enlightened decision-making producing a moral consensus—an account that, in making the Civil War disappear, also presumes a homogenous American "we" that excludes not only the hundreds of thousands of violent defenders of slavery but also the millions of enslaved Americans themselves (who, presumably, wouldn't have needed a couple of hundred years to "make a moral decision"). Directly articulating the ideological premises underlying *An Inconvenient Truth*, Gore's next book, *The Assault on Reason*, does return the Civil War to the picture, framing it as pitting "those who sought to perfect the logic of democracy" against "those who insisted on a perversion of capitalism by fighting to retain the right to own other human beings" (86–87). Even if the premise here that capitalism in its unperverted state would disallow slave labor weren't nonsensical on its theoretical face, it would quickly dissolve in light of the historical evidence that, as Edward Baptist has recently shown, American slavery was absolutely fundamental to the development of industrial and finance capitalism, both in the U.S. and in Europe.

Though it forgets the Civil War, *An Inconvenient Truth* does prominently feature WWII, victory in which, as Gore sees it, brought to his homogenized, national "we" not only "moral authority and vision," but also "the spiritual capacity and wisdom" to "lay ... the foundation for 50 years of peace and prosperity" (11). Especially in a work urging that we face an inconvenient truth, this is a stunningly oblivious representation of postwar history. It proceeds as if the fifty years "founded" by those morally authoritative and visionary, spiritually capable and wise leaders were not a time of extreme, often traumatic events and developments, of normalized violence both fast and slow: the Vietnam War and other postcolonial and cold war acts of massive killing; a nuclear arms race of absurd proportion and the consequent apocalyptic threat and anxiety; extreme and increasing economic disparities, both within industrialized nations and between the developed and the developing world, producing large sacrifice zones of severe poverty; the associated proliferation of authoritarian regimes routinely sponsored or forcibly imposed by Gore's spiritual wise founders themselves; extreme concentrations of corporate wealth and political power. And, of course, those "50 years of peace and prosperity" saw the explosive global escalation of the business-as-usual economic vision—premised on the rapidly escalated burning of fossil fuel, especially oil[23]—that, in defining the natural world as either a "resource" or a trash can, has both produced and forestalled meaningful responses to the climate crisis itself.[24]

Introducing the climate crisis into the mediasphere not as a traumatic questioning of who "we," as "Americans," are but as yet one more occasion to prove the Greatness of who "we've" always been, *An Inconvenient Truth* represents a pivotal moment in the discursive constitution of "global warming," especially the self-congratulatory position that seems to raise the alarm, on the one hand, while, on the other, celebrating the very economic and political orders that generate the dilemma in the first place.[25] We've seen such butchery in the *Times*'s championing of Obama's Climate Action Plan and Clean Power Plan, and we can turn to the *Times* too for a quieter but typically stark instance, a 2014 commentary by David Ropeik—of Ropeik & Associates, consultants in Risk Perception, Risk Communication, and Risk Management—offered by the *Times*'s Dot Earth blogger Andrew Revkin.[26] "Combating climate change," Ropeik initially suggests, "requires nothing less than a radical structuring of how the world makes and uses energy," and he argues that successfully imposing such "sweeping changes on the vested interests profiting by the status quo," and on "a public *comfortable* with the status quo," would require an "overwhelming level of public concern," a feeling that "we were at war—bullets-flying, bombs-dropping, buildings-burning, and body-bags real, live, NOW '*I am in Danger*' war."[27] Because of "the psychology of risk perception," he thinks it's extremely unlikely "we can achieve that level of concern" and—considering "the latest IPCC Working Group 3's" warning that "time is very short before we lock the system into a future [of] much more disastrous damage"—he concludes that "even if it is possible, we are just not going to get there in time."

Just as Ropeik broaches that bleak prospect, however, the traumatic threat of the dilemma is immediately eclipsed by the breezy discourse of "leadership." Since the "bottom up demand" that, in Ropeik's view, we "rely on in a representative democracy" won't work, he concludes "it's going to take enlightened leadership, leaders that take the lead." If that's at least a superficially coherent claim, however, that coherence is swiftly dissolved by what follows: "And they are. ... A world shifting away from carbon is a reality that our leaders have recognized as prudent, and they are moving that way." The "enlightened leadership" that Ropeik, echoing Gore, sees as already taking the lead is exemplified here both by the major industrial and developing nations (taking small actions absurdly inadequate to the problem) and by "many of the world's largest corporations," like Wal-Mart, Apple, Ikea, and "major oil and power companies"—the very "vested interests profiting by the status quo" Ropeik earlier defines as the chief obstacle to the necessary "sweeping changes." If in one breath he might then seem to concede such "leadership" is a sad farce, acknowledging its actions as "far too little and far too late," in the next, with a straight face, he reads it as "a hopeful sign about the capacities of humanity" and mystifyingly concludes that "the serious progress we need to make is still possible," remaining unperturbed by the direness he speaks but does not process. Finally, he thus constructs climate change not as an undoing of culturally central modes of knowing but as a risk to be managed by powerful government and corporate leaders, exemplified by Ropeik & Associates' long list of clients in Government, Industry, and the Academy, like the Office of the White House Communications Director, Entergy Power Corporation, and the Edison Electric Institute (the association representing all U.S. investor-owned electric companies).

***

As Ropeik's allusion to "the psychology of risk perception" suggests, when the dominant constructions of climate change do address the pervasive denialism beyond that of the often scapegoated "skeptics," they typically turn to depoliticized academic discourses like Climate Psychology or Climate Change Communication—again enacting the denial they purport to address from an empirical remove. Here the fantasized detachment is achieved partly by rendering the problem in terms of individual, decontextualized psychology—the abstracted and universalized "human mind"— obscuring the many ways selves are constituted in social, political, and ideological fields.[28] In this approach, humans have what the *Times*'s Revkin calls an "inconvenient mind," a condition he illustrates by linking to work by "behavioral researchers" Matthew Feinberg and Robb Willer, whose experiments, they argue, suggest that "the potentially dire consequences of global warming threatens deeply held beliefs that the world is just, orderly, and stable," that "individuals overcome this threat by denying or minimizing the existence of global warming," and therefore that "less dire messaging could be more effective for promoting public understanding" (34). That the problem of "direness" here is displaced from the geophysical itself to the "messaging" produces the sort of symptomatic failure of coherence by which, as we've seen, much of the dominant discourse of climate change is haunted: in the face of a public that minimizes the threat, the way to "more effectively promote understanding" is ... to minimize the threat. Imagining that "the information [could] be communicated without creating substantial threat to ... individuals' deeply held beliefs" that "the world is fair and stable"—and accepting such denialist beliefs as a natural condition—the authors thus reproduce the denial from which their empirical remove would purport to keep them exempt, their own clinging to their stable disciplinary terms rendering illegible the threat to epistemological business as usual. Sharing their a priori rejection of a discourse of alarm, Revkin himself brandishes the notion of universalized human mind, adding to Feinberg and Willer's analysis the proposal that "those rejecting the alarming visions of a human-unraveled climate are illustrating another solid human trait—skepticism about overwrought claims in the absence of hard evidence" ("Inconvenient Mind")—his own overwrought (and self-evidently dubious) proposal substituting for any engagement with arguments like Risbey's, which three years earlier had firmly rooted a discourse of alarm in the large body of evidence.

The name of Revkin's "Dot Earth" blog suggested the planet as one more virtual domain, equivalent to an Org or a Gov or an Edu system or a Com. Commensurately, beyond the confines of Dot Earth, when the *Times* publishes material addressing the failure to respond to climate change, it constrains itself largely to those knowledge discourses most committed to reducing the radical dilemma to their own normalizing disciplinary narratives, largely premised on those universalizing abstractions like "human traits" and the "human mind." In a 2012 *Times* article, for instance, when Beth Gardiner asks, since "the need to reduce planet-warming emissions has grown urgent ... why, collectively, are we doing so little about it?" she concentrates on experimental research in "the burgeoning field of climate psychology," which studies "the very ways our brains work." Climate change is a very bad "fit with our underlying psychology," she quotes Anthony Leiserowitz asserting, emphasizing his status within the climate-change knowledge industry as "director of the Yale Program on Climate Change Communication."

Elsewhere, Leiserowitz elaborates on this bad fit: "As human beings we are exquisitely attuned to what's happening in our immediate environment ... If you're walking through the woods and you hear the crack of a stick behind you, your body immediately goes into a fear response, a fight or flight response"; climate change, though, "isn't that kind of a problem" ("Interview"). Such explanations of a putatively decontextualized human mind constitute the common sense of much "climate psychology."[29] But to whatever extent it can accurately be said that "human beings" are "exquisitely attuned" to the "immediate environment," it doesn't follow that our "underlying psychology" makes it impossible to attend to what Nixon identifies as "slow violence" (however much a culture of spectacle might make that more difficult). Moreover, though the "fear response" of the generic "you" Leiserowitz sets walking in the woods is proposed as universal, this walker is necessarily someone, not anyone; Little Red Riding Hood won't hear and respond to a cracking stick in the same way as a hungry hunter tracking a next meal, or Helena pursuing Demetrius, or a frantic parent searching for a lost child. Likewise, where for Leiserowitz "our underlying psychology" means that climate change doesn't register as an "immediate, visceral threat," we might suppose that that threat might indeed register somewhat immediately in the viscera of someone who has lost a home—or a person—to the kind of extreme weather event that increasingly characterizes a new normal, even in the global North.

When Leiserowitz turns from the problem of the "bad fit" between the problem of climate change and our "underlying psychology" to the question of how to address the gap between them, his universalized woods-walker is displaced by an ostensibly more heterogeneous vision, grounded in a major Yale Program on Climate Communication report, "Global Warming's Six Americas" (2009). Since "One of the first rules of effective communication is to 'know thy audience,'" that report begins, "Climate change public communication and engagement efforts must start with the fundamental recognition that people are different" (Leiserowitz et al., 1). It thus "identifies Global Warming's Six Americas: six unique audiences within the American public," ranging from the Alarmed, at one end of the spectrum, to, on the other, the Dismissive. The woods-walking "you," that is, isn't just a generic anybody, but one of six generic (American) anybodies.

As the "first rule of effective communication," the imperative to "know thy audience" at once enthrones in the discipline of Communications a universalized Knowledge and disallows scrutiny of what it might mean to "know," its rhetorical form and (with "thy") its diction lightheartedly alluding to the rule's status as beyond question, a Biblical Commandment. If global warming is producing a climate crisis, that is, for the Yale Program, as for the discipline of Climate Communication it prominently exemplifies, that crisis cannot extend to its knowledge system. The status of Expert Knower is achieved by accepting on faith the commandment to "know thy audience," and by constituting the object of such knowledge as precisely what can be quantified as the result of multiple-choice survey questionnaires.

Constituting the Alarmed, the Concerned, the Cautious, the Disengaged, the Doubtful, and the Dismissive as equivalent objects of study, focusing wholly on the "attitudes" that define each category but, like Hulme, identifying with none, "Six Americas" declines to consider which American public might most closely reflect whatever threatening reality might prompt the inquiry in the first place. But if it aims to facilitate "more efficient communication" about climate change in order to address the problem that "climate change remains a relatively low priority among the American public" (2), we might see the report as aiming to convince the merely Concerned, the Cautious, and other publics to join the Alarmed—who are already "fully convinced of the reality and seriousness of climate change and are already taking individual, consumer, and political action to address it" (1). As a pivotal element in the report's attempt to address what the Institute's mission statement calls a "gap between climate science and climate policy and action [that] remains huge" (Yale Program), however, the category of the Alarmed here works mainly to obscure the traumatic threat inhabiting that "gap."

The Alarmed can be legible as "fully convinced" of the problem's "seriousness" only insofar as the problem can be normalized as an "issue" or a "priority," defined within the political structures in which the Project is embedded.[30]

It is thus very difficult to recognize any alarm in the attitudes that here define Alarm. "At the time of the survey," in 2009, "the Alarmed rated global warming as the 4th most important national priority for the President and Congress, after the economy, health care, and the federal budget deficit" (32). Indeed, far from global warming constituting for them an existential emergency, only about half of the Alarmed (55%) see it as even "their most important *environmental* issue" (my emphasis), and a quarter (26%) don't recognize it as an "environmental issue" of even "very high priority." They can thus be described as "fully convinced of the reality of climate change" only by disallowing questions about what that "reality" *is*, as if at stake were simply that binary that structures so many prominent framings of the "issue": is (anthropogenic) climate change "real" or not? "Almost all of the Alarmed hold one of three conceptual models about how the climate system works," the report observes, but only 25 percent hold what the report fails to identify as the most likely correct one, "the threshold model, in which the climate system is stable, but only within certain limits or tipping points" (30). Precisely where a binary approach would seem most apt—will or won't the climate system tip?—most of the Alarmed hold to the more gradualist, linear models. Most of those the Yale Project identifies as Alarmed, that is, do not register the urgency of the threat of a global, ecosystemic collapse.

***

Across a range of climate change discourses, it has been the Yale *Six America*'s non-alarmist "Alarm" that has largely prevailed over more destabilizing definitions like Risbey's—even in the texts that, in examining our pervasive cultural denial, have themselves represented the *causes* for alarm most forthrightly. Hamilton's *Requiem for a Species: Why We Resist the Truth about Climate Change* presents an especially revealing instance. On the one hand, his detailed 2010 consideration of the science leads to a conclusion he recognizes, even then, as "almost too frightening to accept":

> It seems that even with most optimistic set of assumptions—the ending of deforestation, a halving of emissions associated with food production, global emissions peaking in 2020 and then falling by 3 percent a year for a few decades—we have no chance of preventing emissions rising well above a number of critical tipping points that will spark uncontrollable climate change. The Earth's climate would enter

a chaotic era lasting thousands of years before natural processes eventually establish some sort of equilibrium.

(21–22)

On the other hand, in identifying "those who do understand the threat posed by global warming" Hamilton takes the Yale Study at face value, defining those "who do understand" as "the Alarmed and perhaps some of the Concerned in the study of 'Six Americas'" (121). Hamilton's text, that is, itself rehearses the disarticulations in climate change discourse at large, the "almost too frightening" science leaving untouched the normalizing, widely circulated narratives in which, for example, Alarm works to displace alarm.

Similarly, even as *Requiem* locates the "frightening" present in relation to culturally produced modes of thinking rooted in modernity, when the text considers questions of "denial" per se, it largely narrows its focus to "skeptics" and remains constrained within the decontextualized discourses of "climate psychology." Compellingly, Hamilton elaborates how "the prospect of runaway climate change challenges our technological hubris, our Enlightenment faith in reason and the whole modernist project" (31), with entire chapters on economic "Growth Fetishism," "Disconnection from Nature," and "The Consumer Self" articulating ideological premises that, "embodied in our institutions and embedded in our understanding of the world" (118), naturalize a "growth machine [that has] created the types of people who are perfectly suited to its own perpetuation—docile, seduced by its promises and unable to think beyond the boundaries it sets" (48–49). As he turns to "Many Forms of Denial," however, the ideological workings of this "growth machine" abruptly disappear from view. Initially, and for over half its length, his "Denial" chapter focuses on the decontextualized psychological "theory of cognitive dissonance" (96) as it applies to the familiar scapegoats, the overt "deniers" with their "contrarian views" (97). Here, "intense ideological division" (108) refers not to the fundamental conflict between those who remain uncritically identified with that growth machine and those who find it at the root of the crisis itself, but merely to the more narrowly defined partisan conflict between those who "deny" the reality of climate change and those who "accept it," a division Hamilton then nuances only by way of Yale's "Six Americas"—none of which (even, as we've seen, the Alarmed) conceptualize an "outside" to the growth fetish.

If the first of the chapter's "many forms of denial" locate denial not in a culturally dominant mode of thought but in a relatively marginal, though politically influential, contrarianism, the other forms are abstracted from cultural context itself. Thus, Hamilton suggests that "while the skeptics' denial has succeeded in muddying the waters of public understanding," an even "more powerful factor in the reluctance of governments to do what is needed" has been "the strategies routinely used by the public to avoid or downplay the scientific warnings" (119)—"strategies" that reflect "the ways in which" a culturally decontextualized "human psyche has prevented or slowed recognition of the existential threat" (118), partly because of what he imagines to be the "fact" that "humans have evolved to assess and respond to risk through immediate feelings rather than cognitive processing" (119), as if feelings (immediate and otherwise) and cognition didn't necessarily inform each other. In this account, "psychologists are beginning to identify a range of coping strategies used to manage the unpleasant feelings that follow when we open ourselves to the message of climate science" (121), "strategies" like "distraction" (122), "de-problemiti[zation]," "distancing," "wishful-thinking," "pleasure-seeking" (123), "blame-shifting" (126), "shift[ing] responsibility ... to a higher power" (127), and "hope" (128). Where the "message of climate science" elsewhere in the book seems traumatically "almost too frightening to accept," here, from within the normalizing discourse of climate psychology, that "message" stirs not almost unbearable fright but merely "unpleasant feelings," and the strategies deployed to "manage" such unpleasantness are characterized not as "suicidal" or "catastrophic" but merely as "maladaptive" (121). Even as he elsewhere describes our economy as a "growth machine" producing subjects "unable to think beyond the boundaries it sets," that is, Hamilton here resorts to the politically less disruptive, ostensibly non-ideological trope of what Revkin calls our "inconvenient minds." In this way, articulating but then sequestering both the drastic urgency of the climate dilemma and the ideological context maintaining our failure to confront it, *Requiem* compellingly addresses the question raised by its subtitle, *Why We Resist the Truth about Climate Change*, even as it revealingly enacts that "resistance" itself.

In Hamilton's text, that rhetorical sequestration works by severing the question of "why we resist the truth about climate change" from his consideration of the "maladaptive strategies"—deriving from an abstracted "human psyche"—by which that resistance is performed, and he introduces one such strategy for "managing troublesome emotions" (126) by evoking Kari Norgaard's discussion of "blame-shifting." Norgaard's study of climate change denial, however, mounts a very different argument than Hamilton's about the relation between "*why* people [have] failed to respond to climate change," as she puts it, and "*how* nonresponse is ... produced" (94).

Largely breaking with the pervasive cognitive approach to questions of such denial, in *Living in Denial: Climate Change, Emotions, and Everyday Life* she focuses not on managerial "strategies" performed by a universalized inconvenient mind—and not on the oft-scapegoated "skeptics"—but, crucially, on how denial is constructed and enacted within the complex cultural context of a particular Norwegian town.[31] Like Hamilton, Norgaard sees denial deriving from a need to "protect individual identity and ... to maintain culturally produced conceptions of reality" (207) rooted in "our enlightenment sensibilities" (74), but this prompts her to scrutinize the dominant disciplinary understandings of our "nonresponse." Where, she observes, "most existing studies on public response to climate change—coming from environmental sociology, social psychology, or science communication, from survey work on attitudes and beliefs to psychological studies of mental models—use individuals as their unit of analysis" (209), Norgaard, in contrast, focuses on what she calls the "social organization of denial" (211): structured by the enforcement of "cultural norms of attention, emotion and conversation" and the operation of "a series of cultural narratives to ... normalize a particular version of reality," the "public response to global warming is *produced* through cultural practices of everyday life" (207).

Where Norgaard's calls those "existing studies on public response" nonetheless "essential" (209), I've tried to consider how their disciplinary discourses, especially perhaps in their individualistic focus, also themselves represent fundamental instances of how denial "is produced through cultural practices." Producing (expert) knowledge, I've suggested, functions partly to obscure more fundamental questions about what it means to know or about the relation between knowledge and meaning. In contrast to those "existing studies," Norgaard's does work to approach such troubling questions about knowledge. Even when "people care and have considerable information" about global warming, she concludes, they "in some sense don't know *how* to know" (207)—and thus, we might add, they don't know to speak of what they know. "When I brought up the issue of climate change in interviews," Norgaard reports, "it often killed the conversation. People gave an initial reaction of concern, and then we hit a dead zone, where there was suddenly not much to be said" (55).

How does Norgaard's own book "know"? Broaching this question, Norgaard "came to understand that [she] was writing about many things at once," that she was "watching the community of Bygdaby first through one theoretical lens and then another" (208). Encountering the threat that her object of knowledge would thus exceed her proliferating disciplinary framings—grappling with "*how* to know"—she contains this threat by figuring each mode of understanding as an element in a "kaleidoscope of conversations": each "turn [of] the kaleidoscope" (211), in her final chapter, brings into focus a complementary disciplinary knowledge, ranging from psychological accounts of the cognitive or affective roots of individual denial, to sociological, political economic, and ethnographic understandings of how denial (and innocence) is socially constructed and collectively organized. In this way, especially paired with Hamilton's compelling account of the urgency of the crisis, Norgaard's dissection of how the denial of that urgency is produced by cultural structures counters the denialism of the dominant discourses addressing that denial. At the same time, though, I wonder if figuring her work as a kaleidoscope might indicate her own (perhaps inevitable) foreclosures. Just as the multitude of visual combinatorial possibilities is contained within the rigid kaleidoscopic tube itself, what Norgaard calls her "blending" (212) of knowledges operates within the confines of a knowledge system, social science, that itself remains unperturbed.

There's a danger, of course, in subjecting a single conceit to such scrutiny—under sufficient pressure, any metaphor will break—but, insofar as Norgaard's figuring *Living in Denial* as a kaleidoscope does respond to the otherwise unaddressed question it raises about "knowing *how* to know," that response at the same time may obscure an equally fundamental question: how can we know how *not* to know? Her concluding discussion about how we might "break through denial into awareness" thus remains unruffled by traumatic disruption—nothing like what we've seen Gore describe as "the flow of [his] days and hours" having been "abruptly interrupted." As she addresses the question "how do we invigorate political and economic systems" in order to "move forward in the face of enormous uncertainty," the trauma loosed by that enormous uncertainty—and also by what we are relatively more certain about—seems obscured in her call for "a fierce return to the local" (227) (the Slow Food movement, community-supported agriculture, "community groups" that "calculate the carbon footprints of homes, schools, churches," etc. [228]). Conceding that "local political renewal cannot be enough on its own," Norgaard nonetheless suggests "it may be the important next step for individuals in breaking through the absurdity of the double life" and hopes that "as people participate, they will begin to see why the facts of climate change matter to them" (228). In some sense, *Living in Denial* thus ends by averting its own eyes from the rapidly closing window, turning to incrementalism (the "next step") and the discourse of "beginnings" ("they will begin to see").[32] In the Anthropocene, however, what begins is necessarily already pressed up against the horizon.[33] As Yogi Berra is reputed to have remarked, it gets late early these days.

In response to that lateness, Jem Bendell has, in "Deep Adaptation: A Map for Navigating Climate Tragedy," more recently highlighted the failure of academic discourses to help us know how to know the extremity of our moment. Arguing in detail that, increasingly, climate science points toward a "near-term social collapse," he frames his work precisely in relation to that disciplinary failure. He introduces the paper as having been rejected by the *Sustainability Accounting, Management and Policy Journal*, which asked for "major changes" that Bendell considered as either "impossible or inappropriate":

> impossible, as the request to build off existing scholarship on this topic would require there to be publications on the implications of ecologically-induced social collapse, globally, upon which to build. A literature review indicated that there is not such scholarship in management studies. Inappropriate, as a reviewer's request not to dishearten readers

with the claim of "inevitable near-term social collapse" reflects a form of censure found amongst people working on sustainable business.

And he appends to it a letter he wrote in response to that rejection, elaborating the disciplinary failure:

> The trauma from assessing our situation with climate change has led me to become aware of and drop some of my past preoccupations and tactics. I realise it is time to fully accept my truth as I see it, even if partially formed and not polished yet for wider articulation. I know that academia involves as much a process of wrapping up truth as unfolding it. We wrap truth in disciplines, discrete methodologies, away from the body, away from intuition, away from the collective, away from the everyday. So as that is my truth then I wish to act on it as well, and not keep this analysis hidden in the pursuit of academic respect.

Even as he gestures here toward a knowledge that exceeds the neatly wrapped, abstracted, and thus academically respectable sort, we might wonder to what extent "Deep Adaptation" itself manifests an unfolding as opposed to a wrapped truth. Just as in broaching the question of "knowing *how* to know" Norgaard's own knowing, however multiple, nonetheless remains within the stable boundaries of her unifying disciplinary kaleidoscope, the "trauma" to which Bendell here alludes (involving not a collapse of fundamental premises but merely a "dropping" of "some past preoccupations and tactics") leaves unperturbed a terrain that, as in his title, can be wrapped within the confines of "map" that will secure a "navigation" itself not seemingly in question. Thus, where Bendell compellingly parses the normalized denialism inherent in and beyond academic businesses as usual—decrying particularly the ubiquitous argument that "we should not communicate to the public the likelihood and nature of the catastrophe we face," lest "we" promote despair—I wonder if the "deep adaptation agenda" he proposes as a response might itself seem to minimize the extent to which a sufficient response might disrupt the psychic ground on which such adapting might proceed. His modest hope that the agenda's three elements—"resilience, relinquishment and restoration"—could offer a "useful framework for community dialogue," that is, might seem incommensurate to a moment that demands radical action and unwrapped urgency.[34]

The question of how to account both for the fact of urgency and for the necessity of beginnings turns on the question of knowing both how to know and how to not know. Offering an especially revealing encounter with that question, in *A Postcapitalist Politics* J. K. Gibson-Graham introduce the "world problems" to which their book responds as rooted in "increased consumption … bought at the expense of the destruction of the global atmospheric commons we have taken for granted for the past two centuries" (ix–x)—a "matter for urgent discussion" making "crucial" the "rethinking of what constitutes an 'economy'" (x). Tellingly, however, these framing comments are the book's last mention of the climate crisis. "This is a hopeful book written at a time when hope is finally getting a hearing" (ix), the first sentence announces, but, as with the more generalized turn to the local of which this book is an especially elaborated advocacy, that "hope," rooted in its engagement with place-based localism, is thus finally spared any confrontation with the "urgency" the book occludes almost as it introduces. If, aligning themselves with what Eve Sedgwick calls "weak theory," they "refus[e] to know too much" and thus continually try to "act ... as a beginner" (8), such caution—in declining to extend attention from opening gambits to the exigencies of the endgame—remains haunted by a begged question: how can refusing to know too much—refusing to hubristically violate the not-knowing in which any knowledge is embedded—comport with the ethical imperative to refuse to know too little?[35] Again, how can we know both how to know and how not to know?

One way to approach this question, as I've suggested in the introduction to this book, might involve considering what Cathy Caruth has called "the specific point at which knowing and not knowing intersect," the ground, as she has it, where "the language of literature and the psychoanalytic theory of traumatic experience precisely meet" (3). Informed by certain psychoanalytic notions of trauma, then, the next two chapters turn to the question of literary representations of the climate crisis. If, as I've tried to suggest, the dominant discourses of climate function largely to disarticulate the traumatic challenge hurled by our ecocidal present, Chapter 4 reads the way contemporary fiction contributes to that disarticulation, while Chapter 5 considers the extent to which literary discourses might offer important rearticulations—might help us toward that ground constituted by knowing and not knowing both.

Notes

1 See Naomi Oreskes and Erik Conway's *Merchants of Doubt* (2010). More recently *Inside Climate News* has discovered "how Exxon conducted cutting-edge climate research decades ago and then," with the future Secretary of State at the helm, "without revealing all that it had learned, worked at the forefront of climate denial, manufacturing doubt about the scientific consensus that its own scientists had confirmed" (Banerjee et al.). It has also been learned that "the oil giant Shell had a deep understanding, dating at least to the 1980s, of the science and risks of global warming caused by fossil fuel emissions" (Cushman).
2 The distinction I pursue between overt denialism and the more normalized denialism that masquerades as acceptance parallels a distinction Freud observes in his writing about denial, in his papers "Negation" and "Fetishism." Drawing on those papers, Paul Hoggett puts it that

faced with an unpalatable reality, Freud suggested that we may resort to one of two mechanisms—outright rejection, where we simply do not see what is in front of us, and disavowal, where one part of the mind sees while another discounts what is seen.

("Perverse Culture" 59)

To that duo of "rejection" and "disavowal," in the context of the climate crisis itself Sally Weintrobe adds a third term, "denialism," which "involves campaigns of misinformation" (7). Of course, the concept of "denial" has complicated history, and sociologist Stanley Cohen has traced its "original genealogy, in psychoanalysis … and its different version in existential philosophy … and cognitive psychology" (72). And, drawing partly on Cohen, fellow sociologist Kari Norgaard elaborates how what I call normalized denial is socially constructed and organized by daily life (see my discussion of Norgaard below).

3   To whatever extent it's the case that, as Susan Matthews suggests, "the new denialists don't deny climate change—they just refute the fact that it matters enough to require action," this only reformulates the same scapegoating. Matthews illustrates such a position by quoting Trump, as if Obama had taken seriously the imperative to "require action" in a significant way.

4   Perhaps the binary understanding of climate change—is or isn't it real (or anthropogenic, or catastrophic)—will be dislodged by the emergence of the Green New Deal.

5   The Obama administration, while departing from Bush's overt denialism, had for most of his tenure simply excluded climate change from the political agenda, vastly increasingly the likelihood the planet will pass the most cataclysmic tipping point. When, with a possibly suicidal belatedness, he turned a little bit of attention to the crisis, the proposals and actions—like supporting the "historic" Paris Agreement—were blueprints for likely catastrophe. While such proposals received fawning press coverage, little attention was paid to, for instance, how Obama's State Department, under Hillary Clinton, aggressively advocated for the global spread of hydrofracking (see Lee Fang and Steve Horn).

6   As the prospects for preventing the most apocalyptic scenarios dwindle, Obama's ecocidal boasting has continued unabated. In November 2018—the month after the IPCC's most alarming report yet, calling for immediate and drastic greenhouse gas emissions—in reference to "rising energy output under his watch and sudden talk of America's leading role in oil and gas production," he proudly commented, "'That was me, people'" (Klump).

7   For another critique of the Clean Power Plan's gross insufficiency, see David Biello.

8   A more recent instance of how the *Times* domesticates the radical challenge climate change poses to the ideological business as usual for which it operates as house organ involves the 1 August 2018 *The New York Times Magazine*, devoted, for the first time in the magazine's history, to a single article, Nathaniel Rich's 31,000-word "Losing Earth: The Decade We Almost Stopped Climate Change." The magazine "tried to make the release of its … article … as momentous as possible" in various ways, as Robinson Meyer observes, "even produc[ing] a video trailer for it." But if this works to mildly disrupt publishing business as usual, the article's argument per se functions to exempt economic and political business as usual from any such disruption. In the deepest way possible, Rich normalizes the crisis, literally naturalizing it by attributing it, ultimately, to "human nature" (dismissing as a "common boogeyman," for example, the notion that the fossil-fuel industry might bear

significant responsibility). Indeed, Rich insists, "We can trust the technology and the economics. It's harder to trust human nature." In addition to Meyer's, for a few related critiques of Rich's article see Klein ("Capitalism Killed") and Kaufman.

9   Gelbspan articulates "a number of reasons for this" (68), including that fact that the "culture of journalism is, basically, a political culture" and either marginalizes other kinds of stories, like scientific ones, or attends mainly to their short-term political implications and, especially, "the takeover of the news industry by a small number of massive media conglomerates" whose deepest commitments are shared with the energy industry.

10 Hulme does gesture toward situating himself, acknowledging that he "cannot escape the biases of my position" as "an Englishman trained as a geographer ... holding orthodox Christian beliefs" (xxxiv) etc., but what commitments are we meant to ascribe to this perspective? Whatever they are, they don't seem to inform the fantasized detachment he maintains in relation to global warming as an object of knowledge—though we might see his real commitments precisely in that fantasy itself.

11 Just as Hulme's "ideological stage" was a response to Thatcherism, his shift to individual "lifestyle choices" seems to reflect what Stuart Hall sees as the normalization of her brand of neoliberalism in the post Thatcher era, the process of Thatcherism becoming "the 'common sense of the age'" (8).

12 I'll put "Hulme" in quotation marks when referring to the author of the quoted article, as opposed to the author of the book that quotes that article.

13 In his blogpost "Do Scientists Really Believe in Climate Change," George Marshall describes a scene of such chastisement. Asked at a public meeting "If, as you have argued, the Amazon may burn down adding a further *degrees [of warming] to global climate, that's curtains for all of us, isn't it?" Hulme responded, "I do not think it is appropriate or useful for us to bang our drum about this—we need to use this information to generate a dialogue about our future options."

14 Examining the argument that "to discuss the likelihood and nature of social collapse due to climate change is irresponsible because it might trigger hopelessness amongst the general public," Jem Bendell traces it partly to the "paternalistic" and "technocratic attitude that has pervaded contemporary environmentalism."

15 In 2014, two studies concluded that, although it may take centuries, "The catastrophic collapse of the massive West Antarctic Ice Sheet is underway" and has already become "unstoppable" (Oskin).

16 Though Hoggett ultimately "sides" (272) with Risbey's critique of Hulme (discussed earlier), that conclusion doesn't seem to follow from the rest of the article, the brunt of which is an elaboration of Hulme's dismissal of catastrophism.

17 As an example of our having "been here before," Hoggett offers "the terror of nuclear war," and while I do think the climate crisis is indeed in some important ways analogous to the prospect of nuclear war (the aftermath of which would likely produce its own extreme climate change in the form of "nuclear winter"), he can offer that "terror" as an instance of "dangerous" catastrophism only by assuming that that existential threat is over. "Nuclear war never came" (264), he concludes, as if the end of the Cold War meant the end of the danger of thermonuclear exchange. In fact, William Perry, Daniel Ellsberg, and others have argued that the danger is at least as acute now as it was during the Cold War. And, of course, where the prospect of nuclear war is and (at least outside of Japan) was always only a threat, global warming is a catastrophic action that is *in the process* of happening.

18 To the question "when was the last time that CO_2 levels were this high, and what was the climate like back then?" Freedman responds, "there is no single, agreed-upon answer to those questions as studies show a wide date range from between 800,000 to 15 million years ago." Since that response, the CO_2 level has increased from just short of 400ppm to, as of this writing, 415ppm.
19 Compellingly, Ghosh offers a detailed contrast of the normalizing language of the Paris Agreement with the text of Pope Francis's more radical *Laudato Si'* (see pp. 150–59), a document that preceded Paris by only a few months.
20 Focusing on questions of environmental justice, Ziser and Sze also attribute that "sea-change" to Hurricane Katrina (2005), while, examining the recent history of environmental policy, Bluhdorn also sees the Stern Review (2007)—approaching the climate crisis purely in economic terms—and the 2007 IPCC report as elements of the "catapult."
21 Though my critique is centered on *An Inconvenient Truth* in its book form, the analysis applies to the widely circulated film. Both of these derive from Gore's original slide lecture.
22 Paralleling Gore's experience, Bill McKibben's decision to start the activist group 350.org was provoked by his own traumatic encounter. The realization that writing "wasn't enough," he recounts, "happened, I think, after that trip to Bangladesh, where I came down with dengue and watched so many people dying. Something in me snapped" (206).
23 According to Bonneuil and Fressoz, "10 percent of Marshall Plan funds were devoted" to the development of oil and oil-dependence, which "greatly enriched the U.S. oil majors ... from whom three-quarters of the oil financed by the Marshall Plan was bought, at higher-than-world-market price" (244).
24 The period ushered in by Gore's wise men has also been called The Great Acceleration, a hyper-escalation of the forces producing the Anthropocene (or Capitalocene). See, for example, Steffen et al.'s 2015 "The Trajectory of the Anthropocene: The Great Awakening."
25 Eddie Yuen observes that works like Gore's "follow compelling evidence for ecological collapse with woefully inadequate injunctions to green consumption or lobbying of political representatives. The underlying message is that the only available form of political agency lies in being an individual consumer" (29), so that "all inconvenient truths of capitalist exploitation and social inequality [are] swept aside" (32).
26 Revkin's blog in the *Times* ran from 2007 to 2016.
27 Ropeki's commentary is contained within Revkin's blog ("Getting beyond").
28 As I'll elaborate later, in critiquing the frequent focus on individualistic perspectives, Kari Norgaard explores how, in the particular context of a small Norwegian city, such disengagement from the radical meanings of climate change is socially constructed.
29 A different sort of "climate psychology" has emerged from the Climate Psychology Alliance, more interested in psychotherapeutic approaches. "There is value in understanding how grief, loss and mourning can shape our responses to climate change," Caroline Hickman explains on the CPA website, "for if we block out our emotions, then we are unable to connect with the urgency of the crisis—which may be one reason why we have so far failed to act sufficiently quickly."
30 According to its website, the YPCCC

> grew out of a groundbreaking conference on "Americans and Climate Change" convened in 2005 in Aspen, CO by the Yale School of Forestry &

Environmental Studies. Over 100 national leaders representing science, media, religion, politics, entertainment, education, business, environmentalism, and civil society developed an action plan to engage American society.

It was launched, that is, by a collocation of elites representing various businesses as usual, a group akin to those who, on an international scale, congratulated themselves on producing the suicide pact known as the Paris Agreement.

31 Though the study is immersed in the local culture of the pseudonymous Bygdaby, Norgaard sees the social construction of denial there as a "bellwether" for similar processes "in the United States and the rest of the world" (xix).

32 It is not that turning to the local and attending to the lateness of the day might not in fact inform each other. Decrying the "centralized monsters" of large energy providers, both private corporations and publicly owned monopolies, Klein proposes a new kind of utility, "run democratically, by the communities that use them, as 'co-ops' or as a 'commons'" (130). Indeed, she observes that "decentralization delivers ... on the largest scale of any model attempted thus far" (132). Crucially, however, Klein turns to the local only by contextualizing it in relation to a *necessary* centralized power. If "communities, co-ops and farmers" have "the best track record for spurring renewable energy turnarounds," a condition of their capacity to "deliver" is their "working within the context of an ambitious, well-designed national framework" (131–32)—centralized knowledge and local knowledge fulfilling each other.

33 The challenge of representing the question of time has been compounded by the recent appropriation of a discourse of urgency by champions of the very incrementalism that refuses to take that problem seriously: in support of his absurdly inadequate Clean Power Plan, and in the same week Shell started the exploratory drilling for oil in the arctic waters that he had allowed and encouraged, Obama intoned in 2015 that, on the "issue" of climate change, "there is such a thing as being too late" ("GLACIER")—an empty rhetorical gesture itself delayed, perhaps fatally, until seven years after his assuming the bully pulpit.

34 Likewise, Bendell's definition of "relinquishment" as involving the seemingly straightforward process of "people and communities" simply "letting go of certain assets, behaviours and beliefs where retaining them could make matters worse," seems to understate the degree to which "letting go" of "certain beliefs" might involve the traumatic letting go of the selves such businesses as usual partly constitute, a more fundamental relinquishment of the sort to which Bendell's "examples" do indeed half-gesture: "withdrawing from coastlines, shutting down vulnerable industrial facilities, or giving up expectations for certain types of consumption." Emphasizing "restoration" perhaps contributes to this understatement, as if what is called for is as simple as a return to what "we" once had and were, involving "people and communities rediscovering attitudes and approaches to life and organisation that our hydrocarbon-fuelled civilisation eroded."

35 Acknowledging the danger of attending too fully to the knowledge about the future that can be calculated, David Wood stresses that "there is a quite different phenomenon that needs equal treatment, which is that of unexpecting the expected, refusing to do the calculations. Here the problem is not that the future is unknown, but that 'we' live in denial" (281).

References

Banerjee, Neela, et al. "Exxon: The Road Not Taken." *Inside Climate News*, 16 September 2015, www.insideclimatenews.org/content/Exxon-The-Road-Not-Taken.

Baptist, Edward E. *The Half Has Never Been Told: Slavery and the Making of American Capitalism*. Basic Books, 2014.

Bendell, Jem. "Deep Adaptation: A Map for Negotiating Climate Tragedy." *IFLAS Occasional Paper 2*, 27 July 2018, www.lifeworth.com/deepadaptation.pdf.

Biello, David. "How Far Does Obama's Clean Power Plan Go in Slowing Climate Change?" *Scientific American*, 6 August 2015, www.scientificamerican.com/article/how-far-does-obama-s-clean-power-plan-go-in-slowing-climate-change/.

Bluhdorn, Ingolfur. "Locked into the Politics of Unsustainability." *Eurozine*, 30 October 2009, www.eurozine.com/locked-into-the-politics-of-unsustainability/.

Boykoff, Maxwell T. *Who Speaks for the Climate? Making Sense of Media Reporting on Climate Change*. Cambridge UP, 2011.

Caruth, Cathy. *Unclaimed Experience: Trauma, Narrative, and History*. Johns Hopkins UP, 1996.

Chomsky, Noam. "The Prospects for Survival." *Truthout*, 1 April 2014, www.truthout.org/articles/noam-chomsky-the-prospects-for-survival/.

Clark, Peter U. et al. "Consequences of Twenty-First-Century Policy for Multi-Millennial Climate and Sea-Level Change." *Nature Climate Change*, vol. 6, no. 4, February 2016, pp. 360–69.

Clark, Timothy. "Some Climate Change Ironies: Deconstruction, Environmental Politics and the Closure of Ecocriticism." *Oxford Literary Review*, vol. 32, no. 1, 2010, pp. 131–49.

"Climate Signals, Growing Louder." *The New York Times*, 31 March 2014, Editorial, www.nytimes.com/2014/04/01/opinion/climate-signals-growing-louder.html.

Cohen, Stanley. "Discussion." *Engaging with the Climate*, edited by Sally Weintrobe. Routledge, 2013, pp. 72–79.

Cushman, John H. "Shell Knew Fossil Fuels Created Climate Change Risks Back in 1980s, Internal Documents Show." *Inside Climate News*, 5 April 2018, www.insideclimatenews.org/news/05042018/shell-knew-scientists-climate-change-risks-fossil-fuels-global-warming-company-documents-netherlands-lawsuits.

Ellsberg, Daniel. *The Doomsday Machine: Confessions of a Nuclear War Planner*. Bloomsbury, 2017.

Fang, Lee, and Steve Horn. "Hillary Clinton's Energy Initiative Pressed Countries to Embrace Fracking, New Emails Reveal." *The Intercept*, 23 May 2016, www.theintercept.com/2016/05/23/hillary-clinton-fracking/.

Feinberg, Matthew, and Robb Willer. "Apocalypse Soon? Dire Messages Reduce Belief in Global Warming by Contradicting Just-World Beliefs." *Psychological Science*, vol. 22, no. 1, January 2011, pp. 34–38.

Freedman, Andrew. "The Last Time CO_2 Was This High, Humans Didn't Exist." *Climate Central*, 3 May 2013, www.climatecentral.org/news/the-last-time-co2-was-this-high-humans-didnt-exist-15938.

Gardiner, Beth. "We're All Climate Change Idiots." *The New York Times*, 22 July 2012, www.nytimes.com/2012/07/22/opinion/sunday/were-all-climate-change-idiots.html.

html?module=ArrowsNav&contentCollection=Opinion&action=keypress&region=FixedLeft&pgtype=article.
Gelbspan, Ross. *Boiling Point*. Basic Books, 2004.
Ghosh, Amitav. *The Great Derangement: Climate Change and the Unthinkable*. U of Chicago P, 2016.
Gibson-Graham, J. K. *A Postcapitalist Politics*. U of Minnesota P, 2006.
Gore, Al. *An Inconvenient Truth*. Rodale, 2006.
———. *The Assault on Reason*. Penguin, 2007.
Hall, Stuart. *The Hard Road to Renewal: Thatcherism and the Crisis of the Left*. Verso, 1988.
Hamilton, Clive. *Requiem for a Species*. Earthscan, 2010.
Heise, Ursula. *Sense of Place and Sense of Planet: The Environmental Imagination of the Global*. Oxford UP, 2008.
Hickman, Caroline. "What Psychotherapy Can Do for the Climate and Biodiversity Crises." *Climate Psychology Alliance*, 12 June 2019, www.climatepsychologyalliance.org/explorations/papers/357-what-psychotherapy-can-do-for-.
Hoggett, Paul. "Climate Change and the Apocalyptic Imagination." *Psychoanalysis, Culture, & Society*, vol. 16, no. 3, 2011, pp. 261–75.
———. "Climate Change in a Perverse Culture." *Engaging with the Climate*, edited by Sally Weintrobe. Routledge, 2013, pp. 56–71.
Hulme, Mike. "Chaotic World of Climate Truth." *BBC News*, 4 November 2006, http://news.bbc.co.uk/2/hi/science/nature/6115644.stm.
———. *Why We Disagree about Climate Change*. Cambridge UP, 2009.
Klein, Naomi. "Capitalism vs. the Climate." *The Nation*, 9 November 2011, www.thenation.com/article/capitalism-vs-climate/.
———. "Obama Is Beginning to Sound Like a Climate Leader, When Will He Act Like One?" *Democracy Now!*, 4 August 2015, www.democracynow.org/2015/8/4/naomi_klein_obama_is_beginning_to.
———. "Capitalism Killed Our Climate Momentum, Not 'Human Nature.'" *The Intercept*, 3 August 2018, www.theintercept.com/2018/08/03/climate-change-new-york-times-magazine/.
Klump, Edward. "Obama on U.S. Energy Boom: 'That Was Me, People.'" *E&E News*, 28 November 2018, www.eenews.net/stories/1060107557.
Leiserowitz, Anthony, et al. "Global Warming's Six Americas 2009." *Yale Program on Climate Change Communication*, 20 May 2009, www.climatecommunication.yale.edu/publications/global-warmings-six-americas-2009/.
Leiserowitz, Anthony. Interview with Bill Moyers. *Bill Moyers*, 4 January 2013, https://billmoyers.com/segment/anthony-leiserowitz-on-making-people-care-about-climate-change/.
Linden, Eugene. *The Winds of Change: Climate, Weather, and the Destruction of Civilization*. Simon & Schuster, 2006.
Marshall, George. "Do Scientists Really Believe in Climate Change?" *Climate Change Denial*, 22 August 2006, https://climatedenial.org/2006/08/22/do-scientists-really-believe-in-climate-change/.
Matthews, Susan. "Alarmism Is the Argument We Need to Fight Climate Change." *Slate*, 10 July 2017, www.slate.com/technology/2017/07/we-are-not-alarmed-enough-about-climate-change.html.

McKibben, Bill. *Eaarth: Making a Life on a Tough New Planet*. Henry Holt, 2010.
Meyer, Robinson. "The Problem with the *New York Times*' Big Story on Climate Change." *The Atlantic*, 1 August 2018, www.theatlantic.com/science/archive/2018/08/nyt-mag-nathaniel-rich-climate-change/566525/.
Nixon, Rob. *Slow Violence and the Environmentalism of the Poor*. Harvard UP, 2011.
Norgaard, Kari. *Living in Denial: Climate Change, Emotions, and Everyday Life*. MIT Press, 2011.
Obama, Barack. "Remarks by the President on American-Made Energy." The White House, Office of the Press Secretary, 2012, https://obamawhitehouse.archives.gov/the-press-office/2012/03/22/remarks-president-american-made-energy.
———. "Remarks by the President at the GLACIER Conference – Anchorage, AK." The White House, Office of the Press Secretary, 31 August 2015, https://obamawhitehouse.archives.gov/the-press-office/2015/09/01/remarks-president-glacier-conference-anchorage-ak.
Oreskes, Naomi, and Erik Conway. *Merchants of Doubt*. Bloomsbury, 2010.
Oskin, Becky. "Catastrophic Collapse of West Antarctic Ice Sheet Begins." *Live Science*, 12 May 2014, www.livescience.com/45534-west-antarctica-collapse-starts.html.
Oxford Dictionaries. "Disarticulate." www.lexico.com/en/definition/disarticulate.
Perry, William J. Interview with Robert Scheer. "Former Defense Secretary William Perry on the Nuclear Threat." *Huffpost*, 2 September 2017, www.huffpost.com/entry/former-defense-secretary-william-perry-on-the-nuclear_b_59ab04c1e4b0bef3378cd8fc?guccounter=1&guce.
"President Obama's Tough, Achievable Climate Plan." *The New York Times*. 3 August 2105, Editorial, www.nytimes.com/2015/08/04/opinion/president-obamas-tough-achievable-climate-plan.html.
Revkin, Andrew. "An Inconvenient Mind." *New York Times*, 28 November 2010, https://dotearth.blogs.nytimes.com/2010/11/18/an-inconvenient-mind/.
———. "Getting beyond the 2-Degree Threshold on Global Warming." *New York Times*, 3 October 2014, https://dotearth.blogs.nytimes.com/2014/10/03/getting-over-the-2-degree-limit-on-global-warming/.
Rich, Nathaniel. "Losing Earth: The Decade We Almost Stopped Climate Change." *New York Times*, 1 August 2018, www.nytimes.com/interactive/2018/08/01/magazine/climate-change-losing-earth.html?mtrref=www.google.com&gwh=B7185B6A381BC02243D0F7F0D3983805&gwt=pay&assetType=REGIWALL.
Risbey, James. "The New Climate Discourse: Alarmist or Alarming?" *Global Environmental Change*, vol. 18, 2008, pp. 26–37, https://sciencepolicy.colorado.edu/students/envs_4800/risbey_2008.pdf.
Ropeik, David. *The New York Times*, Dot Earth, 16 April 2014, https://dotearth.blogs.nytimes.com/2014/04/16/a-risk-analyst-explains-why-climate-change-risk-misperception-doesnt-necessarily-matter/.
Ropeik & Associates. "Clients," www.dropeik.com/dropeik/clients.html.
Solnit, Rebecca. "By the Way, Your Home Is on Fire: The Climate of Change and the Dangers of Stasis." *TomDispatch.com*, 11 March 2014, www.tomdispatch.com/post/175817/tomgram%3A_rebecca_solnit%2C_evacuate_the_economy/.
Steffen, Will, et al. "The Trajectory of the Anthropocene: The Great Awakening." *The Anthropocene Review*, vol. 2, no. 1, 2015, pp. 81–98.

Stephenson, Wen. "How Pope Francis Came to Embrace Not Just Climate Justice but Liberation Theology." *The Nation*, 9 September 2015, www.thenation.com/article/how-pope-francis-came-to-embrace-not-just-climate-justice-but-liberation-theology/.
Wood, David. "On Being Haunted by the Future." *Research in Phenomenology*, vol. 36, no. 1, 2006, pp. 274–98.
Yale Program on Climate Change Communication. About the Program. www.climatecommunication.yale.edu/about/the-program/.
Yuen, Eddie. "The Politics of Failure Have Failed: The Environmental Movement and Catastrophism." *Catastrophism: The Apocalyptic Politics of Collapse and Rebirth*, Sasha Lilley, David McNally, Eddie Yuen and James Davis. PM Press, 2012.
Ziser, Michael, and Julie Sze. "Climate Change, Environmental Aesthetics, and Global Environmental Justice Cultural Studies." *Discourse*, vol. 29, nos. 2 & 3, Spring & Fall 2007, pp. 384–410.

Chapter 4

Climate change and fiction I
Disarticulations and the Great Derangement

In Russell Hoban's *Riddley Walker*, the "tel woman" Lorna laments to Riddley, "Thats what happens to peopl on the way down from what they ben. The storys go" (17). She is talking about the loss of a particular kind of story, the essence of an oral tradition eroded in that novel by more recently re-emerged forms of narrative and knowing reproducing those that produced the ecocidal history haunting that novel's present. Ursula K. Le Guin, countering what she sees as the dominant Heroic narrative she traces back to "the story the mammoth hunters told about bashing, thrusting, raping, killing, about the Hero," writes that,

> lest there be no more telling of stories at all, some of us ... think we'd better start telling another one, which maybe people can go on with when the old one's finished. Maybe. The trouble is, we've all let ourselves become part of the killer story, and so we may get finished along with it. Hence it is with a certain feeling of urgency that I seek the nature, subject, words of the other story, the untold one, the life story.
> (168)

In a book subtitled *On the Possibility of Life in Capitalist Ruins*, Anna Tsing suggests that "the time has come for new ways of telling true stories beyond civilizational first principles. Without Man and Nature, all creatures can come back to life, and men and women can express themselves without the strictures of parochially imagined rationality," producing "stories [that] might be simultaneously true and fabulous" (vii).[1] And, limning the stakes of such pronouncements, Kate Rigby holds that,

> In a perilously warming world, the kind of stories that we tell about ourselves and our relations with one another, as well as with nonhuman others and our volatile environment, will shape ... whether our responses are geared toward maintaining current systems and relations and practices or whether they are transformative, enabling the emergence of new ways of being and dwelling.
> (2)

I've tried to suggest that the culturally dominant discourses of climate change, often embedded in that "parochially imagined rationality," work partly to disarticulate what Le Guin recognizes as the "urgency" of the moment, failing to grapple with the traumatic challenge to how cultural business as usual makes sense of the world and itself. Understandably, a call for "other" stories often centers on questions of imaginative narrative per se, recognizing the extent to which such stories inform the possibilities of other logics of "rationality," other forms of knowing. At the same time, as Adeline Johns-Putra observes,

> much has been written about the profound challenge that climate change poses to the imagination as an object of enquiry. For Sheila Jasanoff, the temporal and spatial scales of climate change drive "sharp wedges between society's fact-making and meaning-making faculties" (243). "Scale effects," writes Timothy Clark, "impose unprecedented difficulties of interpretation and imagination" (136) when it comes to climate change. It is for this reason that Timothy Morton has labeled global warming a "hyperobject."[2]
>
> ("My Job" 3)

To what extent, then, has imaginative narrative reckoned with this "profound challenge," with the traumatic prospects inherent in changing the story, in opening alternative discursive possibilities by which to help think and confront an existential dilemma often called, as in the subtitle of Amitav Ghosh's *The Great Derangement*, "unthinkable"?

In considering the relation of fiction to the climate crisis, Ghosh's book itself represents one important touchstone. For him, imaginative narrative has for the most part failed to respond to what he calls the Great Derangement of our ecocidal present.[3] "That climate change casts a much smaller shadow within the landscape of literary fiction than it does even in the public arena is not hard to establish" (7), he suggests, a condition he sees as an "aspect of the broader imaginative and cultural failure that lies at the heart of the climate crisis" (8). "Considering what climate change actually portends for the future of the earth," he proposes that "it should surely follow that this would be the principal preoccupation of writers the world over," but "this is very far from being the case." Ghosh mounts a literary-historical argument that addresses why that might be, elaborating how it is "that the age of global warming defies both literary fiction and contemporary common sense" (26), and, without endorsing all of that argument's details, I'd like to elaborate his conclusion, suggesting, indeed, that in some ways it doesn't go far enough—that for the most part fiction itself has contributed to the normalizing disarticulations that, I've argued, structure the discourse of climate change in general.

In doing this, I'll first place Ghosh's sweeping indictment in relation to claims that in the literary scene climate concerns are in fact increasingly prominent, and then more closely examine the nature of Ghosh's argument itself, along with Le Guin's parallel framing of contemporary fiction's failures. This is followed by a detailed consideration of how three particular novels generally lauded for their engagement with climate—Barbara Kingsolver's *Flight Behavior*, Liz Jensen's *The Rapture*, and Kim Stanley Robinson's *Green Earth*—decline the traumatic challenge to literary business as usual and, in that way, in fact contribute to the ongoing derangement.

***

If, as Ghosh has it, the climate crisis "defies both literary fiction and contemporary common sense," his premise itself might seem to defy the common sense of literary criticism. Where, for him, the literary landscape seems so little shadowed by climate change, literary critics tell a very different story, emphasizing how climate change informs a proliferation of all manner of imaginative work. In "Climate Change in Literature and Literary Studies" (2016), for example, Johns-Putra writes: "In the last 5 years, climate change has emerged as a dominant theme in literature and, correspondingly, in literary studies. Its popularity in fiction has given rise to the term cli-fi, or climate change fiction, and speculation that this constitutes a distinctive literary genre" that has produced "a canon of climate change fiction." Most notably, perhaps, Adam Trexler's *Anthropocene Fictions: The Novel in a Time of Climate Change* (2015) surveys a vast archive of over 150 novels and proposes that "as still more novels incorporate the weather, technology, and ideas of the Anthropocene, features of these early climate change novels will be diffused into literature at large" (15).

We might understand such drastically different accounts of climate change in fiction in two ways. First, where in Trexler's ample archive we find many of what are more or less generic fictions, Ghosh can see the literary cabinet as mostly bare by looking primarily at what he calls, as above, "literary fiction" or the "'realist' novel" (23) or "the kind that is taken seriously by serious literary journals" (7).[4] Acknowledging that "there is a new genre of science fiction called 'climate fiction' or cli-fi," he defines it as "made up of disaster stories set in the future," which, for him, "is exactly the rub" (72);[5] considering Margaret Atwood's characterization of science fiction and speculative fiction as concerning "'imagined other worlds located somewhere apart from our everyday one: in another time, in another dimension ... on the other side of the threshold that divides the known from the unknown,'" he finds there "marvelous clarity" about "some of the ways the Anthropocene resists science fiction: it is precisely not an imagined 'other' world apart from ours; nor is it located in another 'time' or another 'dimension'" (72–73).

Of course, as an argument in favor of dismissing science fiction in this context, this is not compelling. As Ursula Heise observes, Ghosh here "fundamentally misunderstand[s] the 'elsewheres' of science fiction," which "of course always addresses its audience's here and now through the detour of imagined futures." Jesse Oak Taylor adds that even as Ghosh "seems to critique the literary history of exclusivity that holds realism as the canonical basis of the novel," at the same time "his own criteria for what substantive engagement with climate change in fiction would look like replay that exclusion, suggesting that only realist novels set in the historical present can fulfill the obligation of rendering the crisis both present and real." There is a difference, however, between endorsing the particular logic of Ghosh's argument about sci-fi per se and sharing his conclusion about the general failure of the contemporary literary imagination. At the heart of that failure Ghosh finds a normalizing "grid of literary forms and conventions" (7), and though his focus remains on what he calls "literary fiction," we might see the genre fiction that in Trexler's account constitutes much of cli-fi as an especially codified element of that "grid" understood in a larger sense. Indeed, considering that, as Andrew Hoberek points out, after "the self-consciously 'literary' appropriation of popular genres in the work of authors like Barth and Pynchon" there has emerged a "newer tendency to confer literary status on popular genres themselves" (238)—a tendency that plays out the logic of Fredric Jameson's 1991 suggestion that "aesthetic production today has become integrated into commodity production generally" (4)—we might see whatever's at stake in Ghosh's sequestering "serious" from "generic" fiction in the first place as mooted by the normalizing function of both. Moreover, if "apocalyptic imagery has saturated popular culture for decades," as Eddie Yuen suggests, so that "the ubiquity of apocalypse in recent decades has led to a banalization of the concept," then the repeated pop cultural iterations of that concept in generic cli-fi can be understood to help maintain the conventionalizing "din," over which truly alarmed "environmentalists" can only "find themselves struggling to be heard" (20). What may be at stake, that is, isn't whether, as for Ghosh, sci fi "addresses its audience's here and now" but, rather, whether the terms of that address respond to the representational challenge with which it is confronted. Extending elements of his critique of realism, we can thus find genre fiction failing that challenge for reasons other than the ones Ghosh himself advances perhaps too casually.[6]

That Trexler and Johns-Putra take science fiction on its own terms points to a second way to understand how a literary scene that seems so impoverished to Ghosh appears to them as thriving. Compelled by what he registers as the urgency of a "deranged" present, Ghosh approaches fiction in light of that urgency, and finds it wanting. More narrowly concerned with literary critical questions per se—and seemingly less compelled by a sense of urgency—they approach an archive of books in some way representing climate change with an intent simply to describe and catalogue, Trexler explaining that, since, "unlike Elizabethan plays or Modernist poetry, Anthropocene fiction has not [yet] been catalogued, sorted, and analyzed" (15), his book is "unapologetically descriptive" (16).

This difference is rooted in very different premises about the nature of climate change itself, and, thus, sharp differences in their understandings of human responsibility and agency. Where for Ghosh it is "the distribution of power in the world" that "lies at the core of the climate crisis" (146), for Trexler, declining any such politically charged framework, "climate change emerges from a host of interrelated sources, including natural effects (solar radiation), industrial processes (car emissions), and scientific practices (climate modeling), but also cultural processes such as popular science writing, policy papers, political speeches, and novels" (25). Denouncing the Paris Agreement, Ghosh finds "enshrined" there "the practices that are known to have created the situation," those proceeding from "the current paradigm of perpetual growth" (154), while, as above, Trexler blunts any such disruptive confrontation with the premises of business as usual and, minimizing the centrality of the human agency by which that paradigm has colonized contemporary common sense, observes how "the best Anthropocene novels … explore how things like ocean currents, tigers, viruses, floods, vehicles, and capital relentlessly shape human experience" (27), including "anthropogenic climate change," just one more element of an endless list of things—"genes, places, local climates [and] findings"—best understood "as hybrids emerging from natural and human agency" (22–23). If Ghosh "differ[s] with those who identify capitalism" as the root of anthropogenic climate change, it is only to the extent that they don't sufficiently locate the crisis as rooted in *both* "capitalism and *empire*" (146, my emphasis), while, for Trexler, "Marxian criticism's blame of corporate capitalism's overweening power, or attention to 'social constructions' more generally, fails to account for climate's distinct, nonhuman agency" (23).[7] Thus where Ghosh responds with alarm to a present he registers as the Great Derangement, indicting "most forms of art and literature" as "modes of concealment" (11), Trexler locates himself above the fray, describing with chilling even-handedness "a moment when scientists and activists make fervent calls for drastic emissions reductions and when other commentators denounce global warming as a conspiracy between big government and big science" (265), just as his approach to the literary archive is "unapologetically descriptive," evincing the same benumbed detachment.[8]

***

In Ghosh's account, "before the birth of the modern novel, whenever stories were told, fiction delighted in the unheard-of and the unlikely" (16), but "the novel takes its modern form through" what Franco Moretti calls "'the relocation of the unheard-of toward the background … while the everyday moves into the foreground'" (17), thus "'rationalizing the novelistic universe'" (19) in accordance with "'*the new regularity of bourgeois life.*'"[9] This rationalizing is rooted in "the Cartesian dualism that arrogates all intelligence and agency to the human while denying them to every other kind of being" (31), one "of the originary impulses of modernity" Ghosh describes, with Bruno Latour, as "the project of 'partitioning,' or deepening the imaginary gulf between Nature and Culture" (68), a "habit of mind that proceeded by creating discontinuities ... render[ing] the interconnectedness of Gaia unthinkable" (56). For Ghosh, insofar as the modern novel is born out of this habit of mind—embodying the "grid of literary forms and conventions that came to shape the narrative imagination in precisely that period when the accumulation of carbon in the atmosphere was rewriting the destiny of the earth" (7)—it cannot account for the extremity produced by climate change, "unheard-of" during the unusual climate stability of the Holocene, but nonetheless a constituting condition of the present and the future.[10] The "essence" of the "Anthropocene," that is, "consists of phenomena that were long ago expelled from the territory of the novel—forces of unthinkable magnitude that create unbearably intimate connections over vast gaps in time and space" (63). Thus, "the age of global warming defies both literary fiction and contemporary common sense" (26), so that "the very gestures with which" the "realistic novel ... conjures up reality are actually a concealment of the real" (23).[11]

Writing, in 1986, without reference to climate change per se but out of a "certain feeling of urgency" that "lest there be no more telling of stories at all" we need "another story ... the untold one," Le Guin offers a very different account of the novel in relation to that "urgency" than does Ghosh. For Ghosh, "before the birth of the modern novel, wherever stories were told, fiction delighted in the unheard-of and the unlikely ... leaping blithely from one exceptional event to another" (as in *The Arabian Nights* or *The Decameron*) (16). Le Guin, too, sees the modern novel eclipsing a narrative tradition that centers on the "exceptional," but where Ghosh stresses the important narrative capacities of that now eclipsed tradition, she finds it problematic precisely *because*, centered around the Hero, it excludes the quotidian, the narrative emergence of which she welcomes. She imagines story emerging from the restless who, in Paleolithic tribes where "the average person could make a nice living in about a fifteen-hour workweek," didn't "have a baby around to enliven their life, or skill in making, or cooking, or singing, or very interesting thoughts to think," and thus "decided to slope off and hunt mammoths." In this version of things, "it wasn't the meat that made the difference" but, rather, "it was the story": "It is hard to tell a really gripping tale of how I wrested a wild-oat seed from its husk, and then another, and then another, and then another, and then another, and then I scratched my gnat bites, and Ool said something funny, and we went down to the creek and got a drink," which "does not compare" and "cannot compete" with "how I thrust my spear deep into the titanic hairy flank while

Oob, impaled on one huge sweeping tusk, writhed screaming ... as I shot my unerring arrow straight through eye to brain"—a story with "Action" and, especially, "a Hero" (165–66). Soon all the other people are "pressed into service in the tale of the Hero. But it isn't their story. It's his" (166). If, against this tradition, "the novel is a fundamentally unheroic kind of story," the dilemma is that "the Hero has frequently taken it over, that being his imperial nature" (168).

If comparing Large Claims about "the novel" or the relation of the (modern) novel to older kinds of stories will to some degree necessarily locate us in the shadow of the Tower of Babel, a close sorting of these two accounts suggests some important complementarity, at least partly centered on the "urgent" need for kinds of narratives other than the ones—either too ordinary or too heroic—each sees as culturally dominant. Suggestively, both of these accounts turn in some way on the question of "containment." For Ghosh, the contemporary imaginative failure in the face of the climate crisis reflects his view that "probability and the modern novel are in fact twins, born about the same time, under a shared star that destined them to work as vessels for the *containment* of the same kind of experience" (16, my emphasis)—of what appears within the framework of the Holocene as improbable; the container functions here to seal off the pressing but ostensibly improbable reality. For Le Guin, that dominant (heroic) narratives have worked *against* containment is itself the problem:

> We've heard it, we've all heard all about all the sticks spears and swords, the things to bash and poke and hit with, the long, hard things, but we have not heard about the thing to put things in, *the container for the thing contained*. That is a new story. That is news.
>
> (167, my emphasis)

For her, though the novel has been colonized by the hero, "the natural, proper, fitting shape of the novel might be that of a sack, a bag ... holding things in a particular, powerful relation to one another and to us" (169).

If opposed senses of the term "contain" operate here—to keep at bay (a cold-war policy of Containment) and to house within ("I contain multitudes," Walt Whitman boasts)—they're both put into the service of a critique of literary business as usual. I'd like to complicate both of those critiques by framing the problem in relation to the representational challenge posed by conceptions of trauma. If the modern novel lets back in those "forces of unthinkable magnitude" Ghosh sees it as having partitioned off, how can it help make those forces partly thinkable? How can Le Guin's fictional carrier bag, made to carry potatoes and oats, respond to those unthinkable forces that would rend the linguistic fabric of the bag itself? In exploring this question in the next chapter, my argument, like theirs, will also turn on a notion of "containment"—though one that, in partly resolving the opposition inherent in their use of the term, can help alert us to how, even in the face of Ghosh's indictment, fictions might open themselves to the challenge of representing the traumatic conditions the climate crisis represents. First, though, I'd like to more closely consider why, even with the emergence of "cli-fi," I find that indictment mostly compelling—indeed, in certain ways not severe enough. Even the few novels Ghosh himself exempts from his indictment, that is, seem to me to participate in the same "concealment" he identifies as the ground of fiction's more general failure.[12]

***

We might see those two works that Ghosh names as exceptions to his general indictment, Barbara Kingsolver's *Flight Behavior* and Liz Jensen's *Rapture*, along with other generally lauded climate fictions like Kim Stanley Robinson's *Green Earth*, as representing the large archive studied by Trexler. If, as Dominick LaCapra suggests, attempts to represent trauma "should" produce "stylistic effects" that would register what he calls "empathetic unsettlement" (723), for the most part, formally, climate fiction remains resolutely *settled*, stylistically unperturbed by the threat it conjures. Summarizing the relationship between climate change and the generic fiction that constitutes much of his archive, Trexler writes,

> Thrillers could describe the countdown to a heroic rescue. Dystopias found a new reason for material scarcity and totalitarianism. Apocalyptic narratives could repurpose greenhouse gases to speculate about the end of time, a novelty to replace nuclear holocausts, pandemics, and the Second Coming.
>
> (223)

Climate change here takes its settled place comfortably within the conventional representational structures, "repurposed" for familiar forms of narrative. It is hard, that is, to see how most climate fiction disrupts the "grid of literary forms and conventions" that, for Ghosh, emerged precisely as a way of normalizing the partition of "culture" from "nature"—hard to see, that is, how it mounts the challenge to literary business as usual for which Ghosh, like Le Guin, so urgently calls.

Kingsolver's *Flight Behavior* centers on the development of its main character, Dellarobia, global warming functioning not as an unsettling of the familiar narrative of individual personal development but, rather, as the source of some of the conflict she has to reckon with and the occasion for her personal growth. In also tracing "the complex circulation of scientific knowledge through a small Tennessee community," as Trexler suggests, and examining how "characters' understanding of climate change is shaped by the complicated terms of their own identity" (227), this novel may accomplish "the good work of literary realism" (228), but that circulating knowledge nonetheless leaves the terms of that "literary realism" themselves unshaken. *Flight Behavior* does critique mass media representations of global warming, especially the TV coverage of the spectacular arrival in Dellarobia's woods of millions of monarch butterflies—the changing climate having driven them from their traditional wintering place, in Mexico—as a "human interest" story. But the critique doesn't go much beyond this easy target. The novel presents a climactic scene in which, interviewed by a TV reporter, the lepidopterist on hand to study the (severely endangered) colony abandons his avowed commitment to public scientific detachment and openly indicts the press for the reductive and trivializing way it "covers" global warming "stories" and for its key role in framing global warming as a scientific "controversy"; the TV camera stops rolling, of course, but another character secretly records the impassioned speech on her phone, and when she posts it to YouTube, this is staged by the book as a triumphant narrative success. But even as the narrative celebrates "the way the Ovid-and-Tina video had gone viral" (374), we might see in the fact that it "came up ninth on the list now, when you Googled 'science'" (375) evidence not of its significant impact but, rather, of the way, like all "content," it is minimized, safely rendered as another element (but in the top ten!) of a familiarizing algorithmic list.

Flight Behavior's critique of the representational limitations of TV as a visual medium is certainly telling, as when the lepidopterist, Ovid Brown, tells the reporter, "We are on top of Niagara Falls, Tina," and asks "Does it strike you as a good time to debate the existence of the falls?" she can only respond, "If this were Niagara Falls, I'd have a decent background. ... I can't do anything with this without a visual" (367). But the triumph of capturing the exchange as a video gone viral itself depends on rendering it precisely as such a "visual"; that it garnered "hundreds of thousands" of views is presented as good news, but we might wonder what it is exactly that is being so massively "viewed," especially when, as a visual image, the exchange itself becomes the social media equivalent of "good TV," effective for the spectacle of conflict itself, not for its substance: "Whatever qualms people had about scientists, they were thrilled to watch one rip into an ice-queen newscaster of some repute" (374). Both in the way the traumatic threat of global warming is domesticated by the (undisrupted) conventions of literary realism, then, and in staging the circulation of a YouTube video as a narrative success, Kingsolver's novel exemplifies how, in evading the representational dilemma, even the most lauded of climate fiction functions to cut the climate crisis down to normalizing narrative size.

Liz Jensen's *The Rapture*, too, cleaves closely to very familiar, rather rigid, narrative conventions, especially those defined by the so-called "eco-thriller." Even if one can't always judge a book by the blurbs tucked behind its cover, in the reviews introducing the paperback edition, presented as "praise," Jensen's novel is, not misleadingly, said to promise the requisite "high-octane action" to "see you through airport delays" (stupefyingly clueless terms of praise for a book ostensibly concerned with the violence inherent in burning fossil fuels). Eco-thrillers, Shawn Schollmeyer writes, "have replaced the Cold War tensions of the classic spy thriller with our struggle to survive ecological threats" (qtd. in Otto, 113), such that, as Eric Otto has it, in this genre "environmental concerns" function largely "merely as background contexts for gripping plots" (119). In *The Rapture*, that gripping plot concerns a psychotherapist, Gabrielle Fox, who begins to see that the visions of her psychotic teenage patient, Bethany Krall, predict with geographic and chronological precision a series of spectacular environmental catastrophes, including a virtually apocalyptic one (the result of an extreme fossil fuel extractive process) about which Gabrielle, climate scientist Fraser Melville (her generically mandated "love interest"), and their cohort of (generically mandated) experts try to raise a global warning. As Otto suggests, "the ecopolitical significance ... fades as Bethany's psychic phenomena take center stage in the protagonist's effort to inform the public about the coming disaster" (116).

In some sense, that is, the novel does focus both on how to know the "disaster" inherent in the fossil economy and on how to represent it. The question of "how to know," however, is reduced to a focus simply on provoking and decoding Bethany's visions—not grappling with a traumatic excess but solving an informational puzzle.[13] And, similarly, the representational problem is reduced to a question of how to distribute in the public sphere such an extreme and apocalyptic warning, a problem neatly and triumphantly resolved in the narrative by means of a technologically ingenious act of geoengineering—"Giant graffiti" (278), written in "dye [that] appears to be organic" (279), that "straddles fifty kilometres of ice cap," each character "at least ten kilometres high and across ... so big you can only see them by satellite" (278). That "they're calling it the world's biggest ever publicity stunt" is staged as a triumph ("Frazier Melville's face is breaking into a grin" [278]), with no sense that the attempt to galvanize world attention, to provoke radical action, has been safely contained within a normalizing media category, as "publicity," and, doubly dismissive, rendered as mere "stunt." Just as *Flight Behavior* poses an ostensible representational dilemma as addressable by fifteen minutes of social media fame, then, *The Rapture* poses a representational problem as primarily a technological one, the adequate solution to which—garnering conventional media "publicity"—is never in doubt within the normalizing conventions that define the eco-thriller's deepest commitments.

Given his dismissal of science fiction as focused on a world "other" than this one, it seems odd that one of the two books Ghosh mentions as overcoming fiction's resistance to climate change relies so heavily on clairvoyant visions containing such precise (and decodable) information about specific future events. A number of other climate novels, having prompted a more serious critical discussion, would seem more likely possible exceptions to his general indictment—though, as I've suggested, that critical discussion has mostly taken such fiction on its own terms, trimming climate change to fit comfortably into the forms of literary business as usual. Kim Stanley Robinson's trilogy *Science in the Capitol* (2004–2007), revised and reissued in the single-volume *Green Earth* (2015), presents a particularly striking case in point.[14] In rebuking Ghosh's dismissal of sci-fi, both Heise and Taylor evoke Robinson, and even as certain elements of it come under some cautious critique, *Green Earth* is roundly treated respectfully as a serious, pragmatically minded and "positive" engagement with global warming, "stand]ing] out among works of cli-fi," Rebecca Evans has it, "for its determined commitment to solutions" and, for Heise, "highlight[ing] the varied kinds of ingenuity, expertise, political engagement, and aesthetic beauty climate change will generate" ("Climate Stories"). Such an approach is typified by Trexler, for instance, who sees Robinson as "imagin[ing] how scientists, politicians, and diverse publics can be assembled into effective agencies," and thus exemplifying how "climate change novels can provide new models of collective organization to address global emissions and local impacts" (26). Especially telling is Johns-Petra's summary:

> The narrative's tone and dénouement are hopeful and happy: the scientists' lives acquire a spiritual depth thanks to their friendship with a group of political exiles from the fictional Buddhist nation of Khembali; lonely misfit Frank finds true—if unlikely—love with a government intelligence agent enmeshed in rogue secret service operations; and romance blossoms between Phil Chase and Diane Chang, who end the narrative as, respectively, President and Presidential Science Advisor.
> ("Ecocriticism" 752)

In that last blossoming romance, culminating in a marriage, Johns-Putra finds "the moral for the trilogy": "only science and politics in concord will save the day; it is such concord that enables the narrative's large-scale scientific interventions, which ultimately mitigate and stabilise the many climate change disasters."

For Johns-Putra, "this summary ... suggests a generic mixing," perhaps "espionage thriller" or "political romance," that, focused on taxonomical questions about genre theory, she finds "provocative." But however extensively they are mixed, the basic building blocks of such commercial genres cannot construct a provocation to literary business as usual itself, and thus no representational challenges impede the lengthy but nonetheless breathless narrative. Indeed, belying Robert Markley's suggestion that the book offers "a visionary reassessment of the assumptions and values that define contemporary science and politics" (8), and Bill McKibben's counting it among those climate fictions offering the "jolts we dearly need" (4), *Green Earth* relies upon the very "Hero" narrative that Le Guin sees as having contributed toward our ecocidally deranged present—whether one identifies the trilogy's hero as an individual character like Frank Vanderwal (whose story Kilgore sees tracing an "heroic odyssey" [97]) or, with Robinson, as "the NSF ... or science itself" (qtd. in Johns-Petra, "Ecocriticism" 757).[15] The "dénouement" that is "hopeful and happy" involves Chase, the newly elected, ostensibly progressive President, committing to a "rescue operation ... so much larger than anything else we've ever done" (940), an America-saves-the-world rescue-project openly celebrated as "Heroic!" (943). Invested in such normalizing narratives (including American Exceptionalism), the book cannot provoke any real challenges to the assumptions on which the heroic (scientific and political) institutions are premised, so that, in articulating his strategy for undertaking the rescue project, the newly elected President (like the actual, "progressive," Paris Agreement) disarticulates results from causes, the need for action from any analysis of the economic or nationalistic forces that have produced the current emergency. Although he says that "capitalism continues to vampire its way around the globe," Chase cannot process the traumatic implications of that vampirism to the political order with which he is identified, and thus, incoherently, rethinks that vampire simply as a neutral force that "we have to harness ... to our cause" (940). Because "we in the United States have the biggest and richest and most powerful government in the world!" (940), he triumphalistically enthuses, we can "aim capitalism in any direction we want ... creating the newest region of maxim profit" by directing the "natural flow of capital." For him, this is great news: "saving the biosphere IS the next investment opportunity! It's massive."

As a result of such neoliberal boosterism, where critics see the book, again, as "committed to solutions," or offering "new models of collective organization to address global emissions," or depicting "interventions, which ultimately mitigate and stabilize the many climate change disasters," or, even, manifesting "a visionary reassessment of the assumptions and values that define contemporary science and politics," its ostensibly happy ending—presumably understood to fulfill these laudatory readings, to show, in Robert Markley's title phrase, "How to Go Forward"—goes all in on massive technological interventions emerging from the very epistemologically hubristic technocratic and economic structures that have produced the dilemma in the first place, primarily a massive project to restart the Gulf Stream by dumping five hundred million tons of salt in the North Atlantic (the "world's first planetary engineering project," financed by re-insurance companies and depending upon the cooperation of the Army Corps of Engineers [KimStanleyRobinson.info]), but also the introduction into Siberia of genetically engineered lichen (designed to increase absorption of atmospheric carbon), the rehydration of the Aral Sea (enlarging it to twice its original size), and other projects meant to contribute to what Robinson calls "terraforming" (his term for what is elsewhere called "geoengineering"), the "conscious and successful management of an entire planet's biosphere" as he puts it (*Imagining* 2), constituting the basis of his celebrated "commitment to solutions."[16] As fundamentally committed to technocratic framings of climate change as it is to conventional literary genres like thriller and romance, then, like *Flight Behavior* and *The Rapture*, *Green Earth* represents how as a body of work climate fiction parallels other climate discourses both in disarticulating the traumatic threat and in thus helping constitute the normalized denial inhabiting contemporary common sense.[17]

Notes

1 Of course, as Kate Rigby cautions, "this does not mean ... that all we need is a 'new story' to budge the entrenched socioeconomic and power-political interests that are keeping us on the path to catastrophe" (177).
2 See Jasanoff's "A New Climate," Clark's "Derangements," and Morton's *Hyperobjects*.
3 Ghosh's title allusively points to how what he calls Derangement is ultimately a form of traumatic social violence. In James Marsh's account of the British expulsion of the Arcadians from Nova Scotia, known as *Le Grand Derangement*, he writes: "Between 1755 and 1763, approximately 10,000 Acadians were deported. They were shipped to many points around the Atlantic. Large numbers were landed in the English colonies, others in France or the Caribbean. Thousands died of disease or starvation in the squalid conditions on board ship."
4 We needn't accept Ghosh's conflation of "literary fiction" with the "realist novel" in order to see a failure of "serious" literature to grapple with the derangement of climate change even across the range of what Andrew Hoberek observes as "the heterogeneity of contemporary fiction" (236).
5 Ghosh's definition of cli-fi here is somewhat anomalous. The term is often used to refer to climate fiction more generally, beyond sci-fi per se, as in Johns-Putra's account, above.
6 It is, of course, possible that a work that is categorizable as a form of "genre fiction" might evoke the conventions of a genre only to unsettle them, functioning to disrupt the "grid of literary forms and conventions" normalizing literary business as usual—as I argue in the next chapter in relation to *The Road* and *Riddley Walker*. In that sense, my discussion here is meant not to stake a claim about the category of "genre fiction" per se, but, rather, to suggest something about the particular kind of popular genre fictions that have defined much of the literary response to climate change.
7 For a wide-ranging critique of the ways that the human agency responsible for anthropogenic climate change is obscured by various discourses locating agency in inanimate entities, see Andreas Malm, *The Progress of This Storm: Nature and Society in a Warming World*. At the theoretical center of these discourses,

Malm locates the work of Bruno Latour, on whom much of Trexler's account depends.
8 If there is some tension between Ghosh's sweeping indictment of contemporary fiction and his acknowledgement that the "challenges" climate change poses to fiction "have been overcome in many novels" (73), perhaps that reflects his sense of political urgency: yes, there are "many" successful climate novels, but they still amount to just a drop in the cultural bucket.
9 Ghosh quotes Moretti's *The Bourgeois*, 381.
10 The Holocene has, of course, seen many individual extreme weather events, and periods of relative climate disruption, often with catastrophic consequences for human societies, though these occurred within the generally stable framework of a climate system that has defined that geologic era, the continued existence of which is precisely what the climate crisis puts at stake. See John Brooke's *Climate Change and the Course of Global History.*
11 A somewhat parallel account is offered by Anna Tsing: since the Enlightenment, the West has for the most part conceived of "Nature" as "grand and universal but also passive and mechanical. Nature was a backdrop and resource for the moral intentionality of Man, which could tame and master Nature. It was left to fabulists, including non-Western and non-civilizational storytellers, to remind us of the lively activities of all beings, human and not human" (xvii).
12 Augmenting Ghosh's suggestion that the "grid of literary forms and conventions" shaping the history of the novel emerged at "precisely the period when the accumulation of carbon in the atmosphere was rewriting the destiny of the earth," we might say that an actionable *understanding* of that process of accumulation emerged just at a period when the forces working to normalize the narrative (and ideological) status quo became especially acute. In Chapter 2, I noted what Klein calls the "bad timing" of the ascendance of neoliberalism (in the wake of the collapse of the U.S.S.R.) coinciding with "governments and scientists [beginning to talk] seriously about radical cuts to greenhouse gas emissions" (18). In the 1980s and 1990s, the U.S. thus saw what Samuel Cohen argues was a "revitalization" of "the triumphalist narrative" (376) by which, as James Berger has shown (in *After the End*), the traumas of U.S. history inhabiting the present were disavowed. The first talk about cutting greenhouse gas emissions thus emerged just as the end of the Cold War ushered in, so it was thought, the End of History, which, Cohen suggests, "provided a model of narrative closure difficult to resist." And though after 9/11 government officials spoke of a "new normal," the attack that day in fact intensified the national commitment to precisely an economic business as usual that demanded massive increases of greenhouse gas emissions. "The speed with which the government sought to return the nation to a pre-9/11 status quo was ... staggering," Kathy Knapp writes:

> Just days after the attacks, for instance, President Bush told the nation that we were engaged in a "fight for our principles," which would require every citizen's "continued participation and confidence in the American economy." Framing the stakes even more explicitly, the president's brother and Florida governor Jeb Bush admonished Americans to "consider it their patriotic duty to go shopping, go to a restaurant, take a cruise, travel with their family," because "frankly, the terrorists win if Americans don't go back to normalcy."
> (197)

Of course, another national response to 9/11 was the inflicting of massive violence on other countries. At just the time when the escalating climate crisis demanded unprecedented global cooperation, that is, the U.S. recommitted itself to the role of Global Avenger.

13   Bethany's visions follow upon treatments of electroconvulsive therapy (ECT), and when it develops that she needs (and craves) higher and higher doses, Gabrielle and the others (reluctantly) apply an almost fatal dose, in an effort to stimulate more visions—to get more information about the coming catastrophe.

14   In "compress[ing] about 1100 pages to about 800," Robinson writes, seemingly without embarrassment, "nothing important was lost" (xiii). If this suggests the original version suffered significant lapses in authorial and editorial attention, the account of the revised edition as "about 800 pages" indicates that it too suffers from such lapses: the revision in fact numbers not "about 800 pages" but, rather, 1069, about the length of the original.

15   John-Putra refers here to Moira Gunn's "Interview with Kim Stanley Robinson."

16   Noting that Robinson's trilogy "was widely applauded for its scientific accuracy and praised for its higher artistic standards relative to the Hollywood film 'The Day after Tomorrow' and Michael Crichton's *State of Fear*," Ernest Yanarella and Christopher Rice analyze his "deep-seated Enlightenment assumptions about modern science and the scientific community" and his granting "license to Science and scientists to utilize industrial-strength geoengineering techniques to refashion ... Earth's ecosystem" (2234). For Robinson on geoengineering, see his "Terraforming Earth." For an elaboration of how geoengineering doubles down on the modes of thinking that have produced the extreme predicament it proposes to address, see Naomi Klein's *This Changes Everything*, Chapter 8, "Dimming the Sun."

17   Beyond its celebration of geoengineering and investment in generic, and heroic, narrative conventions, *Green Earth* remains deeply embedded in a variety of other retrograde ideological and representational businesses as usual, and even when one or another aspect of this is pointed out, it doesn't seem to call into question what seems to be a general inclination to praise the book (perhaps for its ostensibly good intentions). Observing that "critics have hailed cli-fi as literature's contribution to the fight against climate change, praising the genre for combining narrative thrills with practical scientific information and profound ethical interrogations," Rebecca Evans, for example, finds that "*Green Earth's* sheer narrative variety makes it exemplary among works of 'cli-fi,'" even as her description of those ostensibly various narratives would seem to raise fundamental questions about whether being "exemplary" in this regard is a good thing. The "utopian" vision that for her, and others, constitutes one of Robinson's most important contributions—his purportedly useful antidote to the often "dystopian" bent of much cli-fi—seems, for example, a frail cover for the sort of triumphalism we've seen at work in his hubristic investment in geoengineering. Evans finds merely that "this utopianism occasionally rankles," but in what she registers as merely rankling—"Robinson breezes past the major claim of climate justice scholars and activists"—we might recognize a disavowal of the traumatic elements that cannot be accommodated in his technocratic framing of the problem, focused on elite centers of power. Pointing here to "the scene of the cheerful evacuation of [the fictional Asian island nation] Khembalung due to catastrophic sea level rise," in which "helicopters and boats efficiently relocate the entire island in a matter of hours," and noting that "later, the monks use their funds to establish an idyllic new home [in Washington D.C.], and reassuringly explain that their nation has always traveled between different sites," Evans "remain[s] torn over whether the novel should be praised for the mere fact of

depicting climate refugees or taken to task for framing their displacement as so easily resolved," but in such easy resolution, focused solely on a privileged and powerful small group, we might see the process not of "depicting" climate migration but, rather, of effacing the massive trauma such migration reflects and, often, provokes. (Indeed, the only climate refugees in this novel are also power brokers of global reach. They "eventually introduce everybody to the Dalai Lama," Evans writes, "who gives a marriage blessing to the union of the American president and his national science adviser.")

Where Heise recognizes these monks as "functioning as rather grotesque stereotypes of Buddhist wisdom and serenity" (*Sense* 207), such grotesque reductionism characterizes the trilogy as a whole, reflecting its investment in genres like the thriller and the romance. This accords with the central character's involvement with sociobiology. Although Frank Vanderwal is an expert in biomathematics, occupying a powerful position at the NSF, he is so heroically and multiply gifted that, having "a personal interest in sociobiology," in his "free time" (when he is not kayaking, rock-climbing, body surfing, playing frisbee with freegans, hanging with racially mixed group of homeless people, pursuing secret rendezvous with his mysterious, beautiful lover who involves him in spy intrigue with the very highest of democratic stakes) he can manage to "edit ... a journal on the subject" (Kilgore 97); he is himself reduced to a stock character (the impossibly gifted hero of a thriller/romance), just as he reductively types others, "a girl-watcher," as Kilgore (himself reductively) describes him, "who obsessively speculates about women from within the framework of his sociobiological musings" (99), a process less sanguinely characterized in Evans's noting the "frequency with which his penchant for deep evolutionary explanations devolves into unapologetic sexual assessments of his female colleagues."

Often, *Green Earth* seems to imply that the climate crisis arises from humans having departed too far from the deep evolutionary patterns at stake in those sociobiological musings. Approvingly, the novel suggests that, when Frank loses his apartment and decides to build a treehouse and live in Rock Creek Park, this embodies some more primal, Paleolithic Truths about a core nature that "civilization" has forgot—a "wisdom" the novel associates both with the reductive Buddhist presence and with the equally reductive presence of American Transcendentalism Frank encounters mainly in decontextualized snippets of Emerson For The Day delivered by his computer. For him, Markley observes, the planet "has to be terraformed back to a Nature that the Transcendentalists might recognize" (23), as if the landscape of nineteenth-century New England hadn't itself already been massively altered by European settlement, especially its commitment to deforestation (see William Cronin's *Changes in the Land*). But neither these reductive encounters with Wisdom, nor his play-acting as homeless (his credit card easily allows him access to supplies to help build and outfit his high-tech treehouse, he can shower at his private health club), nor his identification with Paleolithic modes of living ("He was Alpine man! [who lived 5,000 years ago]") that he seems, confusingly, to associate both with Buddhism and with Transcendentalism, can perturb his fundamental technocratic premises. For someone ostensibly modelling a "simpler" life, it never seems to occur to him, for example, to wonder about the carbon footprint produced by a globe-trotting worthy of James Bond. A chapter descriptively entitled "Terraforming Earth" finds Frank pursuing that project by flying from D.C., to San Diego, to Beijing, to western China, to Siberia, to London, to New York, and, finally, back to D.C. (for a back-of-his-VW-van tryst with his mysterious spy-lover).

References

Brooke, John L. *Climate Change and the Course of Global History.* Cambridge UP, 2014.

Cohen, Samuel. "The Novel in a Time of Terror: *Middlesex*, History, and Contemporary American Fiction." *Twentieth-Century Literature*, vol. 53, no. 3, Fall 2007, pp. 371–92.

Cronin, William. *Changes in the Land: Indians, Colonists, and the Ecology of New England.* Hill and Wang, 2003.

Evans, Rebecca. "Weather Permitting." Review of *Green Earth*, by Kim Stanley Robinson. *Los Angeles Review of Books*, 19 April 2016, www.lareviewofbooks.org/article/weather-permitting/#!.

Ghosh, Amitav. *The Great Derangement: Climate Change and the Unthinkable.* U of Chicago P, 2016.

Heise, Ursula K. *Sense of Place and Sense of Planet: The Environmental Imagination of the Global.* Oxford UP, 2008.

———. "Climate Stories." Review of *The Great Derangement: Climate Change and the Unthinkable*, by Amitav Ghosh, *boundary 2*, 19 February 2018, www.boundary2.org/2018/02/ursula-k-heise-climate-stories-review-of-amitav-ghoshs-the-great-derangement/.

Hoban, Russell. *Riddley Walker.* 1980. Indiana UP, 1998.

Hoberek, Andrew. "Introduction: After Postmodernism." *Twentieth-Century Literature*, vol. 52, no. 3, Fall 2007, pp. 233–47.

Jameson, Fredric. *Postmodernism, or, The Cultural Logic of Late Capitalism.* Duke UP, 1991.

Jasanoff, Sheila. "A New Climate for Society." *Theory, Culture & Society*, vol. 27, no. 2–3, 2010, pp. 233–53.

Jensen, Liz. *The Rapture.* Bloomsbury, 2009.

Johns-Putra, Adeline. "Ecocriticism, Genre, and Climate Change: Reading the Utopian Vision of Kim Stanley Robinson's *Science in the Capital* Trilogy." *English Studies*, vol. 91, no. 7, 2010, pp. 744–60.

———."Climate Change in Literature and Literary Studies." *Wiley Interdisciplinary Reviews: Climate Change*, vol. 7, no. 2, 2016, doi:10.1002/wcc.385.

———."'My Job Is to Take Care of You': Climate Change, Humanity, and Cormac McCarthy's *The Road*." *Modern Fiction Studies*, vol. 62, no. 3, Fall 2016, pp. 519–40.

Kilgore, De Witt Douglas. "Making Huckleberries: Reforming Science and Whiteness in *Science in the Capital*." *Configurations*, vol. 20, no. 1–2, Winter–Spring 2012, pp. 89–108.

KimStanleyRobinson.info. "Fifty Degrees Below." *KimStanleyRobinson.info*, www.kimstanleyrobinson.info/node/347.

Kingsolver, Barbara. *Flight Behavior.* New York: Harper, 2012.

Klein, Naomi. *This Changes Everything: Capitalism vs. The Climate.* Simon & Schuster, 2014.

Knapp, Kathy. "The Business of Forgetting: Postwar Living Memorials and the Post-Traumatic Suburb in Chang-rae Lee's *Aloft*." *Twentieth-Century Literature*, vol. 59, no. 2, Summer 2013, pp. 196–31.

LaCapra, Dominick. "Trauma, Absence, Loss." *Critical Inquiry*, vol. 25, no. 4, Summer 1999, pp. 696–727.

Le Guin, Ursula K. "The Carrier Bag Theory of Fiction." *Dancing at the Edge of the World*. Grove Press, 1989, pp. 165–70.

Malm, Andreas. *The Progress of This Storm: Nature and Society in a Warming World*. Verso, 2018.

Markley, Robert. "'How to Go Forward': Catastrophe and Comedy in Kim Stanley Robinson's *Science in the Capital* Trilogy." *Configurations*, vol. 20, no. 1–2, Winter–Spring 2012, pp. 7–27.

Marsh, James. "Acadian Expulsion (The Great Upheaval)." *The Canadian Encyclopedia*, 4 September 2013, www.thecanadianencyclopedia.ca/en/article/the-deportation-of-the-acadians-feature.

McKibben, Bill. "Introduction." *I'm with the Bears: Short Stories from a Damaged Planet*, edited by Mark Martin. Verso, 2011, pp. 1–5.

Moretti, Franco. *The Bourgeois*. Verso, 2013.

Morton, Timothy. *Hyperobjects: Philosophy and Ecology after the End of the World*. U of Minnesota P, 2013.

Otto, Eric C. "From a Certain Angle: Ecothriller Reading and Science Fiction Reading *The Swarm* and *The Rapture*." *Ecozon@*, vol. 3, no. 2, 2012, pp. 106–21, www.ecozona.eu/article/viewFile/475/512.

Rigby, Kate. *Dancing with Disaster: Environmental Histories, Narratives, and Ethics for Perilous Times*. U of Virginia P, 2015.

Robinson, Kim Stanley. *Imagining Abrupt Climate Change: Terraforming Earth*. Seattle, WA: Amazon Shorts, 2005.

———. *Green Earth: The Science in the Capital Trilogy*. 2004, 2005, 2007. Del Rey, 2015.

——— "Terraforming Earth." https://slate.com/technology/2012/12/geoengineering-science-fiction-and-fact-kim-stanley-robinson-on-how-we-are-already-terraforming-earth.html.

Taylor, Jesse Oak. "The Work of Fiction in an Age of Anthropogenic Climate Change." Review of *The Great Derangement: Climate Change and the Unthinkable*," by Amitav Ghosh. *boundary 2*, 31 January 2018, www.boundary2.org/2018/01/jesse-oak-taylor-the-work-of-fiction-in-an-age-of-anthropogenic-climate-change-review-of-amitav-ghoshs-the-great-derangement/.

Trexler, Adam. *Anthropocene Fictions: The Novel in a Time of Climate Change*. U of Virginia P, 2015.

Tsing, Anna. *The Mushroom at the End of the World: On the Possibility of Life in Capitalist Ruins*. Princeton UP, 2015.

Whitman, Walt. "Song of Myself." *Leaves of Grass*, edited by Harold W. Blodgett and Scully Bradley. New York UP, 1965, section 51.

Yanarella, Ernest J., and Christopher Rice. "Global Warming and the Specter of Geoengineering: Ecological Apocalypse, Modernist Hubris, and Scientific-Technological Salvation in Kim Stanley Robinson's Global Warming Trilogy." *Engineering Earth*, edited by Stanley D. Brunn. Springer, 2011, pp. 2233–52.

Yuen, Eddie. "The Politics of Failure Have Failed: The Environmental Movement and Catastrophism." *Catastrophism: The Apocalyptic Politics of Collapse and Rebirth*. Sasha Lilley, David McNally, Eddie Yuen, and James Davis. PM Press, 2012.

Chapter 5

Climate change and fiction II
On not eating the baby

If, in exempting works like *Flight Behavior* and *The Rapture*, Ghosh's compelling indictment of contemporary fiction doesn't go far enough, in elaborating how "the age of global warming defies both literary fiction and contemporary common sense" (26) his claim in some ways also goes too far. Or, rather, we might at least refine that indictment by thinking beyond his equation of "literary fiction" with literary realism. We might, that is, consider another strain of modern narrative, one that, pressing against the normalizing "grid of literary forms and conventions" Ghosh stresses, does grapple with those extreme forces that, in his account, literary realism cannot register—does confront the representational challenge posed by the sort of "trauma" that, as Clark again puts it, "entail[s] the deconstruction of multiple frames of reference in multiple fields and modes of thought at the same time" (132).

I'll do that here by taking up four fictions that, centered on that encounter with those deconstructing frames of reference, and riven by the consequent representational impasses, do locate themselves, I argue, at what Caruth, in sketching a geometry of trauma, calls the "point at which knowing and not knowing intersect" (3)—a point maintaining itself only to the extent that knowing can withstand the vaster not-knowing it necessarily conjures and encounters. Grappling with how to know and write in the face of the Holocaust, Art Spiegelman's *Maus* helps define the central elements of that encounter (especially, the centrality of what I elaborate here in terms of "containment"); Cormac McCarthy's *The Road* (2006) and Russell Hoban's *Riddley Walker* (1980) stage it in relation to anthropogenic climate change itself (though, revealingly, as I'll suggest, not to global warming per se), at the heart of which both books locate a cultural logic of paedophagy; and, perhaps approaching one kind of limit case for a text interrogating the discursive possibilities on which it must rely, Peter Dimock's *George Anderson: Notes for a Love Song in Imperial Time* (2012) wrestles with how to speak and know national trauma in a discursive context so thoroughly defined by the language of nationalist and imperial triumph.[1]

***

As we've seen (in Chapter 1), like cultural trauma theory itself, such narratives have roots in attempts to grapple with "the problem of aesthetics 'after Auschwitz'" (Luckhurst 13). Considering the crucial role of witnessing in the process of trying to apprehend the Holocaust, Shoshana Felman and Dori Laub, for instance, approach "literature and art as a precocious mode of witnessing—of accessing reality—when all other modes of knowledge are precluded" (xx), and Michael Rothenberg describes how such works respond to the difficulties in "grasp[ing] the Holocaust as an event that fundamentally challenges traditional disciplinary divisions and knowledge" (6). Central to that difficulty is how those traditional divisions, like Ghosh's normalizing grid, operate to domesticate disruptive threats to common sense. Once again, in Spiegelman's *Maus* Pavel puts the dilemma most starkly:

> Look at how many books have already been written about the Holocaust. What's the point? People haven't changed. ... Maybe they need a newer, bigger Holocaust. Anyway, the victims who died can never tell THEIR side of the story, so maybe it's better not to have any more stories.
>
> (*II* 45)

In defining the representational dilemma that haunts the text, however, Pavel's lament itself is also crucial to how *Maus II* tries to negotiate that dilemma, staging the lament within a book that survives it—a process, I'll suggest, akin to how some climate fictions do engage the "unthinkable" in ways Ghosh doesn't account for. Early on in *Maus II*, in "Time Flies," Spiegelman represents himself, as Artie, in his drawing studio, trying to work on the very volume in which the scene appears. But he is stuck. While *Maus I* shows Artie gathering and narrating what he calls "great material" (23) from his father, Vladek, to tell the "story" about Vladek's experiences during the Holocaust, in "Time Flies" we see him paralyzed and "depressed," rendered unable to continue on the second volume both by his becoming overwhelmed—empathetically unsettled into silence—by the traumatic force of a history that had for him initially been mere "material" for his book, and by the implications of that book, by virtue of such suffering, having become a "critical and commercial success" (41). It is Artie's discussing his writerly impasse with his "shrink," Pavel, that prompts Pavel's lament—an expression of a feeling of futility that, seeming to endorse Artie's own, might seem to threaten to stop the conversation in its tracks. But just as Artie's impasse provokes Pavel's lament, that lament in turn prompts not the cessation of Artie's words but his evocation of literary tradition: "Beckett once said: 'Every word is like an unnecessary stain on silence and nothingness'" (45). This might in fact seem to stop the conversation, for in the panel that follows neither of them speaks. What immediately precipitates that silent panel, however, isn't Beckett's sentence itself but, rather, Pavel's verbal response to it; just as Artie's evoking Beckett is a way of responding to Pavel's lament, in the same panel Pavel responds to that evocation not immediately with silence but with a word: "Yes." In this way, the chain of responses both defines the representational dilemma at the heart of traumatic experience and exemplifies how that dilemma might be negotiated, how trauma might be partly worked through. By virtue of its being *said*, that is, Pavel's "yes" means "yes and no"; he both acknowledges Beckett's repudiation of language and, in that very process, enacts the *capacity* of language, in this case to acknowledge a shared sense of things, including a shared sense of the presence of what cannot be shared, like the "side of the story" that "the victims who died can never tell."[2] The silent panel that follows thus appears not as the failure of words in the face of trauma but, rather, as the culmination of a conversation in which such a shared sense of things is mutually constructed. Artie and Pavel sit in companionable silence, each contemplating what they've come to recognize together, a shared sense both of knowing and of not knowing, a companionship evinced by the visual imagery of the panel: they sit facing each other, the space between them traversed by the parallel slats of the Venetian blinds, nonverbal lines of connection; both are smoking, smoke rising from each figure forming parallel lines as wavy as the narrative in which they play such a pivotal role.

Where Artie had been at a loss for words, unable to continue his book, the conversation with Pavel arrives at a scene of a very different kind of wordlessness, which, in turn, returns him to work. Just as in the next panel Artie breaks the companionable silence by exclaiming, about Beckett's disavowal of words, "On the other hand, he SAID it," Artie's traumatized silence is staged by the book itself. *Maus*, that is, both suffers and SAYS the representational dilemma that necessarily inhabits its attempt to narrate a traumatic history.[3] As I've suggested, the book stages the *condition* of this saying as a particular kind of conversation about the dilemma itself—a kind of conversation "Time Flies" sets in relief against the kind of mock-conversation that immediately precedes it. As Artie sits in his studio, in a present paralyzed by the intrusion of a past that won't stay in the past tense (a heap of emaciated bodies lies on the floor, suggesting also crumpled, discarded pages, failed attempts to write or draw what he's overwhelmed by), he is invaded by a TV crew, the violence of whose work is suggested by the words we hear before their speaker appears in person: "We're ready to shoot!" (41). The entrance of the crew in the following panel clarifies that, for them, "shoot" refers not to a gun but to a camera, but their next words nonetheless constitute a form of (rhetorical) violence: "Tell our viewers what message you want them to get from your book?" (42). The media, that is, wants to kill off the book itself, to reduce its complex encounter with traumatic history to an easily consumable and commodifiable soundbite (akin to the "Ovid-and-Tina video" in *Flight Behavior*)—which is a way of commodifying Artie himself, rendering his own experience invisible and unacknowledged (just as the crew, intent on getting the soundbite, stands obliviously atop the pile of bodies by which Artie is haunted). Haltingly, he attempts to really respond, to articulate why he resists thinking in terms of a "message," only to be interrupted by the next reporter. "Many younger Germans have had it up to HERE with Holocaust stories," that reporter begins, in ironic anticipation of Pavel's lament, and then asks: "Why should THEY feel guilty?" Again, Artie's attempt to take the question seriously—"Who am I to say? But a lot of the corporations that flourished in Nazi Germany are richer than ever. I dunno ... maybe EVERYONE has to feel guilty. EVERYONE! FOREVER!"—cannot be acknowledged, as the next reporter, failing to register even Artie's distress, much less the disruptive implications of his words, says simply "Okay" and changes the subject once again. Finally, the reporters themselves are interrupted by a businessman who wants to commodify *Maus* not as media soundbite but as a marketing strategy: "*Maus*: You've Read The Book, Now Buy The Vest!" Able to hear Artie's nonplussed "Huh?" only as a negotiating ploy, he counters, "So, whaddya WANT–a bigger percentage? Hey, we can talk." Artie's dilemma, though, is precisely that, in a public sphere where "talk" is reduced to an exchange of numbers, he *cannot* talk. Here, he can only cry: "WAH!"

If making *Maus I* has rendered Artie a kind of witness to traumatic history, the representational dilemma that emerges in "Time Flies" is thus partly constituted by a public sphere that cannot hear his testimony. The threat represented by Artie's attempt to offer witness, that is, cannot be recognized by those who come to shoot. As we've seen, the resulting mock-conversation sets in relief the very different kind of "talk" enacted with Pavel, immediately following, who offers a discursive context in which Artie's paralyzing representational dilemma, inherent in his attempt to witness his father's testimony, can itself be negotiated—negotiated precisely insofar as his attempt to witness is itself in turn witnessed. Studying survivor testimony, Dori Laub describes something like Artie's impasse: "While historical evidence to the event which constitutes the trauma may be abundant ... the trauma—as a known event and not simply as an overwhelming shock—has not been truly witnessed yet, not been taken cognizance of." It is only in the presence of someone who can hear it, he writes, that "the 'knowing' of the event is given birth to," so that "the listener, therefore, is party to the creation of knowledge *de novo*" (Felman and Laub 57)—a process dependent partly on "*listen[ing] to and hear[ing] the silence*" (58), as in the panel above, where Artie and Pavel sit wordlessly. Tracing an analogous process of attending, in a pedagogical context, to texts that evoke traumatic events, Felman suggests that "the question for the teacher"—the one who tries to listen and respond to the student's response—is "on the one hand ... how *not to foreclose* the crisis, and, on the other hand, how to *contain it*" (54), a question grappled with, too, by some of the texts that provoke that crisis, as with *Maus*.

As we've seen, Le Guin calls for the novel to *be* a container, but, insofar as for her that involves renewed attention to the quotidian and routine, we might see in this a risk precisely of such foreclosing of the crisis (the extremities that would rend the linguistic fabric of the "carrier-bag"). Ghosh bemoans that the novel is *already* a container, which, in partitioning off the ostensibly improbable, already functions to perform such foreclosure. But considering "containment" in relation to the process of witnessing trauma points to how it might help *attend to* the crisis—how it might be possible to speak or think trauma without either foreclosing its unspeakability or dissolving into its totalizing intensity. Revealingly, what Laub articulates as the process of "bearing witness" to attempts to represent, and thus to know, traumatic experience parallels the process of primitive subject formation W. R. Bion elaborates as a process of what he too calls "containment." For Bion, an infant's overwhelmingly intense internal states, especially those of anxiety, fear, and rage, need to be made tolerable by the primary caretaker's taking them in and returning them in a more bearable form. By helping to establish both a distinction and a relationship between inside and outside (and thus between past and present), this exchange—either originally or later, in a psychoanalytic context—forms the basis for the construction of a self that can experience and think such threatening emotions without being utterly overwhelmed by them, giving rise to the possibility of experiencing meaning. Ideally, Bion writes (adopting Melanie Klein's reduction of the mother to "the breast"),

> the relationship between the infant and the breast permits the infant to project a feeling, say, that it is dying into the mother and to reintroject it after its sojourn in the breast has made it tolerable to the infant psyche.

However,

> if the projection is not accepted by the mother the infant feels that its feeling that it is dying is stripped of such meaning as it has. It therefore introjects, not a feeling of dying made tolerable, but a nameless dread.
>
> (*Second Thoughts* 116)

Insofar as the failure of containment adumbrates the way trauma is produced, calling the result "*nameless* dread" locates a verbal impasse at trauma's heart. Bion describes what is initially a nonverbal exchange, but—if it is this exchange that enables dread to be named and, to a degree, thereby experienced and known—the traumatic dilemma appears precisely as the failure of containment to operate finally in language. When a patient of Bion's was "trying to 'contain' his emotions within a form of words," the words that would have "represented the meaning the man wanted to express were fragmented by the emotional forces he wished to give only verbal expression: the verbal formulation could not 'contain' his emotions" (*Seven* 94).

In *Maus*, "Time Flies" can thus be understood as staging the process of containing Artie's trauma without foreclosing the crisis. Where his initial interlocuters cannot hear his distress, by hearing and sharing it Pavel returns it to Artie in more bearable (and speakable and drawable) form. The licensing agent calls Artie "Artie baby," an insincere term of endearment, but cannot notice that Artie, his subjectivity coming undone, is in some ways indeed becoming a baby, physically shrinking in size, blurting "I want my MOMMY!" and, again, crying out "WAH!" (42). Only after his exchange with Pavel, ironically referred to as his "shrink," does Artie grow back up and continue his own work of witnessing.

In a psychoanalytic account parallel to Bion's, D. W. Winnicott also locates the construction of subjectivity in an intersubjective process. Optimally, Winnicott writes, when

> the baby ... looks at the mother's face ... what the baby sees is himself or herself. ... In other words the mother is looking at the baby and *what she looks like is related to what she sees there.*
> (112)

Although he calls the mother's face a "mirror," it is also responsive to what it reflects, so that the baby gets back not merely itself (a passive reflection, an echo) but also the mother, a process akin to what Laud describes as witnessing, or to Wordsworth's conjecture about the "Babe ... Upon his Mother's breast, who when his soul / Claims manifest kindred with an earthly soul / Doth gather passion from his Mother's eye!" (109), his emerging subjectivity constituted by those enlivening "mute dialogues" (110), the basis for a subsequent worded one. For Winnicott, such early experiences of the coming together of internal and external worlds establishes a "potential space" of "play," or a "transitional" zone between them, the intersubjective field in which language can function as a form of, always provisional, knowing.[4] As with Bion's description of containment and its failures, then, in this account language is made meaningful partly by how it is received, and trauma names precisely the failure of such responsiveness, the collapse of potential space, and thus the failure of signification itself.[5]

***

If, as I've suggested, fictions over the past decades have largely declined to represent the climate crisis as a traumatic threat to representation itself, I'll draw partly on such psychoanalytic accounts, and on *Maus* as a paradigmatic literary formulation of the processes at stake there, to consider how some fictions might be read as exceptions to that failure.[6] Importantly, attempts to grapple with the representational dilemma posed by trauma have in some sense always involved works of imagination. "If Freud turns to literature to describe traumatic experience," Cathy Caruth argues, "it is," again,

> because literature, like psychoanalysis, is interested in the complex relation between knowing and not knowing. And it is at the specific point at which knowing and not knowing intersect that the language of literature and the psychoanalytic theory of traumatic experience precisely meet.
>
> (3)

For Roger Luckurst, in trauma theory's turn toward the literary the aesthetic is imagined as a space that "rehearses or restages narratives that attempt to animate and explicate trauma," a "space of (serious) play," a "transitional mode where knowledge and meaning can be constantly disarticulated and reassembled" (79). Although Luckhurst grounds this understanding in the work of Jacques Derrida and of Isobel Armstrong—for whom the aesthetic "mediates a life-creating, culture-modifying space which is at once transgressive and communal," where one can "*play* with contradiction" (qtd. in Luckhurst 79–80)—we might recognize it as itself a "rehearsal or restaging" of Winnicott's "potential space" (41). What Winnicott calls that "third" space (2) between the internal and external worlds—constituting a "transitional" realm of "play" (40), of "cultural experience" (95) itself—enables "the perpetual human task of keeping inner and outer reality separate yet related" (2), a task we might see as seeking and maintaining the containing ground on which knowing and not knowing can remain in productive relation. Psychoanalysis and literature thus both traffic in knowledge that announces itself as only provisional—offering vantage points thereby from which what might feel like the absolute condition of traumatic dread, an irrevocable rupture, can be understood as itself contingent, contextualized in relation to alternative possibilities.

It is true that neither *The Road* nor *Riddley Walker* concerns global warming per se, taking up instead another form of anthropogenic climate change, that of the "nuclear winter" scientists imagine might follow a thermonuclear war (the smoke and dust from which would, it is thought, likely sharply diminish the amount of sunlight reaching the earth's surface, lowering the global temperature and thus fundamentally disrupting the climate system). Crucially, however, central to these texts (as I read them) is less the particular physical cause of the disrupted climate than the cultural logic by which both global warming and nuclear war are produced and the climatic collapse they both entail. In this, they engage the representational challenge inherent in any attempt to speak or write, and thus come partly to know, the traumatic conditions prevailing in the wake of that collapse.

Nuclear war is more explicitly the cause of climate collapse in *Riddley*, named there as the "1 Big 1," than in *The Road*, where the catastrophic event is described only very briefly. The exact nature of that catastrophic event has occasioned much critical speculation, "with answers," Hannah Stark notes, "ranging from divine intervention, a meteor colliding with the Earth, nuclear winter and climate change" (72). Dana Phillips, for example, argues that what the text describes is more like the collision of a meteor than the descent of a nuclear missile (177). But to whatever extent that's true, nuclear explosion still remains the most obvious cause of the catastrophe. If a massive meteor were headed to earth, people would know about it in advance and presumably respond in some way (moving far away from the site of likely impact, storing up supplies, etc.), but the catastrophic event comes to the unprepared characters as a shock. Moreover, in the geopolitical world of the early twenty-first century—where, as former defense secretary William J. Perry warned in 2017, "We stand today ... in greater danger of a nuclear catastrophe than we faced during the Cold War"—the chances that a climate-smashing catastrophe would come not as a thermonuclear exchange but as a meteor (or an asteroid) would simply be too remote to consider: although meteorites do occasionally strike the earth, the last time the impact was significant enough to cause catastrophic climate collapse was sixty-five million years ago, when, it is thought, an asteroid impact caused the extinction of the dinosaurs and most other then-extant forms of life. In 2006, it would then not seem possible to represent an apocalyptically altered climate system without at least implicitly conjuring an anthropogenic cause, whether thermonuclear explosion or global warming. *The Road* "owes much of its cultural impact to climate change," Adeline Johns-Putra can thus observe, evoking Andrew O'Hagan's "oft-quoted endorsement of the novel" as "the first great masterpiece of the globally warmed generation" and George Monbiot's description of it as "the most important environmental book ever written" (520).

Reading *The Road* in relation to climate change, Johns-Putra writes that

> at the heart of climate-change discourse resides an anxiety about whether we have cared enough, not just about and for each other and the planet but about and for the future. It is, furthermore, children who—not unproblematically—serve as shorthand for the future and therefore as a particularly emotive marker of the problem of climate change.
>
> (520)

If the novel reflects an "anxiety" about having cared "enough," however, it also reflects a concern about what it *means* to care, especially in the face of traumatic circumstances that might seem to dissolve the ground on which such caring might be enacted. Such concern, that is, reflects the representational dilemma loosed by (and defining) the novel's attempt to articulate trauma; like Artie, the traumatized boy finds himself at a verbal impasse, and like Pavel, the man has to contend with a sense that language has been rendered futile. In response, like *Maus*, *The Road* stages processes of containment, reconstituting a ground on which to some degree language, and thus the possibility of caring, is restored to life.

From the novel's start, the traumatic present is for the man a world of utter detachment, where, "Everything uncoupled from its shoring" (11), the once taken-for-granted ground of meaning has dissolved. The narrative thus "powerfully stage[s] a largely completed process of signs becoming irrevocably divorced from the things they represent," Donovan Gwinner observes, leaving "a dying state of signification of meaning" (143), in which the man "tried to think of something to say but he could not," as the "names of things slowly follow[ed] those things into oblivion" (88). Words uncoupled from their referents, they are encircled by a "nameless dark" (9), and although he desperately appeals to an imagined Other (named "God") to help contain that threat—"Are you there?" (11)—he gets back nothing, leaving him a world of Bionian "nameless dread." Images of unshored language thus permeate the text, emblematic of the collapse of any context in which shared meaning might anchor itself.[7] The man muses that, with that utter collapse, "old and troubling issues [are] resolved into nothingness" (28), and later, after emptying his wallet, lays all the items (written forms of ID, currency, a picture) flat on the road, "like gaming cards," and leaves them there (51). Later still, as he remembers his old life, a memory of his book- and paper-laden table is interrupted by a more recent, postapocalyptic memory— an almost literal staging of Pavel's lament—of his standing in the "charred ruins" of a "library ... blackened books lay[ing]" in "pools of water. Shelves tipped over. ... Rage" at the "lies arranged in their thousands, row on row." He "picked up one of the books and thumbed through the heavy bloated pages" (187). All those books, and what was the point? They could not matter in the face of the logic justifying both the existence and the use of massive and absurdly redundant stockpiles of nuclear weaponry. And in the ashen land that is the consequence of that logic, even the pretense that all those words could mean or matter has been obliterated.

Two of the man's adult interlocutors insist on this futility. In "times like these the less said the better," offers the old man whose name isn't Ely, registering the sense that the world to which their language once might have referred—and comprehension of which language might once have thereby helped facilitate—has been traumatically ruptured: if "something had happened and we were survivors and we met on the road then we'd have something to talk about. But we're not. So we dont" (172). Tellingly, it is the word "survivor" itself that here exemplifies the unshoring of existing language from its referents, just as earlier, when in an attempt to dissuade his wife from suicide the man tells her that they're "survivors," she incredulously refuses the word (55). For her, their desperate circumstances have rendered moot the very process of talking itself; the shared ground underlying the possibility of meaningful exchange has given way, and thus, while the man resorts to empty rhetorical gestures about taking a stand, for her there is "no stand to take" and, so, no basis for speech (57). When, as she goes off to commit suicide, he asks if she will say goodbye to the boy, she curtly responds that she will not (58).[8]

Just as "talk" appears here as futile, the boy repeatedly arrives at a verbal impasse. Conversation with his father is at the center of his world, but in the wake of each of a series of traumatic encounters he stops talking. When he is captured by one of a cannibalistic gang, whom the father then shoots, they desperately flee the rest of the gang—the man carrying the stunned boy, splattered with gore—and when they seem to be temporarily safe, the father cannot get the boy to respond to him (68). Later, when coming on a hastily abandoned campfire they discover what proves to be a "charred human infant, headless" and "gutted" and "blackening on the spit" (198), the man wonders whether his son will ever speak again (199). And when his conception of his father and himself as "the good guys" is traumatically undermined by what the boy sees as the father's needlessly killing a man who tried to steal their supplies, again the boy cannot speak, though his father repeatedly pleads for him to do so (261, 267).

Such verbal impasses reflect the boy's experience of the world as fundamentally unresponsive, as a zone of "nameless dread" inhabited by Bionian "bizarre objects" (*Seven* 99)—as his description of a nightmare suggests. In it, there appears a mechanical toy penguin, propelled by a winder, but when it appears in the dream version of the boy's original home, "The winder wasn't winding" (36–37). It isn't only that the dream house of the self is invaded by a mechanical substitute for a possibly responsive living creature, but it's also that that mechanical presence, as a bizarre object, has an, utterly alien, agency of its own, abrogating any possibility that the boy's intense distress might be recognized and responded to—a dream dread that registers their real world, we learn later, when the man and boy spy a phalanx of armed men with enchained captives who march with a "swaying gait like wind-up toys" (91).

For the boy, however, the verbal impasses that register such traumatic encounters are not final. Like *Maus*, *The Road* stages the representational dilemma that defines trauma but also stages a response to that dilemma as kind of containment or witnessing. Declaring about their relationship, "I don't care. It's meaningless" (56), the man's wife poses (the absence of) "care" as the condition for (the absence of) "meaning," an equation *The Road* elaborates in constituting the man's care for the child as a matter of prompting more talk—the recoupling of language to some shoring enacting the recoupling of the speakers. As in the process Bion calls containment, this recoupling begins with the father's attunement to the child's overwhelmed state. After their close escape from the cannibal gang, the man is anxious to gather wood for a fire, to get them through the night without freezing, but the terrified boy won't let him go. The man first tries, and fails, to reason with him, but then he "realized [the boy] was shaking," and, empathizing with the intensity of the child's fear, he responsively accommodates it with a familiar acknowledgment: "Okay … Okay" (72). When after a while the father does venture into the dark for wood, the responsive exchange made possible by such acknowledgment proves essential for his returning from the dark as, when he calls out, the boy guides him safely back with his voice. The fire built, the text then separates out each act of the man's physically caring for the boy: he "washed [the gore from] the boy's face and his hair," "dried him with a blanket," "wrap[ped] him" up, "carried him to the fire," "kicked holes in the sand for the boy's hips and shoulders where he would sleep" and "sat there holding him … tousl[ing] his hair before the fire to dry it" (74). On the basis of this attentive care, a day later the man initiates a conversation in which the two of them can to some degree give words to the traumatic encounter that has silenced the boy. "I should have been more careful," he begins, and when the boy doesn't respond, he persists:

> You have to talk to me.
> Okay.
> … My job is to take care of you … Do you understand?
> Yes … Are we still the good guys? …
> Yes. We're still the good guys.
> And we always will be.
> Yes. We always will be.
> Okay.
>
> (77)

Similar containing conversations repeat throughout the text—often punctuated by an exchange of that affirmative "Okay"—the man taking in the boy's intense state and returning it in more "tolerable" form and, in this attentiveness, establishing a ground on which, in their post-apocalyptic world, "talk" can re-shore itself. This ground, that is, comprises an intersubjective field, something like Winnicott's "potential space" comprised by "play," as when they find a deck of cards, and the man, having forgotten the rules for Old Maid and Whist, not only invents new games but gives them new names (53), an act of posttraumatic resignification centered on play and elaborated in the man's frequently telling the boy stories. Later, written language, too, is in some ways re-shored. When, near starvation, they find a hidden bunker stocked with cans of food, the man asks the confused and disbelieving boy if he can read one of the labels:

>   Pears. That says pears.
>   ... Yes it does. Oh yes it does.
>
>   (139)

Ultimately, it is by virtue of the process of containment establishing a ground of meaning that the boy can go on being after his father dies. Glossing Bion's description of this process, Hanna Segal writes,

> When an infant has an intolerable anxiety he deals with it by projecting it into the mother. The mother's response is to acknowledge the anxiety and do whatever is necessary to relieve the infant's distress. The infant's perception is that he has projected something intolerable into his object, but the object was capable of containing it. ... He can then reintroject not only his original anxiety but an object modified by having been contained. He also *introjects an object capable of containing* ... anxiety. The containment of anxiety by an external object capable of understanding is a beginning of mental stability.
>
> (134–35, my emphasis)

The boy thus takes in not only the disturbing, though no longer traumatizing, feeling that his father will die but also *the presence of the attentive caretaker*, the experience of the father's care in and beyond language—an experience that will persist as long as the boy does. Close to death, the father alerts the boy to this presence already inside of him. If "I'm not here you can still talk to me. You can talk to me and I'll talk to you," he tells the boy, and, responding to the boy's question, "Will I hear you?" he replies "Yes. ... You have to make it like talk that you imagine. And you'll hear me" (270). As throughout their history of trying to talk in the face of trauma, the boy's taking in here of both his father's death and his continuing and containing presence is signaled by a familiar exchange—"Just don't give up. Okay?" "Okay." "Okay." And because he has experienced such talk, grounded in the field of their presence to one another, the boy can bear its loss: "It's okay, Papa. You don't have to talk. It's okay." He can lose his father and his father's talk, that is, precisely because he has been given them in the first place. After the father's death, then, the woman who cares for him would sometimes tell him about "God," but the "best thing was to talk to his father" and he "did talk to him and he didn't forget" (286).[9]

Again, such talk—the tentative recoupling of words to their referents—depends upon the process of (re)establishing a shared context, dramatized as a process of containment, but also as what I've described above as the construction of what Winnicott calls "potential space." For Winnicott, crucial to that construction is the nature of the caretaker's looking: again, to know itself as a self and the world as a world, the baby "looks at the mother's face" and, optimally, that look is returned, confirming the baby's sense of being. The mother is in this sense a "mirror," but, crucially, more than a mirror; she reflects back what she sees, but adds something of herself to it, reflecting but also responding, so that the baby gets back not only confirmation of its own being but also something of the mother's responsive presence—a coming together of internal and external worlds that, like containment, makes both seem real.

In this context, we can understand the traumatic break in *The Road* as itself constituted as a failure to see. Launching nuclear weapons would seem thinkable only according to a binary vision of the world that remains blind not only to the reality of the millions of the "enemy" (and the nonhuman creatures) who would die, but also to the fact that, sharing the planet with them, obliterating their world means obliterating one's own. Further, it enacts a failure to see the present as perforce connected to the future—a failure to recognize those who will inherit the ruined earth (a premise for nuclear war and for global warming both). Just as *The Road* stages repeated scenes of containment, then, it is also pervaded with concerns about adequate looking—about how looking and seeing might, in the face of the traumatic dissolving of the ground of meaning, help reconstitute it as a kind of potential space.[10]

The book begins by coupling an act of physical connection, the man reaching toward his son, with the act of "looking toward the east for any light" (3) and closely scanning the landscape for signs of danger. When the boy awakens, the man almost immediately engages him in this project of looking, inviting him to "Take a look" (6), a phrase that echoes through the rest of the narrative, much of which, as Hannah Stark observes, "is devoted to the description of watching" (75).

The existential stakes of responsive seeing are acutely dramatized when the man and boy "take a look" (105) in and around a plantation house they come upon. When in the yard, the man finds a cauldron, over ashes and charred wood, with a wagon beside, the narrator comments, "All these things he saw and did not see" (109). He perceived, that is, without really attending, failing to register this evidence of the cannibalism they then discover when they explore further (enchained captives, some of whom are missing body parts), and thus endangering their lives. (That the enchained captives are imprisoned within a "tall and stately" house with "white doric columns" [105], a place once served by "chattel slaves," connects the postapocalyptic violence in the novel to the normalized violence of American slavery, so crucial both to the establishment and thriving of the U.-S. economy, and, as Donna Orange suggests, to the contemporary failure to register the scope of environmental destruction.)

For the most part, however, the man's seeing is a form of responsive attentiveness, a kind of seeing that, repeatedly instructing him to "take a look," he nourishes in the boy (who eventually can see what the man cannot, like a farmhouse barely visible from the road [202]). Teaching him to attend to the outside world, the man commensurately attends to the boy's inner world also—constructing a potential space connecting those worlds—as he encourages him to take a look at the stories and dreams and thoughts he has inside of himself, beyond those he has been told (267). When the boy says he doesn't know how to locate the "fire" he has been told the two of them are carrying, the man tells him that it remains inside the boy himself and revealingly adds that he can see it (279). Near death, he alerts the boy to how that inside space can retain what he takes in, including his father's presence. If we can take the possibility of the consequent exchanges with the dead as constructed by the process of containment, it's also thus constructed by the father's history of sympathetic looking. This history culminates in the representation of the man's last hours as a scene of extended mutual watching. As he dies, he is absorbed with looking at the boy (277), just as the boy is three times described as "watching" his fading father (277, 280), and practices the "talk that you imagine" by first "watch[ing]" his father and only then "clos[ing] his eyes" and "talk[ing]" to him and "listen[ing]" (280).

Where his previous traumatic experiences were signaled by his wordlessness—reflecting the generalized decoupling of words, in a postapocalyptic context, from shoring—in the wake of his father's death the boy is impelled to speak: he "knelt beside his father" and "held his cold hand" and "said his name over and over" (281). And soon, indicating that his father's words are also still alive, he gets up to, once again, "take a look," and returning to the road, "looked down" one way and "looked back" the other. However implausible it might be that this look would be returned, a man appeared and "look[ed] at him"—a looking that, as the scene transpires, both gives back the boy's own look and adds the man's presence to it, recapitulating the construction of a potential space that survives traumatic emptying out of meaning. When the boy asks this man if he is "carrying the fire," the man can hear the words beyond their literal meaning, acknowledging the distress they convey ("You're kind of weirded out, aren't you?"), and, when the boy answers "No," returns it in modulated form ("Just a little") and offers a familiar containing affirmation ("That's okay"), so that the boy can acknowledge and bear that now-contained distress ("Yeah"). Only when he has acknowledged the boy's condition in a way the boy can recognize, both reflecting and augmenting the boy's "taking a look," does the man respond to the repeated question on its (the boy's) own terms: "So are you? What, carrying the fire? ... Yeah. We are" (283–84).

If the father's caring for the son stands in opposition to the normalized failure to see the Other—the mode of thought underlying anthropogenic climate collapse—with the emergence of the second man, *The Road* suggests that the father's own responsive recognition of the child is itself implicated in that catastrophic failure. Focused so exclusively on his child, the father's care consistently manifests what Johns-Putra describes as a "brand of parental care" committed to "saving one's offspring at the expense of others" (532), a form of what Gwinner calls "survivalist insularity" (153). Throughout the novel, this insularity is set against the boy's more wide-ranging concern for others, what Andrew Hoberek sees as his "commitment to versions of the social beyond the father-son dyad" (496), a "democratic care ethic," Johns-Putra writes (533), that is "defined against the father's exclusionary" one. While the boy consistently wants to care for others, the narrative remains so fully, and (until the end) exclusively, immersed in the father's point of view that we're unlikely to join the boy in questioning his harsh calculus: helping others (especially sharing food) diminishes the already slim chances of their survival (though even that harsh dismissal of others has its limits: the man won't eat other people or feed them to the boy). If the father's exclusive care does prepare the boy to bear his death, however, finally the boy can survive only by virtue of the more "democratic care ethic" enacted by the man and woman who take him into their family. Earlier, despite the boy's repeated entreaties, the man will not consider taking in another little boy. Ultimately the boy is saved, that is, precisely by an act of care that his father would not take.

As it stages processes of containment and democratic care, then, we might read *The Road* as grappling with the representational challenge inherent in understanding the climate crisis in terms of trauma, and thus as disrupting the "grid of literary forms and conventions" that, for Ghosh, underlies fiction's failure to confront the urgency of our moment. For this reason, if, as Tim Blackmore has it, "the book shares the postapocalyptic genre with over 400 texts" (22) or, as Stark observes, it "has been positioned as part of the remerging sub-genre of dystopian literature called climate fiction" (71), it evokes those categories mostly to unsettle them, to register precisely their inadequacy in the face of the dissolution of forms of knowing. While Blackmore proposes that, among its over 400 generic mates, "closest to *The Road* are J. G. Ballard's *The Drowned World* (1962) and Russell Hoban's *Riddley Walker* (1980)," those three books are "close" mainly in that each responds to its postapocalyptic premise as a challenge to generic forms themselves, a formal challenge each meets in its own, very particular, way. Suggesting that while "minimalism, pragmatism, or naturalism ... may come close to identifying McCarthy's stock in trade in *The Road*," Phillips foresees that "none are likely to stick for long" for in it "the labelling impulse itself is called into question," and he notes "the book's sheer particularity," seeing it as "something of a literal misfit and oddball" (178). Johns-Putra sketches how, although Lawrence Buell has described apocalypse as "the single most powerful master metaphor that the environmental imagination has at its disposal" (525),[11] *The Road*, in "forego[ing] the appeal of spectacle" in the form of "disaster," declines what "according to [Ursula] Heise is one of the 'most dated and formulaic clichés' of apocalyptic narratives" (526), even as it also "rejects the sense of posttraumatic relief and postmodern opportunity that comes with the postapocalypticism described by critics such as [James] Berger and [Virginia] Heffernan)." And this "sheer particularity" on the narrative level is matched in *The Road* by the peculiarity of its diction, all those defamiliarizing "misfit and oddball" words that, originating mostly in lost discourses, manifest both that traumatic condition where words float uncoupled from their shoring and the possibility of textual groundings that might still survive the dissolutions that define the book's ecocatastrophic present.[12]

***

Within the first few pages of Russell Hoban's *Riddley Walker*, set in southeast England, or "Inland" as it is then called, around 3000 years after a nuclear holocaust, Riddley interrupts the narrative of his "naming day" to write down a story, "Hart of the Wood," the first of many representations in the novel of the traumatic history centered around an apocalyptic nuclear war, in his time sometimes called the "1 Big 1" (19), including the nuclear winter that would follow. "Every 1 knows about Bad Time and what come after," he tells us—"Bad Time 1st and bad times after" (2). In this, the story offers an earlier figuration of the premise of *The Road*:

> Not many come thru it a live.
> There come a man and a woman and a chyld out of a berning town they sheltert in the woodlings and foraging the bes they cud. Starveling were what they wer doing. … Snow on the groun and a grey sky overing and the black trees rubbing ther branches in the wind. … The man the woman and the chyld digging thru the snow they wer eating maws and dead leaves which they vomitit them up agen. Freazing col they wer nor dint have nothing to make a fire with to get warm. Starveling they wer and near come to the end of ther strenth.

And, as in *The Road*, in "Hart of the Wood" some of those few still alive, starving and freezing to death, enact the paedophagic logic of their ratiocinations. Without food or fire, the man and woman meet a "clevver looking bloak" who offers them a deal:

> "Iwl tel you what Iwl do. Iwl share you my fire and my cook pot if youwl share me what to put in the pot." He wer looking at the chyld. The man and the woman thot: 2 out of 3 a live is bettern 3 dead. They said, "Done."
> They kilt the chyld and drunk its blood and cut up the meat for cooking.
>
> (3)

Framing the book, the question of child-eating returns at its end when, at an analogous moment of cultural instability, Inland's ideological business as usual in the process of dissolving, Riddley mounts a Punch and Judy puppet show centering on Punch's repeated attempt to eat their "babby," Riddley's way to "think on" the question with which his narrative leaves us: "Why wil [Punch] all ways kil the babby if he can?" (220).

Just as *Riddley* and *The Road* both recognize at the heart of anthropogenic climate change the process of the present consuming the future, a form of intergenerational violence both figure as paedophagia,[13] both grapple with the representational dilemma posed by trying to speak, and thereby perhaps to interrupt, that trauma in process. And thus, once again, in *Riddley* we hear a permutation of Pavel's lament. The narrative defines itself as Riddley's own attempt to grapple with representing what Lorna, the "tel woman" (4), introduces to him at the start (ironically, on his "naming day") as "some thing in us [which] dont have no name … lorn and loan and sheltering how it can" (6), and that first chapter ends with his writing, "Thats why I finely come to writing all this down. Thinking on what the idear of us myt be. Thinking on that thing whats in us lorn and loan and oansome" (7). But eventually, confronted with the traumatic excess of the history of the 1 Big 1 and of Bad Time 1st and bad time after—and with the way that history both inhabits, and is in the process of repeating in, the present—that process of writing-as-thinking arrives at a familiar impasse: "I dont have nothing only words to put down on paper. Its so hard. Some times theres mor in the emty paper nor there is when you get the writing down on it" (161).

Just as *Maus* stages both Beckett's representational dead end, where "every word is like an unnecessary stain on silence and nothingness," but also the process of containment by which that dead end can itself be spoken, Riddley's impasse is itself staged within a text by which it is survived. As we've seen, in *Maus* that process is figured as an initially nonverbal exchange, akin to a Wordsworthian "mute dialogue." In *Riddley*, while the feeling that writing stains the silence of the blank page is figured as an isolating failed exchange—"You try to word the big things and they tern ther backs on you"—he also then imagines the dilemma beginning to resolve by means of being invited into a mute dialogue: "Yet youwl see stanning stoans and ther backs wil talk to you" (161). This wordless talk, stirring a vision of an animated physical world in which even the stones participate, then prompts the utterance, still wordless but now voiced, by which Riddley continues the exchange: "I opent my mouf and mummering only dint have no words to mummer. Jus only letting my froat make a soun." Finally, it is by means of this wordless exchange that, after being stymied by the feeling that "theres mor in the emty paper nor there is when you get the writing down on it," he can return to that empty page, now with a new kind of writing. Soon after his "mummering," Riddley writes: "This nex what Im writing down it aint no story tol to me nor it aint no dream. Its jus some thing come in to my head" (163). Taking the form of a genre that itself has no name (neither a "story" nor a "dream," just "some thing"), the words that "come into his head," comprising a text he entitles "Stoan," themselves reflect upon their origin in wordlessness, meditating on the mute dialogue in which they are rooted. "Stoans want to be lissent to," "Stoan" begins:

> Them big brown stoans in the formers feal they want to stan up and talk like men. Some times youwl see them lying on the groun with ther humps and hollers theywl say to you, Sit a wyl and res easy why dont you. Then when youre sitting on them theywl talk and thywl tel if you lissen.
>
> (163)

Again, this story, of how a representational impasse is negotiated by contextualizing it in relation to an originary mute dialogue, is itself embedded in a narrative by which it is survived. And crucially, that narrative itself originates in a scene of wordless exchange. We've seen how, at the start, Riddley frames his "writing all this down" as a means of "thinking on" what Lorna has told him, as his written response to their conversation ("Loran said," "I said," "She said," "I said," etc. [6–7]). But just as "Stoan" is rooted in a mute dialogue, that instigating verbal exchange itself rises out of a wordless one. When Riddley first asks, "Lorna, will you tel for me?" she responds by inviting a nonverbal exchange: "Riddley, Riddley, theres mor to life nor asking and telling. Whynt you be the Big Boar and Iwl be the Moon Sow" (5). It is only after they then "freshent the Luck up there on top of the gate house," as they are "lissening to the dogs howling aftrwds and the wind wuthering and wearying and nattering in the oak leaves," and "looking at the moon all col and wite and oansome" (5–6)—as they lie, that is, in a post-coital state of heightened attentiveness to the sounds and sights of the elemental world—that Lorna begins to speak: "You know Riddley there some thing in us is it dont have no name" (6).

Of course, as Peter Schwenger observes about this scene, "Speaking about what has no name ... is another form of naming" ("Circling" 257). It isn't until he has learned and thought much more about the traumatic history inhabiting Inland's present, however—when, as we've seen, his written words appear to him as less expressive than the blank page that precedes them—that Riddley feels the full force of that paradox. Exploring how, in response to that and other "paradoxes of nuclear representation" Hoban's novel enacts a narrative "circle around a point designated zero" (251), Schwenger attends to a key moment in the "Eusa Story": when asked by Eusa, "Wut is the idear uv yu?" (34–35), the Littl Shynin Man the Addom replies, "I aint the noing uv it Im jus only the showing uv it"

(35). The novel thus exemplifies how "it is possible ... to show something one does not know," Schwenger suggests (259), in Riddley's circling narrative itself but also, I'd add, in his own staging of the puppet show to which he commits himself at and beyond that narrative's end—what he calls a "New Show" (208).

As the culmination of the novel's attempt to show beyond knowing, to negotiate the representational dilemma perforce presented by any attempt to speak and thus intervene in an unfolding traumatic history, Riddley's "New Show" focuses precisely on the possibility of such intervention—as we've seen, on the possibility of preventing Punch from eating the babby. I want to examine how the show does this, but as important as what the show stages is how it itself is staged—how the conditions of its emergence frame the show as an explicit attempt to forestall the repetition of a particular traumatic history. Throughout, the novel rehearses the characters' various attempts to understand and represent those traumatic events that have so severely conditioned their Stone Age present. In many of those accounts, the 1 Big 1 was produced by a figure called Eusa, who afterward, in some versions, was for revenge blinded and castrated. Near the end, Riddley and his partner Erny approach the walls of a settlement, Weaping Form, intending to perform their new show, with a set of Punch and Judy puppets ("figgers") Riddley has been given (to this point, presenting puppet shows—the dominant form of media—has been the prerogative of the state, and its major form of propaganda). This is their attempt to help shape the future, at what is a volatile political moment: gunpowder has just been reinvented (at first thought to be the technology of the 1 Big 1, then understood as only, perhaps, a first step, the "1 Littl 1"), the government (the Ram) has fallen, and thus, as Riddley puts it,

> The way things are now it aint jus only you don't know whos going to go bang nex [set off a gunpowder explosion] you dont even know where the arrer myt come from with your name on it. ... It use to be if you wer agenst the Ram youwd be agenst the forms [farms, as opposed to smaller hunting and gathering groups] becaws you knowit they wer all 1 thing only jus like a body and its head. Now the head myt say 1 thing only you dont know what the body will do.
>
> (203)

Because Weaping Form's Big Man, Rightway Flinter, sees them as agents of "clevverness" (technological knowledge) and thus implicated in the recent explosion that he associates with the 1 Big 1 and Bad Time, he reads Riddley and Erny as Eusa. When they approach, his first thought, shaped by one particular account of the traumatic history, is thus to make them pay in kind for the traumatic violence he ascribes to them—to repeat the trauma. "Time back way back," he tells them, every place as seen Eusa helt the bailey dint they. Every 1 as seen him pourt the ounts of judgd men dint they. Howd Eusa come back to Cambry he come back blyn and bloody ... he wernt a man no mor he wer what wer lef. ... He done clevverness and fetching the same. So he had to pay for it dint he. ... You see what it is Erny youve got to pay for 1 thing befor you go on to the nex. You and your yung partner here youre Eusa ... youve got things youwd like to do nex only befor you get to them youwll have to pay for the las things what you done.

(212)

Just as Eusa "had to pay," Riddley and Erny have "got to pay," by being blinded and unmanned.

But Riddley's aesthetic intervention—introduced as an act of "saying"—breaks the literalizing chain. Punch is in his pocket and, faced with Rightway's threat, Riddley "thot Mr Punch myt have some thing to say":

I ternt my back to the gate and Mr Punch come up looking at them over my sholder. He wer waving his stick he made his cock fessin noys. Rrrrrrrrrrrrrr. He said, '*Ah putcha putcha putcha.*' Which he begun to beat me with his stick.

(212)

Initially, "Them on the gate begun to larf," but the laughter doesn't last long:

I cud feal ther eyes on Punch and I wer hoaping hewd say some thing funny. He dint tho. He stoppit beating me and he wer looking up at them. He wer staring at them and waving his stick. Dint say a word. ... Them on the gate looking at Punch and Punch staring back and waving his stick. Not saying a word.

And Punch's staring and waving has the desired effect:

Nex there come Rightway Flinters voice he said, "You myswel come in and do your show. Whats on you is on you. ..." So we dint dy at Weaping Form nor we dint get cut off nor blyndit. We livet and we kep our eyes and our cocks and balls that time any how.

The novel's concluding "New Show," then, can happen only in the aftermath of a mute dialogue. Though he "Dint say a word," Punch does beat Riddley with a stick, make inarticulate sounds (his "Rrrrrrrrrrrrrr ... *putcha putcha putcha*" recalling the wordless "mummering" that precedes Riddley's writing "Stoan"), and engage "them on the gate" in a silent exchange of looks. Riddley's word for what we call puppet is "figger," and if he cannot word precisely how Punch's intervention negotiates the impasse—the threat of a violent disruption of his going-on-being—it is nonetheless "figgered" in other ways (narratively, theatrically) that make it available for interpretation (or, in Riddley's terms, for "thinking on it").[14] Indeed, the process of interpretation itself—displacing the literal with the figural—itself here figures how Punch's intervention functions as a process of containment. Something uncontained (or unthinkable) is at large at Weaping Form: the culture's ground of meaning is dissolving as, as we've seen, the political order has shattered, and gunpowder has been newly reinvented and explosions have started, loosing an intense anxiety inhabited by the traumatic history of nuclear war and its aftermath. This is the condition of violence, the failure of terms that might shape or structure or interpret or figure—terms that Riddley's "figger-al" intervention then precisely provides. In a sense, Rightway himself sets the conditions for this intervention when, as Riddley and Erny first approach, instead of immediately proceeding with the butchery, he articulates to them the traumatic logic of why they must be disarticulated—wording the anxiety, as it were, rather than simply enacting it. Taking in this anxiety and returning it in modulated form, Riddley contains it by having his figger make it figural: revenge is taken, but metaphorically, as Punch beats him with his stick, then simply waves his stick and stares at those on the gate. Earlier, when Riddley was getting to know his figgers, he recounts that "Punch says to me, '*What am I?*'" (205); at the gate of Weaping Form, Punch's gaze silently repeats this question to those poised to continue the chain of traumatic violence, inviting them to consider, rather than enact, the part of the self that wields the stick. In this way, by reworking the threat of a literal acting out as a symbolic action, by a literal restaging, Riddley contains the loosed anxiety, figuring the mute dialogue out of which representation might emerge renewed—the conditions of being for the newness of the New Show he can proceed to mount.

The show Riddley and Ernie are eventually allowed to perform itself confronts Weaping Form with an occasion to consider rather than enact its traumatic inheritance. Indeed, Rightway continues to read figuratively: "theres moren 1 kynd of crookit. Theres crookit on the out side and theres crookit on the in side. Which Im beginning to think may be this here humpy figger [Punch] is some kynd of a nindicater" (215). And many of the others, too, accept and interact with the show as a "nindicater"; Pooty (Judy) leaves Punch alone with the "babby," asking the audience to "Give us a shout wil you if he dont mynd that babby right" (217), and when it looks like Punch is going to eat the babby—he sings

> *There were a little babby*
> *A piglet fat and juicy*
> *Who ever got ther hans on him*

They cudnt tern him lucey
Ah yummy yummy yummy
Ah slubber slubber sloo
Ah tummy tummy tummy
Ah piggy piggy poo

—they're eager to warn her: "Pooty! Pooty! Come up qwick!" (218). As a response to Pavel's lament, the show thus defines itself as one pole of a conversation, as establishing an affective field birthed and sustained only dialogically and figuratively.

In contrast, Rightway's brother, Easyer, remains constrained within the literal (in Rightway's terms, the "out side," rather than the "in side"). Left alone again with the babby, Punch once more moves to eat it—"Punch says, '*O so juicy o so terbel juicy!*' He grabs the babby"—and Easyer this time literally breaks the containing figurative frame, launching an attack:

> No sooner does Punch get his hans on that babby nor in comes a big hairy han which it grabs Punch and my han inside Punch.
> Its Easyer he yels, "You little crookit barset I tol you not to try nothing here!"
> Over goes the fit up [the stage] and me and Punch and the babby and Easyer with it.
>
> (219)

Riddley's hand animates the literal materiality of that wood and cloth puppet from an inside for which Easyer fails to account, and thus Easyer's own hand work ("grab[ing]" Punch with his "big hariy han") simply repeats Punch's own ("get[ting] his hans" on the baby)—his literality reproducing Punch's reduction of the other to a single, fixed, material meaning.

In the context of the novel, that reduction is framed as inherent in the purely technical mode of, quantifiable, knowing designated in Inland as "clevverness," which, again, is embodied in the figure of Eusa—an "out side" knowing, fantasized as absolute, that disavows its embeddedness in a not-knowing that necessarily exceeds it. Until the political order unravels, the government had been driven by an obsessive pursuit of the technology such a definition of knowing produces, the possession of which has, for the government, itself defined the superiority of the past (of "what we ben") and the Goodness of the "Good Time" (48) it had wished to recreate. That that pursuit depended partly on a complex regime of torture (provoking a violent backlash) suggests how that definition of Good, as "clevverness," aligns Eusa with Punch's commodifying reduction of other lives (and in "Hart of the Wood" the man who first suggests eating the baby is described as "a *clevver* looking bloak" [3]). Indeed, it is the literalizing logic of that pursuit—defining knowledge, constituted wholly by numbers, utterly in terms of technological power—that, as in the uncontested account offered in "The Eusa Story," produces nuclear catastrophe. There, Eusa, a "noing man" whose, purely technical, knowing consisted in his "noet how tu bigger the smaul & ... how tu smauler the big," is for the purpose of finding the "numbers" of the ultimate weapon, called the "1 Big 1," sent to "fyn the Littl Shynin Man the Addom" (30). He thus "smaulert his self down tu it," entering into matter, to find the Addom/atom, from whom he demands those numbers, torturing him by "pulin on" his "out strecht arms" until Addom "begun tu come a part." Through the splitting of the atom, figured here as a scene of interrogation by torture, Eusa gets the numbers he seeks, and from them makes the 1 Big 1, puts "the 1 Big 1 in barms" and, with "Mr. Clevver"—the "Big Man uv Inland" for whom Eusa works—"droppit so much barms thay kilt as menne uv thear oan as thay kilt enemes" (33), producing what is later called "Bad Time" and what we could call catastrophic climate collapse:

> the lan wuz poyzen frum it the ayr & water as wel. Peapl din jus dy in the Warr thay kep dyin after it wuz over. ... Evere thing wuz blak & rottin. Ded peapl & pigs eatin them & thay pigs dyd. Dog paks after peapl & peapl after dogs tu eat them the saym. Smoak goin up frum bernin evere wayr.

Easyer's literalizing violence thus figures Punch's attempt to eat the baby, which itself figures the violence at the heart of the reductive "clevverness" that traumatically undoes the present, inaugurating a chain of violence that consumes the future. And Rightway's understanding of Punch as "some kynd of a nindicater," prompted by Riddley's trying to show what he knows he cannot know, figures the prospect of breaking that traumatic chain.[15]

Whose mode of reading will most shape the future, Rightway's or Easyer's? In formulating this question, *Riddley Walker* elaborates the possibility that inherited trauma may not be passed forward. Will the emergence of gunpowder inaugurate a repetition of the history that had produced the ecocatastrophic 1 Big 1 and Bad Time? Will we go on eating the baby?[16] As Rightway and others from Weaping Form join Riddley and Erny, taking to the road, the book's final gesture, like that of *The Road*'s, is toward the emergence of a new, anti-paedophagic social order, brought into being precisely by the process of trying to confront and thus disrupt the traumatic history that has brought the present to the brink.

As we've seen, in a present so committed to the disavowal both of the traumatic history on which it is founded and of the traumatic violence it is in the process of inflicting on itself and on the future, the possibility of such anti-paedophagic disruption is confronted with how to speak beyond the normalizing grid of literary conventions Ghosh sees as having made fiction complicit in this condition of great derangement. *Riddley Walker* wrangles with that dilemma, as I've argued, by staging Riddley's own wrangling with it. But the novel does so also in the way that staging is itself staged. Just as Riddley enacts a newness, in the first place by writing his narrative (an unprecedented act in his oral culture) and finally by mounting his "New Show," *Riddley* constitutes itself in a "new" kind of language (evident in the passages quoted above, with their odd spellings and constructions), disrupting the normalizing representational conventions in a fundamental way.[17] The novel's language, that is, constitutes a posttraumatic field, where old representational structures have been fragmented and are in the process of being reformulated. And at the heart of such extreme defamiliarizing lies what we've seen as the book's resistance to the literal, to the violent logic enacted by literalizing forms of reading and knowing. Quite insistently refusing the one-word-to-one-referent, reductive logic of "clevverness," words and phrases here mean multiply. In commenting that "As much as possible I tried for more than one meaning in the words," Hoban illustrates with a typical example: in the aftermath of his father's death, "when Riddley says …'I wer the loan of my name' he means that he is the lone carrier of his name" but also that he is "living on borrowed time," that his embodied life, marked by his bearing a name, is only "loaned" to him for a while (233). Often, the polysemantic thrust of a word or phrase unsettles a material, literalizable, meaning by drawing it together with a more abstract one. Thus, with the "Littl Shynin Man the Addom" the elements of matter itself cannot be disarticulated from the Biblical origin story. Similarly, "Wud" means "wood as in forest," Hoban has commented, but also "would" as in "intention, volition, or desire," and "hart" means both "heart" and "stag" (235), so that Eusa's encounter with the "Hart uv the Wud" (31) is an encounter both with the stag of the wood and with "the essence of one's wanting" (235). And, as Jeffrey Porter points out, "when Riddley calls inhaling 'breaving' we are asked by wordplay to recombine 'grieving,' 'breathing,' and 'bereavement' into an anomalous whole" (450). If isolating and dissecting such examples in this way belies the density of the text's polysemantic field, it nonetheless does point to how, in its fundamental commitment to discursive defamiliarization, Hoban's novel works against the disarticulations of discursive business as usual. In response to a traumatic history informing a present itself in the process of determining a traumatic future, *Riddley's* fundamental project is rearticulation.

***

Grappling with how to speak a present inhabited by, and perpetuating, a disavowed traumatic history, *Maus*, *The Road*, and *Riddley Walker* pursue their rearticulations, as I've tried to show, at least partly by staging both the representational impasse inherent in their attempts and the processes of containment that (re)contexualize language and narrative within an intersubjective field. The afterlife of language in these texts, that is, depends on returning to its relation to the nonverbal—on its being rooted in a dialogue that is mute. And, in a discursive context structured by that normalizing grid of literary forms and conventions Ghosh sees as deranging contemporary fiction, such response to Pavel's lament, as we've seen, perforce produces what Schwenger (like others) calls an "antinarrative," which "sweeps away the comfort of established structures of apprehension" that help define Ghosh's grid and "demands that we find our own way—in the narrative experience as in the political one" ("Narrative" 1177). In these three texts, the most explicit stagings of the traumatic impasse take shape only eventually. But I'd like to conclude this chapter by considering a text that takes that impasse as its very starting point. Like *Maus, The Road,* and *Riddley Walker,* Peter Dimock's *George Anderson: Notes for a Love Song in Imperial Time* (2012) responds to that impasse both by trying to locate language within a containing intersubjective field and by constituting itself as an "anti-narrative," but, following from its premise, it draws these elements together in an especially concentrated way, offering an especially acute definition of and response to the traumatic present.

If *George Anderson* addresses global warming even less literally than do *The Road* and *Riddley Walker,* it is even more explicit in its attempt to rearticulate the sort of traumatic meanings disarticulated by the prevailing climate discourse. For Dimock, the predominance of an "historical narrative of national triumph" has, in the face of the atrocities central to U.S. history and present (especially slavery, militarist empire, and the post 9/11 torture regime) produced a pervasive "national narrative failure" (159), the larger context, I suggest, for the sort of representational failure Ghosh sees in the face of global warming. Examining how the Paris Agreement reflects a commitment to "the maintenance of the status quo" (145), Ghosh writes that "within the current system of international relations, there is no language in which questions related to the equitable distribution of power can be openly and frankly addressed" (146); expanding that insight beyond international relations itself, Dimock suggests that "the dominance exercised by the triumphant narrative of a redeeming national American greatness" has meant that "Americans lack a language adequate to the history we are living." It is that dominant narrative, working partly through the partitioning grids Ghosh examines—and, as we've seen framing Al Gore's introduction of "global warming" into the mediasphere—that has rendered the ecocatastrophic structure of that history unspeakable. Again, Donna Orange's formulation makes the claim most forcefully: "Unconscious and silent about the U.S. history of settler colonialism, ignorant and mute about our crimes of chattel slavery and racial domination, neither governments nor citizens can seriously tackle climate injustice until we confront this 400-year history" (37).

Responding to the rhetorical impasse constituted by the "lack [of a] language adequate to" that history, with *George Anderson* Dimock "invent[s] ... a form that purports to create the internal imaginative condition for the refusal of American national triumph"—and thus aims "to speak without compromise from the ground of that refusal" (159–60). As it is, "the words in which the history of the present we are living first comes to us, we have to assume, are unreliable," the narrator realizes, and thus "the betrayal built into the syntax in which most experience is steeped makes spontaneous speech un-useable for [achieving] reciprocity" (20). Crucial to this framing of the dilemma is the premise that a language that would be "adequate to the history we are living" would be a language of "reciprocity." Responding to the national "lack" of such a language, the narrator thus proposes a meditative "historical method" by which, he hopes, "a person rids the self of its inordinate attachment to empire"—a process equivalent to what Orange calls "conversion" (55)—and, with another person who has undertaken the method, can speak beyond that "betrayal" in a way that "creates reciprocity," the "basis for a just society of equal historical selves" involving a "way of being" that is an alternative to "the abundance of capitalism" (22).

In a discursive context where "betrayal" is "built into the syntax" of experience itself, speaking outside of the consequent "national narrative failure" involves reworking the basic syntax of how experience is processed. And a text that at least purports to attempt such reworking will by definition seem, as Dimock acknowledges, "estranged or estranging" (160). Operating outside of the prevailing grid of literary conventions, *George Anderson* virtually dispenses with plot itself. Instead, the novel presents itself as a long letter (with some relevant documents appended) from Theo Fales to David Kellen, a fictionalized version of the Justice Department lawyer, who—despite having subjected himself to waterboarding, in order to provide an experiential basis for his opinion—signed the legal document that in effect legalized the post 9/11 torture regime. Knowing their paths will cross in a few months (at an event both are scheduled to attend), Fales hopes to talk with him then—on a common ground of refusing the narrative of national triumph—and so "learn to live [his] complicity honorably."[18] Fales does explain the context and background for his request for a meeting, but the letter is structured mainly as a day-by-day description of the meditative "historical method" he proposes both of them follow, as a way of making possible speech outside of empire. Much of the letter thus consists of formulaic, repeated recitations of the sequential elements, or mental "exercises," of that method, or of the content of Fales's own practice of it: juxtaposing the chosen "master narrative" to the corresponding "governing scene" and to the "historical subject" occupying that scene; making that scene "present" by "the promptings of a pair (one of a prescribed sequence of four) of constructive principles," each pair "contain[ing] one positive principle, one negative" (36) (the positive and negative pairs are listed and described [39–42]); bringing to the scene one of "seven truths" listed in Table Three (36–37); and offering a "colloquy" that meditates on the resulting mental construct. With the content of the examples Fales provides from his own practice, the novel manifests its preoccupation with the disavowed history of American slavery as a torture regime. Crucially, however, that "content" appears in the text only by way of *example*. George Anderson, that is, remains structured not by any narrative of events but, rather, by the obsessive delineation of Fales's *method*, a species of anti-narrative, and if the repetitive result, in its preoccupation with formulaic exactitude, might, according to the prevailing conventions, indicate a somewhat "unreliable" narrator, it is just those conventions of "reliability" that structure the impasse the book takes as its premise. The risk of unreliability thus appears as a necessary condition of an attempt to speak in the face of what Dimock sees as that catastrophic American "lack [of] a language adequate to the history we are living."

The novel stages that "lack" partly by appending to Fales's estranging letter two of the documents that provoke that letter into being—texts whose inadequacy appears, in this context, as a function of their rhetorical and generic conventionality. Where Fales's letter is riven by the tension between, on the one hand, the urge to speak the trauma inherent in "the history we are living" and, on the other, the estranging excessiveness of his attempt to contain that threat within the byzantine scaffolding of his formulaic "method," the appended documents—both real—represent precisely the unified, normalizing discourse against which Fales defines his effort. One is the entirety of Kallen's 35-page "Memorandum Opinion for the Deputy Attorney General," the carefully constructed, conventional legal document whose dispassionate, ostensibly rationalistic rigor belies the extreme violence it renders legal—appearing to disallow waterboarding as torture but, by means of a single footnote, in fact making "torture the official policy and accepted practice of [the] government" (9) and thus "perpetuat[ing] war crimes" (11–12).[19]

The other appended document, also real, is a 1925 newspaper article from the Trenton *State Gazette*, from which Fales takes both his "master narrative" (one key element of the meditational "method" he proposes to Kallen) and his "governing scene" (another core element). Recounting in a breezy, human-interest style, the life of George Anderson, a 108-year-old former slave it condescendingly refers to as "Uncle Georgie," the article exemplifies the sort of triumphalist narrative that has helped construct the "lack of a language adequate to the [traumatic] history we are living," and it does so, like Kallen's "Memorandum," by normalizing a regime of torture. But where in the legal document the disarticulated trauma inheres all but invisibly in a single, seemingly innocuous footnote, in the newspaper that trauma is disturbingly evident, in a single paragraph, even as, crucially, that paragraph remains in its way invisible to the rest of the narrative.

Just as, in *Inconvenient Truth*, Gore adduces the ending of slavery as inspiring evidence that America history is a record of "the capacity to do great things" (290),[20] in the *Gazette* article, as "time went marching by, leaving in its wake ... the greatest triumphs of a scientific age," it "also brought the abolishment of slavery, treasure of treasures for the storehouse" that is Anderson's memory (115). The point of slavery as it is introduced here, that is, is its role in contextualizing the (1925) present, as a storehouse of treasures, in relation to a narrative of national triumph. Thus, though "Uncle Georgie" lives in a "shabby" house, and "if he wanted a dollar this very minute it is extremely doubtful if he could find it anywhere in those worn old clothes of his," the article introduces him as "one of Trenton's very richest men," possessing those treasures in the "storehouse of memory": just as it is introduced here in relation to a narrative of the accumulated "treasure," the way slavery shapes a subsequent history of African American poverty (not to mention how fundamentally the vast national wealth depended on enslaved labor) is here obscured, by defining "riches" without regard to material or economic conditions.

While slavery is introduced primarily in relation to Anderson's possessing the "treasure of treasures" of the memory of its abolishment, when the article does consider his enslavement before that point, it is hard to see why that abolishment would have amounted to so rich a treasure. "If his lot was a hard one," Anderson "did not realize it"—not because he had a kind or enlightened owner, but, the article explains, simply because for him "slaves were slaves and masters were masters, and between them there was no question of freedom for the black man. He was owned as his master's mules and other stock were owned" (116). He understood (the apparently self-evident fact) that "slaves were meant to be beaten if they deserved it," and although he "witnessed beatings time and again," and "saw how the slaves suffered under the lash," still, as the article summarizes Uncle Georgie's apologist view, "always there was an excuse back of the flogging, the colored man had stolen or committed some other misdemeanor, or he had shirked at his labor."[21] Whatever outrage or fellow-feeling observing the routine brutalities of slavery might have stirred in the actual George Anderson, the article's Uncle Georgie responds only in terms of his personal self-interest, telling himself "if I do what I am told ... and never do the things the other folks are punished for, they'll never need to beat me." As a result, he "made himself the most docile of servants" (117). Indeed, he is so docile that "when he heard of the war being fought to give slaves their freedom," it "didn't interest him much," for, again, "he was reasonably satisfied with his lot" and, like the other enslaved people who shared that lot, "never gave freedom a thought" (117–18). Even after the "disturbing news" that the South had lost the war, Uncle Georgie remains unmoved by the question of freedom, and it's not until "several weeks" after "great droves of [now free] negroes passed the plantation singing ... FREEDOM" that he learns from his master that "he is no longer a slave" (118)—though even then the news is unremarkable, since "life went on much as before except that now and then the Negroes received a small sum of money" (119). Whether or not life going on as before still involved "beatings" administered "time and time again" isn't thought to be worth mentioning.

While the article's initial claim, that what makes Uncle Georgie the richest man in Trenton is the treasure of the memory of slavery's abolishment, seems to prepare us for a story of extreme hardship followed by joyous liberation, what in fact the article thus offers is a picture of slavery as a "reasonably satisfying lot," not even, to him, as he experienced it, a "hard" one. Even as the article would substitute a triumphant national history for a traumatic one, however, it remains riven by what it would exclude. Though he "wishes he could forget" one particular episode of his enslaved life, Anderson nonetheless cannot not speak of it:

> One day my brother stole something. It was not the first time; he had been punished for it before, and the master said that this time he should have a lesson he would never forget. So they began to beat him early in the morning, and when his back was all cut open they put salt on it and pounded it in with a paddle. Then they whipped him again, and when the overseer's arm would get tired the master would take the whip. By and by, late in the afternoon, my brother did not cry out anymore, but swayed from side to side, side to side, going lower all the time until he went down and did not come up again. "That ought to settle him for good," said the master. "He'll never steal again." My brother didn't, for they had beaten him to death.
>
> (117)

This scene of atrocity might seem to shatter the article's apologist narrative. But just as it cannot be repressed (Uncle Georgie "wishes he could forget" it but must speak it anyway) neither can it be accommodated—remaining at once the heart of the article and utterly discontinuous with the rest of it. Indeed, even as the horrific scene is elaborated in some gruesome detail, the text works to try to foreclose on the traumatic memory by which it has been invaded, especially on the outrage such a scene might provoke, as, immediately after the awful description, the next paragraph quite desperately and directly insists on reframing the traumatic event as utterly unremarkable: "Uncle Georgie said he did not feel any special resentment against the master. He had known slaves to be beaten to death before and his brother was only another one."

In taking it as the source of both the "master narrative" and the "governing scene," the meditative bringing together of which is the first work of his "method," Fales attempts to join elements that remain in the *Gazette* article ostentatiously disjointed—the triumphant public narrative of George Anderson's life (the "master narrative" that narrates his life as if from the perspective of Anderson's "master") and the traumatic history that narrative would disavow. And in demonstrating the work of that meditation he elaborates the context of the traumatic "governing scene" in a way that bears directly on the question of intergenerational violence central to *The Road* and *Riddley Walker*. "It is well known by everyone present" at the fatal whipping, Fales writes, "that Robert [George's brother] is the master's son" (26). Again, while *George Anderson* doesn't explicitly broach the way the discursive regime of "empire" (that it defines itself as trying to resist) is implicated in the climate crisis per se, the filicidic thrust of Thales's "governing scene" does, in the context of working toward "a language adequate to the history we are living," point toward how the living of that history constitutes a war against the ecological conditions that might make the future even partly viable—how the present disarticulates itself both from its traumatic history and from the trauma it is in the process of inflicting on the future.

Just as, against the normalized eating of children and others, *The Road* sets a democratic "ethic of care" and Riddley's concluding show locates in the audience the responsibility to "mynd that babby right," in *George Anderson* Fales is prompted to compose his "method" by something like the very opposite of a filicidic act. Articulating the need for that method—for the obsessive pursuit of the possibility of speaking reciprocity, of speaking from the ground of the refusal of empire—his letter to Kallen begins by describing a "vision": "I came to the end of myself and found other people standing there—and knew that the present was a gift of time in which to sing a true history of equal historical selves" (9). Crucially, in this instigating vision he "was suddenly four years old again standing behind my mother," as Fales recounts it, when "High above ... appearing in the doorway, was a woman's radiant face":

> The woman's eyes were already looking for mine, as my mother's body politely blocked her entrance. ... The woman's eyes found mine there where I stood behind my mother's skirt. They asked without using words—without fear—(they assured me she was willing to bear the knowledge of whatever answer I gave without restraining the reach of my infant terror and glory)—"How are you?"
>
> It was the first empirical question I understood as important. I knew it was urgent beyond sentiment or calculation. In the event ... I answered with my gaze ... that I was valuable and full of light because she came back.
>
> (15–16)

The possibility of a reciprocal exchange, beyond the logic of empire—the finding of "other people"—is thus here rooted in an early experience of mutual, attentive looking, a Winnicottian exchange by which the child comes to feel both itself and the world as real, by virtue of the caretaker's responsive gaze inaugurating, as Winnicott describes it, "a two-way process in which self-enrichment alternates with the discovery of meaning in the world of seen things" (112–13). Central to such a possibility here, moreover, is the woman's being able to "bear" and thus, as for Bion, contain the child's "infant terror," a premise on which the possibility of generative mute dialogue itself rests.

That the woman "came back"—affirming the child's sense of what Winnicott calls "going-on-being," moving him to feel "valuable"—points to what Fales later learns from his mother's diary: "the woman in my vision ... was Melisande Chandless, a Jamaican nurse who cared for me as an infant when my mother couldn't take care of her newborn for the first thirteen weeks of its life" (85). The instigating vision, that is, figures both a traumatic failure of the possibility of reciprocity—of what might ensure that sense of going-on-being, or of feeling real—and also its apparently timely-enough restoration. In her diary, Fales learns that his mother "turned to the wall and would not speak when her baby was offered her to hold" because "she was mourning a first child who had died nine months before this new birth," and in the vision itself his mother is interposed between him and the woman "in the doorway" with "the radiant face" who "came back" (and whom, we learn, the mother will not invite inside). But as the mother enacts the trauma of losing a previous child by abandoning the new one, that traumatic chain reaction is (as in *Riddley*) interrupted, initially by Chandless's caretaking presence and later by her returning to ask, wordlessly with her eyes, "How are you?"—the memory of which provokes in the adult Fales the imperative to live "the present as a gift of time in which to sing a true history of equal historical selves."

Of course, in light of how the adult Fales is haunted by the atrocity of slavery in the Americas, that Chandless is Jamaican also suggests how the possibility of the "reciprocity" he consistently opposes to "empire" depends on a re-emergence of the traumatic history of racial and colonial violence—a "true history" disarticulated by the triumphalist narrative that defines the bounds of intelligible public speech, just as Chandless herself cannot be admitted into the house. But even as the discursive impasse figured in her remaining unhoused persists, it is also broken, as her rearticulating gaze radiates across the threshold, "flood[ing] the doorway" (15). Indeed, that gaze breaks young Fales's own impasse. Though he "had just turned four" (16), he "had not yet begun to speak," and Chandless's gaze prompts him to "answer with [his] own gaze," ushering him across a threshold into a reciprocal mute dialogue, a kind of silent speech that—as for Artie, the boy in *The Road*, and Riddley—subtends the speaking with words. Later, she comes back again—or her coming back comes back—in the "vision" that, again, provokes him, this time into the language that is the letter to Kallen, constituting the book itself as an attempt to rearticulate what has remained outside of the house of national narrative. In the vision that inaugurates the letter, Fales "came to the end of [him]self and found other people standing there"—people who are "othered," like Chandless and George Anderson—and thus "knew that the present was a gift of time in which to sign a true history of equal historical selves." If the book's premise is that "Americans lack a language adequate to the history we are living," this inaugurating vision helps to define an "adequate language" here as a language of reciprocity, one that, as such, refuses the denialist logic and language of an empire in which Fales knows himself complicit. And if in that "lack" we can, with Orange, see disarticulations involving not only the traumas of racial history and of the contemporary torture regime but also of the normalized destruction of the climate system, we might see how, in the act of addressing the atrocities in the true histories we have lived and are living, *George Anderson* also addresses the unthinkable violence we are in the process of inflicting on lives to come.

In a discursive context where even most climate fictions help normalize the Great Derangement, works like *The Road*, *Riddley Walker*, and *George Anderson* might stand both as refusals of that deranging discursive businesses as usual and as attempts to speak "from the ground of that refusal." They discover that ground as the ground where knowing can limn its traumatic relation to the not-knowing that dominant discourse disavows, and in staging that estranging relation as a reciprocal exchange, they work toward ways of registering and responding to the present both as "gift of time" and an as-of-yet unabated assault on the future.

Notes

1. In trying to "refine" Ghosh's argument, I don't mean to qualify what I think is his crucially important conclusion about "the broader imaginative and cultural failure that lies at the heart of the climate crisis." In this regard, that neither of the climate-fictions I consider here addresses global warming per se points to how, even in the face of his problematic conflation of "serious fiction" with "realism," his conclusion remains compelling.
2. As the historical trauma of the Holocaust is in *Maus* bound up with Artie's own traumatic experience, one of the "victims who dies [who] can never tell their side of the story" is his mother, Anja, who, though she survived Buchenwald, years later committed suicide, leaving no note, as Artie repeatedly stresses, and whose wartime journals Artie's father Vladek, in a fit of grief after her suicide, burned, leaving Artie with only Vladek's version of the story.
3. Luckhurst sees in "the relationship between trauma as a devastating disruption and the subsequent attempts to translate or assimilate this disturbance" what he calls "a fundamental tension between interruption and flow, blockage and movement" (79). But if we might see in Artie's both suffering and saying the

impasse a paradigmatic instance of that "tension," we also here see that the possibility of "flow" is itself conditioned on the "new mode ... of listening" that, for Caruth, "the language of trauma, and the silence of its mute repetition of suffering, profoundly and imperatively demand" (9).

4 In turning toward Bion and Winnicott, to an extent I'm going somewhat against the grain of trauma theory as it has been taken up in some influential critical theoretical discourses operating largely within a framework established by Freud and inflected by Jacques Lacan. Though Freud was repeatedly prompted to understand trauma in relation to an event (a seduction, a war), he repeatedly turned from that position, as James Berger argues (23), to locate trauma as inherent within the psyche. And Lacan saw the construction of subjectivity as by definition a process of alienation, premised upon a "primal Discord" (4). Winnicott and Bion understand "Discord" as other than necessarily primal—or at least as other than necessarily only alienating. In "Mirror-Role of Mother and Family," Winnicott ambiguously acknowledges that Lacan's mirror stage "has certainly influenced me," but immediately adds, with characteristic understatement, "However Lacan does not think of the mirror in terms of the mother's face in the way I wish to do here" (111).

5 Geoffrey Hartman points toward this process when he sketches contrasting understandings of "the relationship between trauma and the symbolic." For Lacan, "the symbolic ... is not a cure of the real," he writes, "but is itself a kind of trauma." For Winnicott, "if the mother-child ... develops *transitional* objects that are 'a symbol of the union of the baby and mother'—that is, objects located at that point ... where separation or contiguity replaces union or continuity—then trauma occurs when such symbol-making is disabled" (561).

Writing about the severe "depression" that is often the manifestation of such traumatic collapse of "symbol-making," Julia Kristeva puts it that "melancholy persons are foreigners in their maternal tongue" (53).

6 Of course, in considering "exceptions" to a literary scene structured by that "grid of literary forms and conventions" evoked by Ghosh, I'm pointing to what might seem simply an alternative set of conventions. My "exceptions," that is, might in one way themselves seem unexceptional, might themselves be understood as grouped within a category, one constituted precisely by attempts to grapple with the sort of representational challenge defined by cultural trauma studies, especially as it emerged in relation to attempts to speak the Holocaust—though the category of such "trauma narratives" also includes responses to a range of other historical and cultural traumatic events. In this account, such "exceptions" take their categorical place alongside works like Toni Morrison's *Beloved*, D. M. Thomas's *The White Hotel*, W. G. Sebald's *Austerlitz*, Han Kang's *Human Acts*, Zoë Wicomb's *David's Story*, and many others. And this genre of "trauma narrative" itself bears a complex relation to other categories, like Postcolonial Narrative and the Neo-Slave Narrative, and, premised on an interrogation of the transparency of language, to larger literary-historical ones like Modernism or Postmodernism. That novels can be categorized together, however, doesn't in itself mean that they exemplify a species of representational business as usual, and if such works are bound together in responding to a representational challenge, the most notable ones do that each in its own unconventional way. At any rate, to whatever extent we can speak of the genre of "trauma narrative," that category has remained marginal, at best, in relation to climate fiction in general.

7   For Kenneth Lincoln, McCarthy's "writing settles into a postholocaust grammar of scree, shards, smoke, fractals, bits and pieces of charnel, dead flesh, and sallow bone" (165).
8   Just as there is no basis for speech, there seems to be no basis here for processing meaning through narrative form itself. Rebekah Sheldon writes: "When the Man asks her to think of them as survivors, she retorts that they are not survivors but rather 'the walking dead in a horror film' (55). Their competing figurations point to the generic nature of their argument. They can't agree on which type of story they have been thrust into" (87).
9   In alluding to "the boy's rejection of the basic therapeutic method to work through trauma," Francisco Collado-Rodriguez might be seen to emphasize the boy's verbal impasses at the expense of those scenes of restored "talk."
10 Hannah Stark argues that "interrogating the metaphor of vision is central to considering [*The Road*] as climate fiction" (71), but where for her this is "because [vision] positions the human as the chosen witness to the end of the world," for me it reflects not just the fact of such witnessing but also an engagement with how witnessing can respond to the ethical and representational questions inherent in understanding the "end of the world" specifically in its traumatic aspect.
11 Johns-Putra is quoting from Buell's *The Environmental Imagination*. Below, she cites Heise's *Sense of Place* (the quotation is on Heise's p. 206, not the p. 204 Johns-Putra cites).
12 The persistent defamiliarizing diction involves both unusual forms of familiar words ("granitic," "envacuuming," "illucid," "shoring" itself, for instance [3, 191, 116, 11]) and, especially, words likely, for most readers, to be ostentatiously unfamiliar (for example "discalced," "siwash," "claggy," "chert," "patterans," "gimballed," "travois" [24, 68, 75, 129, 180, 230, 249]).
13 In an earlier instance of such figuration, Edward P. Mean writes in his 1842 "The Steam King"—a reaction against the industrial revolution's growing reliance upon steam power, and thus upon mining and burning coal—that the Steam King's "bowels are of living fire, / And children are his food" (qtd. in Malm, *Fossil* 241).
14 On the back cover of the Indiana University Press edition of the novel, the author photo has Hoban with his back to the camera and Punch confronting us eye to eye, over Hoban's shoulder—simply repeating Punch's challenging gaze at Weeping Form, rather than blurbishly reducing it to a static meaning, offering a showing rather than a knowing.
15 My argument here counters readings of the ending offered by Jeffrey Porter, for whom the book "ends with the dark promise of a never-ending cycle of ... destruction" (453), or Clair James, who sees the novel as "cynical, even fatalistic" (1175).
16 The prospect of continuing the traumatic cycle is figured in the story of Abel Goodparley, who, as "Pry Mincer," is driven by his obsession with recovering the "clevver" knowledge that produced technological progress, especially the power to make the 1 Big 1. As the agent of traumatic violence—one way he searches for that knowledge is by means of institutionalized interrogation by torture ("helping the qwirys" [79])—he repeats his own traumatic history. When he is "but ten years old," as Ronald Granofsky summarizes it, "the nomadic settlement of his people" is destroyed by "a raiding party" who "kill his father and carry off his mother" (174) in a scene that Granofsky associates with the Holocaust and that we might associate with the various descriptions of Bad Time: "'Wite smoak and arnge flames upping in that grey morning and the dogs coming for the dead'"

(131). A few years later, he is subjected to brutal sexual violence. And just as we can see the adult Goodparley replaying the violence to which he is subjected as a child, that violence he perpetuates in the present is itself repeated, as, eventually, his victims blind and castrate him—a literal enactment of the revenge that, as we've seen, Riddley, with Punch, renders figural.

17 Jeffrey Porter offers a particularly compelling examination of *Riddley*'s language, reading what he calls its "quantum wordplay" as participating in a tradition of twentieth-century works that, in attempting to "reinvent language in the future in order to challenge the conditions of normal discourse in the present" (449), offer what "M. A. K. Halliday has called an 'antilanguage,' an alternative ... speech [incorporating] elements excluded ... by normal discourse" (450). Such works "project verbal counterrealities wherein the values and norms of official language are criticized and ultimately disrupted." Although initially Porter introduces *Riddley* as one of a number of books invested in such "antilanguage," I think the intensity and density of its linguistic reinventions, comparable, he (a little hyperbolically) suggests, only to *Finnegans Wake*, render it more than usually resistant to such stabilizing classificatory maneuvers—which is more or less the point.

18 Fales identifies himself, like Kallen, as a relatively powerful purveyor and beneficiary of American empire, both by birth and by his active part in disseminating the narrative of national triumph. An "expert by formal training in our national narrative," in his "long career as an [book] editor," he has "helped regulate a bourgeois ethical monopoly over the words by which we know ourselves" (43), especially his having edited and given "rhetorical shape" (82) to a best-selling memoir by the ex-Director of the CIA, in which, during the rise of the post 9/11 torture regime, the Director is presented as "the conscientious family man keeping the country safe by all means necessary" (59). Within the frame of the history we are now living, this editorial act "makes forgiveness meaningless" (82).

19 The real document, dated December 30, 2014, was signed by Daniel Levin, the acting head of the Office of Legal Counsel at the Justice Department (the model for Dimock's Kallen).

20 As I show in Chapter 3, above, Gore attributes the abolishment of slavery to the country's finally making a moral decision that slavery was wrong, framing out in his account any mention of the Civil War. Similarly, the *Gazette*'s account elides the traumatic violence of that war, attributing slavery's end merely to the march of time.

21 In fact, as Edward Baptist has shown, on cotton plantations whipping operated not only to punish "misdemeanors" or "shirking" but as a routine method of coercing increased productivity (131–44). For each person picking cotton, an initial daily quota was established, and if the person fell short, they were beaten. Once the person could make the quota regularly, it was increased, and the torture cycle would repeat. For this reason, it was often the most productive workers, those who could pick the most, who were whipped most frequently (since their quotas would increase more rapidly). In this way, by means of a business plan that took torture as a core element, between 1800 and 1860 per capita production for enslaved people picking cotton increased 400 percent (125–31). It is often pointed out that "torture doesn't work," but while that is true if the goal is extracting "intelligence," it obscures that fact that, as a management method for increasing labor productivity, the *effectiveness* of torture was central to the growth of the American economy.

References

Baptist, Edward E. *The Half Has Never Been Told: Slavery and the Making of American Capitalism*. Basic Books, 2014.
Berger, James. *After the End: Representations of Post-Apocalypse*. U of Minnesota P, 1999.
Bion, Wilfred R. *Second Thoughts: Selected Papers on Psycho-Analysis*. Heinemann, 1967.
———. *Seven Servants*. Jason Aronson, 1977.
Blackmore, Tim. "Life of War, Death of the Rest the Shining Path of Cormac McCarthy's Thermonuclear America." *Bulletin of Science, Technology & Society*, vol. 29, no. 1, February 2009, pp. 18–36.
Buell, Lawrence. *The Environmental Imagination: Thoreau, Nature Writing, and the Formation of American Culture*. Princeton UP, 1995.
Caruth, Cathy. *Unclaimed Experience: Trauma, Narrative, and History*. Johns Hopkins UP, 1996.
Clark, Timothy. "Some Climate Change Ironies: Deconstruction, Environmental Politics and the Closure of Ecocriticism." *Oxford Literary Review*, vol. 32, no. 1, 2010, pp. 131–49.
Collado-Rodriguez, Francisco. "Trauma and Storytelling in Cormac McCarthy's *No Country for Old Men* and *The Road*." *Papers on Language & Literature*, vol. 48, no. 1, Winter 2012, pp. 45–69.
Dimock, Peter. *George Anderson: Notes for a Love Song in Imperial Time*. Dalkey Archive, 2012.
Felman, Shoshana, and Dori Laub. *Testimony: Crises of Witnessing in Literature, Psychoanalysis, and History*. Routledge, 1992.
Ghosh, Amitav. *The Great Derangement: Climate Change and the Unthinkable*. U of Chicago P, 2016.
Gore, Al. *An Inconvenient Truth*. Emmaus: Rodale, 2006.
Granofsky, Ronald. "Holocaust as Symbol in *Riddley Walker* and *The White Hotel*." *Modern Language Studies*, vol. 16, no. 3, Summer 1986, pp. 172–82.
Gwinner, Donovan. "'Everything Uncoupled from Its Shoring': Quandaries of Epistemology and Ethics in *The Road*." *Cormac McCarthy: All the Pretty Horses, No Country for Old Men, The Road*, edited by Sara Spurgeon. Continuum, 2011, pp. 137–56.
Hartman, Geoffrey H. "On Traumatic Knowledge and Literary Studies." *New Literary History*, vol. 26, no. 3, Summer 1995, pp. 537–63.
Hoban, Russell. *Riddley Walker*. Indiana UP, 1980, 1998.
Hoberek, Andrew. "Cormac McCarthy and the Aesthetics of Exhaustion." *American Literary History*, vol. 23, no. 2, Fall 2011, pp. 483–99.
James, Clair. "Narrative against Nuclear War?" Letter. *PMLA*, vol. 106, no. 5, October 1991, pp. 1175–76.
Johns-Putra, Adeline. "'My Job Is to Take Care of You': Climate Change, Humanity, and Cormac McCarthy's *The Road*." *Modern Fiction Studies*, vol. 62, no. 3, Fall 2016, pp. 519–40.
Kristeva, Julia. *Black Sun: Depression and Melancholia*. Translated by Leon S. Roudiez. Columbia UP, 1989.
Lacan, Jacques. *Écrits: A Selection*. Translated by Alan Sheridan. Norton, 1977.

Lincoln, Kenneth. *Cormac McCarthy: American Canticles.* Palgrave, 2009.
Luckhurst, Roger. *The Trauma Question.* Routledge, 2008.
Malm, Andreas. *Fossil Capital: The Rise of Steam Power and the Roots of Global Warming.* Verso, 2016.
McCarthy, Cormac. *The Road.* Vintage, 2006.
Orange, Donna. *Climate Crisis, Psychoanalysis, and Radical Ethics.* Routledge, 2017.
Perry, William J. Interview with Robert Scheer. "Former Defense Secretary William Perry on The Nuclear Threat." *Huffpost,* 2 September 2017, www.huffpost.com/entry/former-defense-secretary-william-perry-on-the-nuclear_b_59ab04c1e4b0bef3378cd8fc?guccounter=1&guce.
Phillips, Dana. "'He Ought Not to Have Done It': McCarthy and Apocalypse." *Cormac McCarthy: All the Pretty Horses, No Country for Old Men, The Road,* edited by Sara Spurgeon. Continuum, 2011, pp. 173–88.
Porter, Jeffrey. "'Three Quarks for Muster Mark': Quantum Wordplay and Nuclear Discourse in Russell Hoban's *Riddley Walker.*" *Contemporary Literature,* vol. 31, no. 4, Winter 1990, pp. 448–69.
Rothenberg, Michael. *Traumatic Realism: The Demands of Holocaust Representation.* U of Minnesota P, 2000.
Schwenger, Peter. "Circling Ground Zero." *PMLA,* vol. 106, no. 2, March 1991a, pp. 251–61.
———. "Narrative against Nuclear War?" Letter. *PMLA,* vol. 106, no. 5, October 1991b, pp. 1176–77.
Segal, Hanna. *The Work of Hanna Segal.* Aronson, 1981.
Sheldon, Rebekah. *The Child to Come: Life After the Human Catastrophe.* U of Minnesota P, 2016.
Spiegelman, Art. *Maus I: My Father Bleeds History.* Pantheon, 1986.
———. *Maus II: And Here My Troubles Began.* Pantheon, 1992.
Stark, Hannah. "'All These Things He Saw and Did Not See': Witnessing the End of the World in Cormac McCarthy's *The Road.*" *Critical Survey,* vol. 25, no. 2, 2013, pp. 71–84.
Winnicott, Donald Woods. *Playing and Reality.* Routledge, 1971.
Wordsworth, William. "The Two-Part Prelude." *The Essential Wordsworth,* edited by Seamus Heaney. HarperCollins, 1988.

Coda
"Don't you see?" The burning child's reproach

In *The Interpretation of Dreams*, Freud introduces what has come to be known as the dream of the burning child. If, as Adeline Johns-Putra has it, there is "little surprise ... that climate-change discourse circulates around representations of children" (523), and if, as I've suggested, *The Road* and *Riddley Walker* might be said to broach how that discourse also circles around a representational impasse, then we might hear Freud's burning dreamchild both as confronting us with knowledge of and as trauma, and, from the ground of that impasse, as nevertheless sounding a desperate appeal.

Of course, evocations of the child have themselves become formulaic, central to the normalized denialism of mainstream climate discourse. "If you've got a spare month some time, google *global warming* and *grandchildren*," Bill McKibben writes, and you'll find hundreds of "essentially identical and anodyne responses" (11). I'll consider how the dream of the burning child might be heard as rearticulating the trauma disarticulated by such anodyne repetitions. Then, I'll contrast the urgency of the dream's address to the ways that, even in the process of imagining the future indicting the present, such normalizing discourse repeats its fundamental disavowals.

Whose dream, whose child?

Someone once had a dream of a burning child calling out to his father. It makes its way to us through Freud, who introduces it at a crucial point in *The Interpretation of Dreams*:

> A father had been watching beside his child's sick-bed for days and nights on end. After the child died, he went into the next room to lie down, but left the door open, so that he could see from his bedroom into the room in which his child's body was laid out, with tall candles standing around it. An old man had been engaged to keep watch over it, and sat beside the body murmuring prayers. After a few hours'

sleep, the father had a dream that *his child was standing beside his bed, caught him by the arm and whispered to him reproachfully: "Father, don't you see I'm burning?"* He woke up, noticed a bright glare of light from the next room, hurried into it and found that the old watchman had dropped off to sleep and that the wrappings and one of the arms of his beloved child's dead body had been burned by a lighted candle that had fallen on them.

(509)

Freud finds that "The explanation of this moving dream is simple enough": fulfilling the father's wish, the child has come back to life, is again capable of speech. Since the dream is related to him by a patient who heard it at a lecture, Freud has no access to the dreamer's associations, yet asserts without qualification that "the explanation ... was correctly given by the lecturer." While he later adds the suggestion that the dream also fulfills the father's wish to continue sleeping—"his sleep, like the child's life, was prolonged by one moment by the dream" (571)—and acknowledges that "Other wishes, originating from the repressed, probably escape us," this doesn't disrupt Freud's perhaps too confident claim that the dream "raises no problem of interpretation" (510).

Among the questions begged by Freud's puzzlingly reductive reading of the dream is: aside from the literal burning corpse, what else is at stake in the child's burning and in his address to the father? Freud does glance hastily at this question, noting only that "'*I'm burning*' may have been spoken during the fever of the child's last illness, and '*Father, don't you see?*' may have derived from some other highly emotional situation of which we are in ignorance" (510), but the possibility of such a "situation" doesn't seem to bear on his reading the dream as "simpl[y] enough" explained in terms of two of the father's wishes. In this, I suggest, Freud seems himself to replay the father's failure to see or appreciate the child's burning. (Indeed, as I'll argue, we might see in the dream the father's own burning disappointment at his failure to be seen as a son.) And so the dreamchild's reproach still sounds, Freud's account provoking a number of returns to the story of this dream of burning.[1] As Amy Clampitt writes of it, in "The Burning Child," "The dream redacted cannot sleep."

Clampitt's poem stresses how, even as Freud originally represents the dream in relation to a traumatic event in the dreamer's life, it retains only the most tentative relation to any set of "particulars":

Dreamwork, the mnemonic flicker
of the wave of lost particulars—
whose dream, whose child, where, when, all lost
except the singed reprieve, its fossil ardor
burnished to a paradigm of grief.

Quoting as epigraph from Freud's account only the fact of the father's sleep and the brief dream itself, Clampitt herself trims away the few particulars Freud does offer (the vigil, the dead body ringed with candles, the old watcher, the burning corpse), but even in its first redaction (Freud's), the dream is only very tenuously moored to a particular context. Indeed, from the outset the dream floats free from any specific dreamer, relayed to Freud through an unknown number of degrees of separation. It was reported to him "by a woman patient who had herself heard it at a lecture on dreams" and thus, he insists, "its actual source is still unknown to me" (509). (The situation is made even murkier when Freud adds that the dream "made an impression on the lady ... and she proceeded to 'redream' it, that is, to repeat some of its elements in a dream of her own," introducing the possibility that Freud's redaction of the dream is inflected by his patient's imitation.[2]) Loosed from its "actual source," the dream thus confronts us both with the loss of particulars—"whose dream, whose child, where, when, all lost"—and with the "burnished ... paradigm" that remains.

For Clampitt, what remains is a "paradigm of grief," sounding not only from whatever particulars were originally at stake but, proleptically, from an entire century "lurid / with recurrences of burning," with "people herded from the cattle cars / first into barracks, then to killing chambers." But just as such "grief" exceeds what Freud first described as mere "reproach," we can also hear in the child's cry a burning *appeal*. It calls us, that is, not only to see and grieve what is already traumatically burnt and lost, but to attend to what is in the very process of burning now and not yet lost, and thus to what we might yet stop from burning. In this sense, at this moment the dream of the burning child not only cries back a history whose traumas we are reproachfully called to witness, but also reaches us from a future whose history is still at stake.

The dream thus sounds a call to awaken, and such a call is central to Cathy Caruth's compelling reading of Lacan's reading of the dream. But if reading in the Lacanian grain helps amplify some aspects of the child's call, it may also muffle aspects of its urgency. Lacan does prompt Caruth's central insight: at "the center of Lacan's reinterpretation of Freud's narrative of the burning child" is "this listening to another who addresses us" (9). Indeed, such a scene of listening constitutes the animating trope of Caruth's *Unclaimed Experience* as a whole:

> It is this plea by an other who is asking to be seen and heard, this call by which the other commands us to awaken (to awaken, indeed, to a burning) that resonates in different ways throughout the texts [her book] attempts to read.

Caruth articulates this scene of listening as necessarily inhabited by a trauma that forecloses the possibility that the plea "to be seen and heard" may to some significant degree be responded to. "As a response to the child's ... plea to be seen," she writes, "the father's awakening represents ... a missing, a bond to the child that is built upon the impossibility of a proper response" (100). Thus, "*awakening*, in Lacan's reading of the dream, *is itself the site of a trauma*, the trauma of the necessity and impossibility of responding to another's death" (100), and the "bond to the child ... is in its essence tied to the impossibility of recognizing the child in its potential death," a "bond that the dream reveals, exemplarily, as the real, as an encounter with the real established around an inherent impossibility" (103).

If the father is called to awaken to the impossibility of a traumatic loss, however, this needn't be understood as exhausting the possibilities inherent in the dreamchild's plea. Caruth's reading operates within the bounds of a Lacanian discourse in which the self's encounter with the other constitutes by definition a (traumatic) alienation—as in Lacan's description of the "mirror-stage," where subjectivity is constituted in relation to a rigid otherness that necessarily grounds the self in a "primal Discord" (4). But in what Caruth calls its engagement with "the complex relation of knowing and not knowing" (3) psychoanalysis has offered other visions, more attuned to the possibilities that a scene of listening may yield a scene of responsiveness.[3] D. W. Winnicott counters Lacan's mirror, for instance, with his articulation of the mirror as the mother's possibly responsive face; both see the self as coming into being in the field of the other, but where for Lacan that encounter must define a "primal Discord," for Winnicott the mother may to an important extent see, empathize with, and respond to the infant's being, trauma registering the failure of such "mirroring."[4] If the dreamchild commands the father to awaken to a trauma that has already occurred—as for Lacan, Caruth, and Clampitt—it also, then, beseeches him to attend to a trauma that might yet be forestalled: the trauma of not being seen, of one's burning alive going unrecognized.

At stake in the child's cry, that is—beyond the reference to the corpse afire—is both the unbearable intensity of the child's internal world and the intensity of his need to have that intensity recognized, shared, and thus made bearable. In this, the dream sounds a cry for the process (of self-construction) articulated by W. R. Bion as "containment." Bion suggests that an infant's overwhelmingly intense internal states, if they are to be made tolerable, need to be taken in by the primary caretaker and returned in more bearable form. By thus helping to establish both distinction and relationship between inside and outside, this intersubjective process forms the basis for constructing a self that can experience difficult emotions without being traumatically dissolved into them. Again, in the optimal case the "relationship between the infant and the breast," Bion writes "permits the infant to project a feeling, say, that it is dying into the mother and to reintroject it after its sojourn ... has made it tolerable to the infant psyche" (116). Leonard Shengold has teased out how the child in the dream burns with Freud's own complex intensities (he is "burning with desire for his mother," but also "burning with ambition" and "burning with the blazing light of his intellect" [51]), but we can supplement this Freudian reading with a reading focused on the burning need for such intensities to be seen and contained—a burning urgency that the father awaken not only to what cannot be known of the other (as in Lacan and Caruth) but also to what is partly knowable, that he see what can indeed be seen.[5]

Understanding "knowing" and "seeing" here in terms of (Bion's) containment helps address a crucial aspect of the child's dilemma. If "burning" involves a dense nexus of psychic intensities, the burning we are called upon to "see" is invisible, and containment figures a way of resolving this apparent impossibility, of "seeing" precisely these invisibilities. It is thus illuminating to consider the dream of the burning child as a reworking of an earlier attempt to formulate the dilemma of invisibility. Early in Mary Shelley's *Frankenstein*, Victor Frankenstein recalls what he considers a pivotal boyhood encounter with his father. When young Victor happens on a volume by Cornelius Agrippa, he tells us, "A new light seemed to dawn upon my mind; and, bounding with joy, I communicated my discovery to my father" (44). He is, we might say, burning with the passion of a new discovery, but also, as he immediately tries to share this discovery with his father, burning with the need to have that burning recognized and shared. Alphonse, however, does not see his son's burning. Asleep to Victor's intensity and to the need for that intensity to be contained, seeing only what Victor has read (a work of alchemy he considers outmoded by modern science), not Victor himself and how what he read has fired his being, Alphonse "looked carelessly at the titlepage of [Victor's] book, and said, 'Ah! Cornelius Agrippa! My dear Victor, do not waste your time upon this; it is sad trash.'" Victor himself, that is, remains invisible, and he thus reproachfully emphasizes the inadequacy of his father's looking (he "looked carelessly") and the anxiety such careless looking fails to address: "the cursory glance my father had taken of my volume by no means assured me that he was acquainted with its contents." He is left on his own, to "read with the greatest avidity" (44), an avidity which recalls what Walton, a kind of double, calls "the burning ardor of my soul" (35).

The story of the dream of the burning child is the story of three generations—child, father, aged watcher—and if, as Freud notes, "it is quite possible that [the father] had taken into his sleep his anxiety lest the aged watcher should not be equal to his task" (509), we might say that the child's cry repeats in a more intense register the father's own anxiety about the adequate attention of the one he hopes will watch. As a figure in the father's dream, that is, the child can be read as an aspect of the father's own psyche—his sense, perhaps, that his own burning grief is not recognized by the aged watcher with whom he had tried to share his burden. This story of an unseen son who is also an unseeing father—of a sleeping father whose dreamchild's plea is also his own—is precisely the story of

Frankenstein.⁶ For just as Alphonse repeatedly fails to see a burning Victor, Victor repeatedly turns away from the being he has brought into the world. At the moment the creature comes alive, Victor "rushed out of the room" into his "bedchamber," where, having been "deprived of sleep and rest," he falls asleep (that he is soon awakened by a troubling dream alerts us to how closely the elements of this scene—the recent sleeplessness, the abandonment of the body, the departure to a sleeping room, the dream that troubles and awakens—anticipate those of the story of the burning child). When Victor awakes, the first thing the just-made creature seeks is a returned look of recognition—"his eyes," Victor recalls, "were fixed on me. He jaws opened ... while a grin wrinkled his cheek" (58)—an appeal from which Victor precipitously flees. Indeed, literalizing Victor's own dilemma, the creature's predicament throughout the novel is precisely that his loving looks cannot be returned, that his own intense but invisible desire goes unrecognized. He burns to be seen but cannot be, and the frustration of this desire is itself formulated as an (uncontained) burning as, shunned by the De Laceys, he is overcome by a "rage of anger" (119) that "burst all bounds" (120) and sets ablaze the cottage that had embodied his hopes for recognition. Such burning doesn't exhaust the creature's own intensities. At the end of *Frankenstein* he bounds away, only to repeatedly return, to continue to haunt a (popular) narrative tradition by which, in rendering him monstrous, his invisibility is perpetuated—just as "the dream [of the burning child] redacted cannot sleep."⁷

Whose reproach?

As the burning child reproaches his father's failure to see, we might also hear his cry as indicting the way that the voices of children and grandchildren have been conscripted into those "hundreds of essentially identical and anodyne responses" observed by McKibben. While the scene of future generations questioning those in the present has itself become a formulaic trope, that is, his cry might be heard as an attempt to restore the desperation rendered anodyne by such repetitions.⁸

In the very process of imagining the future address the present, such scenes regularly obscure the traumatic threat structuring that present. James Hansen's *Storms of My Grandchildren*, for example, is prompted by his not wanting his "grandchildren, someday in the future, to look back and say, 'Opa understood what was happening, but he did not make it clear'" (xii)—as if the issue wasn't a normalized denial of the existential threat science has defined to cultural businesses as usual but, simply, that that science hasn't been communicated with sufficient "clarity," the clear facts apparently being sufficient to inspire radical change (a fantasy belied, as we've seen, by the account in Hansen's book itself). In a more elaborated instance of imagining the future looking back to the present, Naomi Oreskes and Erik Conway's *The Collapse of Western Civilization: A View from the Future* presents itself as an imagined work of academic history, marking "the occasion [of the] tercentenary of the end of Western culture (1540–2093)" (ix), in which the "future historian, living in the Second People's Republic of China, recounts the events of the Period of the Penumbra (1988–2093) that led to the Great Collapse and Mass Migration (2073–2093)" (x). From the vantage point of 2393, the historian focuses on a seemingly paradoxical failure: "It is clear that in the early 21st century, immediate steps should have been taken to begin a transition to a zero-carbon world. Staggeringly, the opposite occurred" (9)—in spite of "just how much these people knew" about "what was happening to them" (2). But in representing a time after the Great Collapse, the vantage point Oreskes and Conway construct is premised on the very structures of knowing that prevailed—and failed, and, despite the Collapse, survived—in that "staggeringly" obtuse historical period. The very rhetorical premise of the book preserves the failed academic discourses of the institutionalized knowledges of that suicidal time, as, in building her argument, the future historian refers not only to other "historians" of the day but also to "archeologists and synthetic-failure paleoanalysts" (1), suggesting a highly developed, stable, technologically advanced cultural context that can support highly specialized academic disciplines, akin to those that structured how "people knew" in the early twenty-first century.[9] In crucial ways, that is, the book represents not the "collapse" of key elements of Western Civilization but the *continuity* of the very epistemological structures that defined how "people knew" in that obtuse time—the historian herself remaining immune to the collapse she would "know."[10]

Indeed, we might see the historian's account not as an engagement with a traumatic undoing but, rather, as a species of triumphalism. From her position, the "dark ages" she describes seem already safely located in the past, and what has emerged from them is a clear *improvement* on the late twentieth- and early twenty-first-century culture that staggeringly failed to act: observing that, in the 1970s, "it was the rare man ... who in fact understood that he was in fact studying the limits of planetary sinks," the historian notes that "in those days sex discrimination was still widespread" (3); and to "evaluate well-being in a state," where "most countries" in the early twenty-first century "still used the ... concept of a *gross domestic product*, a measure of consumption," in the historian's 2393 such a by-then "archaic" measure has been superseded by "the Bhutanian concept of gross domestic happiness" (8).

As with other aspects of the way the prevailing discourses of climate change sequester its traumatic meaning, Al Gore's *An Inconvenient Truth* provides a stark instance of the anodyne evocation of future generations reproaching the present. There Gore stages a "brief conversation with our children and grandchildren as they are living ... in the year 2023": "What were you thinking?" he has them ask—"Didn't you care about the future? Were you really so self-absorbed that you couldn't—or wouldn't—stop the destruction of Earth's environment?" (11).[11] Like the historian in *The Collapse of Western Civilization*, these children seem to fully realize how the "destruction of the Earth's environment" was produced by their ancestors' failure to "think" or to "care," as if a scientific and ethical understanding of the nature of anthropogenic global warming itself stayed miraculously undestroyed by that utter "destruction." The contrast with Freud's burning child here is revealing. Where, as Clampitt has it, the agonized reproach of Freud's dreamchild functions as "a paradigm of grief," Gore's grown descendants, though angry and perplexed, remain relatively self-possessed; where the dreamchild both addresses the father and voices his own burning distress, they voice not their own state of being but only their (grand)parents' failure; where, operating in the present tense, the child desperately demands an ameliorating response, they speak retrospectively, from a position apparently beyond the possibility of meaningful action. Where Freud's dreamchild, that is, prompts an awakening to the traumatic urgency of the present moment, Gore, speaking from within that same moment, reframes it as already "safely" in the past: his children speak not as the children they now are but as the articulate adults they have survived to become, not from an agonized present but from an angry, resigned future. And, crying "Don't you see?" where the dreamchild indicts the father's fundamental failure to pay adequate attention, and thus to empathize, they define the present on which they look back merely in terms of its inadequate "thinking."

Perhaps we can hear something like the dreamchild's cry, "*Father, don't you see I'm burning?*" echoing in Pope Francis's admonition that, in responding to the ethical demands of the climate crisis, those in power must "hear *both the cry of the earth and the cry of the poor.*"[12] A few months after his Encyclical, the same dominant powers that have produced the crisis euphorically congratulated themselves on the Paris Agreement, the sacred text of normalized denial. But in that euphoric celebration, as in the text itself, no response to the cry of the earth and the poor can be discerned. No "cry," that is, can be permitted to disrupt what Ghosh calls the Agreement's fundamental commitment to "the maintenance of the status quo" (145). As he observes, in its "naming of the conditions it is intended to remedy ... the Agreement speaks only of the *adverse impacts* or *effects* of climate change," while "the word *catastrophe* is never used and even *disaster* occurs only once" (only "because it figures in the title of a previous conference"), and the text as a whole "contains no clause or article that could be interpreted as a critique of the practices that are known to have created the situation that the Agreement seeks to address" (154).

If "at core of the text" of the Agreement, as Ghosh summarizes it, "the current paradigm of perpetual growth is enshrined" (154), then its signatories must remain oblivious to the burning dreamchild as a "paradigm of grief" sounding in the "cry of the earth and the cry of the poor"—and, we might add, in the cry we might imagine from those in the future on whom we're in the process of inflicting an unthinkable violence. Insofar as the dominant discourses of global warming, that is, remain disarticulated from the traumatic knowledge by which they nonetheless remain inhabited and haunted, the cry of the burning child, the future's desperate appeal to an already burning present, remains unheard and unheeded.

***

I'd like to end by acknowledging that, in light of such desperation, a book like this—haunted by Pavel's lament—might itself seem fundamentally unresponsive to the very traumatic urgencies by which it is provoked into being. In the face of the rapidly closing window—the few years we (might) have left before we will have made certain that our already catastrophically less-fucked future will become apocalyptically more-fucked—a book might seem a pretty frail stay. Initiating his poetic epic, *The Changing Light at Sandover*, written against the prospect of nuclear war, James Merrill concedes:

> Admittedly I err by undertaking
> This in its present form. The baldest prose
> Reportage was called for, that would reach
> The widest public in the shortest time.
> Time, it had transpired, was of the essence.
> Time, the very attar of the Rose,
> Was running out.

If I proceed with a similar generic error, it's partly because the "baldest prose reportage" that Merrill tentatively entertains as a less errant form itself functions, as I've argued, as a dominant mode of disarticulation. Of course, there are other perhaps less errant ways of responding, beyond reportage, like, for instance, intervening against the building and operating of fossil fuel infrastructure—though much of the point of such activism is itself to generate "reportage," by which, again, attempts to unsettle business as usual are normalized as "news stories." It's hard to speak unerrantly. Emily Dickinson advises that the overwhelming "Truth" can be told only "slant," can be arrived at only through "Circuit,"[13] and if responding to the dreamchild's cry must involve (seemingly) direct activism, perhaps more self-evidently slant-wise forms of approach might also count as necessary—necessary, though, of course, hardly sufficient: in the traumatic conditions imposed by the climate crisis, even a circuitous approach is up against a looming deadline. At any rate, my hope is that, in the face of that deadline, this book might help register in the dreamchild's remonstrant cry not only the reproach of future generations for the contemporary failure to see, but also the burning appeal that might disrupt that failure—that the child's cry might yet burn through the prevailing normalizations that constitute our filicidic present. In that sense, speaking through my own redaction, the dreamchild gets the last word: *"Father, don't you see I'm burning."*[14]

Notes

1. See, for example, Caruth, Clampitt, Felman, Gallop (178–84), and Shengold.
2. Leonard Shengold repeats speculation about "whether this dream might not have been Freud's own in the first place" (43).
3. The following discussions of Winnicott and Bion repeat some of what is elaborated more fully in Chapter 5, above.
4. See Winnicott's "Mirror-Role of Mother and Family in Child Development," in *Playing and Reality*. Jane Flax offers the fullest elaboration of the crucial distinction between the ways Lacan and Winnicott revise Freud (126–32).
5. In the context of global warming more directly, David Wood warns that, in resisting Enlightenment claims of epistemological mastery, theoretical evocations of the vastness of our necessary unknowing ought not to preclude the imperative to "do the calculations" (275): what we don't or can't know shouldn't obscure what we do or can.
6. I've elaborated this argument in "*Frankenstein*, Invisibility, and Nameless Dread."
7. Himself the product of an utterly rationalist world view, Victor cannot imagine that his technophilic project might produce a creature with a mind and intense passions of his own. In this way, the creature might be understood as a figure for global warming itself—the ultimate "unintended" (but hardly unpredictable) consequence of modernity's fantasy of remaking a world reducible to its (calculable) terms. And, uncannily, this figure emerges at precisely the historical period when the industrializing economy began to premise itself on steam power, inaugurating the deadly rise in atmospheric greenhouse gas.
8. My evocation of the burning child (and the eaten child) thus offers a corrective to Lee Edelman's prominent polemic, in *No Future*, against the fetishized discourse of "the Child whose innocence solicits our defense" (2), the linchpin of what he calls "reproductive futurism" (4), a "Ponzi scheme" that, in his account, puts beyond debate the dominant structures of (patriarchal, heteronormative) power in the present. Refining Edelman's critique, in *The Child to Come* Rebekah Sheldon addresses both the appeal to "The Child" in environmental discourse per se and also "the slide from child in need of saving to the child who saves" (2), though, like Edelman's, her work "positions itself against the imperative to rescue the future through the child" (4). I'm hoping that my own dependence on the figure of the child, even as it might itself join in the critique of those fetishized (and "anodyne") brandishings of The Child, might also help us see beyond the ideological Child to the actual child whose presence functions not as a legitimizing of "our" power to "save" it but as an indictment of a current order committed to its obliteration. Rejecting reproductive

futurism, that is, needn't mean (*pace* Edelman) repudiating an ethical relation both to futurity itself and to real children—needn't mean, in Claire Sagan's apt phrase, "throwing out the baby with the bathwater, the living and lived child with the fetishized, normative Child" (156).

9 Similarly, Ghosh imagines, or "presumes," that our understanding of geohistory and its relation to ideological paradigms will have remained unperturbed (and perhaps will have advanced) in a future he otherwise calls "unthinkable": "knowing what they presumably will know about the history of their forbearers," future humans will "surely understand" that only very briefly during our time on Earth was it thought that the planet was "inert" (3). And the cultural heritage of that brief time will likewise remain immune from the ravages of that unthinkable world; when "sea-level rise has … made cities like Kolkata, New York, and Bangkok uninhabitable," somehow it will still be possible for "readers and museum-goers" to "turn to the art and literature of our time" to look for "traces and portents" (11) of what happened (as if, when cities like New York are submerged, there would still be museums and access to literary archives).

10 Contrast this with the way that in *Riddley Walker*—where from the vantage point of the far future, the very ways of knowing that produced the traumatic collapse are the subject of central debate in the book's present—those advocating a recovery of technological "cleverness" are at odds with those concerned with recovering a "first knowing." See Chapter 5, above.

11 Revealingly, in 2006, when *Inconvenient Truth* appeared, 2023 is imagined as a time when, apparently, it is too late to stop the "destruction of Earth's environment." Of course, most projections at that time actually underestimated the pace at which warming and consequent climate disruption would occur.

12 While in this staging of a desperate appeal the "child" is supplanted by "the earth" and "the poor," I think the virtually automatic presence of (grand)children in such scenarios—all those "anodyne responses"—means that it cannot not be "the child" who is also voicing the "cry." At the same time, it's troubling that, while Francis's is certainly the most prominent sounding of an urgent challenge to ecocidal business as usual, that prominence reflects his position as the head of an extremely powerful globalized institution that has for decades, as a matter of its own business as usual, *itself* silenced the cry of children suffering at the hands of its own powerful officials.

13
>   Tell all the truth but tell it slant—
>   Success in Circuit lies
>   Too bright for our infirm Delight
>   The Truth's superb surprise
>   As Lightning to the Children eased
>   With explanation kind
>   The Truth must dazzle gradually
>   Or every man be blind—

14 Both the plea of the burning child and its utter unintelligibility to those to whom it is addressed were spectacularly staged in Greta Thunberg's September 21, 2019 address to the U.N. Summit, where, barely able to contain her rage and astonishment, she admonished those world leaders for their "empty words." In the face of the extremity of the crisis, and how little time is left for adequate action, she tells them, "all you can talk about is money and fairy tales of eternal economic growth. … How dare you pretend that this can be

solved with just 'business as usual' and some technical solutions?" ("Speech at the U.N. Climate Action Summit"). In response, those present didn't begin to weep, or fall upon their knees, or offer apologies. They applauded and cheered. And then proceeded to fulfill Thunberg's prediction that whatever plans would be proposed that day would have no relation to the size and speed of greenhouse gas reductions the IPCC identifies as necessary to prevent a catastrophic tipping point. Similarly, when in January 2018 she spoke at the World Economic Forum at Davos, pleading with her audience to "act as if our house is on fire. Because it is," they applauded enthusiastically and proceeded to carry on with ecocidal business as usual ("Our House Is on Fire").

References

Bion, Wilfred R. *Second Thoughts: Selected Papers on Psycho-Analysis*. Heinemann, 1967.
Caruth, Cathy. *Unclaimed Experience: Trauma, Narrative, and History*. Johns Hopkins UP, 1996.
Clampitt, Amy. *The Collected Poems of Amy Clampitt*. Random House, 1999.
Dickinson, Emily. *The Poems of Emily Dickinson: Reading Edition*. Edited by Ralph W. Franklin. Harvard UP, 1999.
Edelman, Lee. *No Future: Queer Theory and the Death Drive*. Duke UP, 2004.
Felman, Shoshana. *Writing and Madness: Literature/Philosophy/Psychanalysis*. Cornell UP, 1985.
Flax, Jane. *Thinking Fragments: Psychoanalysis, Feminism, and Postmodernism in the Contemporary West*. U of California P, 1990.
Francis, Pope. *Laudato Si': On Care for Our Common Home*, 2015, http://w2.vatican.va/content/francesco/en/encyclicals/documents/papa-francesco_20150524_enciclica-laudato-si.html.
Freud, Sigmund. "The Interpretation of Dreams." *The Standard Edition of the Complete Psychological Works of Sigmund Freud*. 24 vols., vol. 5. Hogarth, 1953–1974.
Gallop, Jane. *Reading Lacan*. Cornell UP, 1985.
Ghosh, Amitav. *The Great Derangement: Climate Change and the Unthinkable*. U of Chicago P, 2016.
Gore, Al. *An Inconvenient Truth*. Rodale, 2006.
Hansen, James. *Storms of My Grandchildren*. Bloomsbury, 2011.
Hoban, Russell. *Riddley Walker*. 1980. Indiana UP, 1998.
Johns-Putra, Adeline. "'My Job Is to Take Care of You': Climate Change, Humanity, and Cormac McCarthy's *The Road*." *Modern Fiction Studies*, vol. 62, no. 3, Fall 2016, pp. 519–40.
Lacan, Jacques. *Écrits: A Selection*. Translated by Alan Sheridan. Norton, 1977.
McKibben, Bill. *Eaarth: Making a Life on a Tough New Planet*. Henry Holt, 2010.
Merrill, James. *The Changing Light at Sandover*. Edited by J. D. McClatchy and Stephen Yenser. Knopf, 2011.
Oreskes, Naomi, and Erik Conway. *The Collapse of Western Civilization: A View from the Future*. Columbia UP, 2014.
Sagan, Claire. "Capitalist Temporalities as Uchronia." *Theory and Event*, vol. 22, no. 1, January 2019, pp. 143–74.

Sheldon, Rebekah. *The Child to Come: Life after the Human Catastrophe.* U of Minnesota P, 2016.
Shelley, Mary. *Frankenstein.* Edited by Johanna M. Smith. Bedford, 1992.
Shengold, Leonard. *Father, Don't You See I'm Burning?" Reflections on Sex, Narcissism, Symbolism, and Murder.* Yale UP, 1991.
Thunberg, Greta. "Our House Is on Fire." www.theguardian.com/environment/2019/jan/25/our-house-is-on-fire-greta-thunberg16-urges-leaders-to-act-on-climate.
———. "Speech at the U.N. Climate Action Summit." www.theguardian.com/environment/video/2019/sep/23/greta-thunberg-to-world-leaders-how-dare-you-you-have-stolen-my-dreams-and-my-childhood-video.
Winnicott, Donald Woods. *Playing and Reality.* Routledge, 1971.
Wood, David. "On Being Haunted by the Future." *Research in Phenomenology*, vol. 36, no. 1, 2006, pp. 274–98.
Zimmerman, Lee. "*Frankenstein*, Invisibility, and Nameless Dread." *American Imago*, vol. 60, no. 2, Summer 2003, pp. 135–58.

Index

1.5 degrees C of warming 34, 35–36n1
2 degrees C of warming 15, 27, 34, 35–36n1
9/11 18, 83–84n12, 112, 113, 122n18

academic detachment 44–46, 52–55, 59–60
Adler, Ben 34
Alarm *see* "Global Warming's Six Americas"
alarmism 2–3, 9n8, 17, 22n6, 45–48
Alley, Richard B. 7n2
American Association for the Advancement of Science 8n2–3, 41
American Geophysical Union 2
Anderson, Kevin 3, 8n5, 28, 37n13
Angel of History *see* Benjamin, Walter
Anthropocene 4, 28–29, 36n5–6, 59, 64n24; and fiction 72, 74–75
Apple 51
Armstrong, Isobel 94
Asafu-Adjaye, John 29
The Assault on Reason (Gore) 50
Atkin, Emily 23n11
Atwood, Margaret 72

Ball, Karyn 21n1
Ballard, J. G. 102
Banerjee, Neela 61n1
Baptist, Edward E. 50, 122n21
Barnosky, Anthony 7n2
Baumann, Nick 15
BBC News 46
Beckett, Samuel *see Maus* (Spiegelman)
Bendell, Jem 8–9n6, 9n8, 59–60, 63n14, 65n34
Benjamin, Walter 13

Berger, James 20, 22n5, 83n12, 103, 120n4
Biello, David 62n7
Bion, W. R. 15, 120n4; containment 92–93, 97, 99, 118, 128–29; nameless dread 12, 92, 96, 97
Blackmore, Tim 102
Blair, Tony 46
Blitzer, Jonathan 9n7
Bluhdorn, Ingolfur 20, 35, 49, 64n20
Bonneuil, Cristophe 29, 36n5, 37n10, 64n23
Bows, Alice 3, 8n5
Boykoff, Maxwell T. 43
Breakthrough Institute *see* "An Ecomodernist Manifesto" (Asafu-Adjaye)
Brooke, John L. 83n10
Brooks, David 34
Buell, Lawrence 102, 121n11
"The Burning Child" *see* Clampitt, Amy
business as usual 1, 3–4, 8n4, 9n8, 15, 29, 31, 43, 49, 51–52, 62n8, 83n12, 135n12, 135–36n14; literary 72, 76–77, 80, 82n6, 111

Calderone, Michael 15
cannibalism 97, 98, 100; eating of children 97, 103–4, 106, 109, 110, 117, 121n13
capitalism 5, 20, 30, 33, 35, 36n7, 37n10, 41, 49, 50, 74, 81, 131; conflation with modernity 6, 9n10, 29, 30; industrial capitalism 6, 16, 30–33, 35, 36n7, 49, 50; reliance on fossil fuel 31–33
Capitalocene 4, 29, 36n7, 64n24
Caruth, Cathy *see Unclaimed Experience* (Caruth)

The Changing Light at Sandover (Merrill) 133
Chomsky, Noam 41, 42
Civil War 50, 122n20, 115–16
Clampitt, Amy 126–128, 132, 134n1
Clark, Peter 22n3, 36n2, 48
Clark, Timothy 6, 12, 35, 43, 71, 88
Clean Power Plan (Obama) 42, 51, 62n7, 65n33
Climate Action Plan (Obama) 41–42, 51
Climate Crisis, Psychoanalysis, and Radical Ethics (Orange) 15–16, 20, 23n7, 100, 112, 113, 119
climate fiction (cli-fi) 72–73, 77, 78, 80, 82, 82n5, 84n17, 102, 120n6
Climate Psychology Alliance 23n7, 47
Climate Trauma (Kaplan) 14–15, 18
Clinton, Hillary 62n5
Cohen, Samuel 23n13, 83n12
Cohen, Stanley 61n1–62n2
Cohen, Tom 13, 22n2
Collado-Rodriguez, Francisco 121n9
containment 76, 88, 92–93, 96, 97, 99, 100–2, 104, 108, 112, 128–29
Conway, Erik 61n1, 131
Copenhagen Accord (2009) 27
Corn, David 22n4
Crichton, Michael *see The Day after Tomorrow* (film)
Crist, Eileen 20, 36n6, 37n9
Cronin, William 85
Cushman, John H. 61n1
cynicism 2, 4

The Day after Tomorrow (film) 84n16
deep adaptation *see* Bendell, Jem
Deep Ecology 37n9
Democratic Party 41
denial 1, 17, 40, 42, 43, 47, 52, 56–57, 61–62n2, 62n3; normalized denial 1, 5, 15, 16, 22n2, 34, 40–43, 52, 55, 60, 61n2, 62n2, 82, 125, 130, 132; social construction of 57–58
Derrida, Jacques 22n2, 94
Dickinson, Emily 133
Dimock, Peter *see George Anderson: Notes for a Love Song in Imperial Time* (Dimock)
disarticulation, in butchery 20, 40; discursive 4, 6, 16, 20, 21, 27, 28, 42, 48, 56, 61, 71, 81, 94, 108, 111, 112, 114, 117–19, 125, 133

Dunlop, Ian 8n2, 9n6
dystopian narrative 14, 84n17, 102; *see also* genre fiction and film

"An Ecomodernist Manifesto" (Asafu-Adjaye) 29
Edelman, Lee 134n8
Edison Electric Institute 52
Einstein, Albert 6
Ellsberg, Daniel 63n17
empire 30–31, 37n10, 112–13, 117–18, 122n18
Entergy Power Corporation 52
Evans, Rebecca 80, 84–85n17
Exxon 61n1

Fang, Lee 62n5
Feinberg, Matthew 52–53
Felman, Shoshana 89, 91–92, 134n1
Flight Behavior (Kingsolver) 72, 77–78, 79, 82, 88, 91
Fossil Capital: The Rise of Steam Power and the Roots of Global Warming (Malm) 9n9, 31–33
Francis (Pope) 8n4, 41, 135n12; *Laudato Si'* 8n4, 33, 34, 40, 64n19, 132
Frankenstein (Shelley) 129–30, 134n6
Freedman, Andrew 48, 64n18
Fressoz, Jean-Baptiste 29, 36n5, 37n10, 64n23
Freud, Sigmund: on denial 61–62n2; dream of the burning child 7, 125–29, 132, 134n2; on trauma 15, 19, 22n5, 23n13, 94, 120n4
Frost, Robert 12

Gallop, Jane 134n1, 136
Galtung, Johan 23n9
Gardiner, Beth 53
Gelbspan, Ross 43, 63n9
General Electric 49
genre fiction and film 14, 72, 73, 79, 80, 82n6, 84n17, 102; dystopian narrative 14, 84n17, 102; ecothrillers 78–79; science fiction 20, 72–73
geoengineering 79, 81–82, 84n16–17
George Anderson: Notes for a Love Song in Imperial Time (Dimock): American empire and triumphalism 112–13, 115, 117; American slavery 114–16, 118; reciprocity 117–19; representational impasse 88,

112–14; torture regime 113–16, 132n19
Ghosh, Amitav *see The Great Derangement: Climate Change and the Unthinkable* (Ghosh)
Gibson-Graham, J. K. 5, 60–61
"Global Warming's Six Americas" 54–56
Glover, Leigh 29
Gore, Al 16, 34–35, 112, 131–32; *The Assault on Reason* 50; economic business as usual 49–50, 65n25; *An Inconvenient Truth* 48–51; trauma 49, 59; triumphalism 50–51, 115, 122n20
Granofsky, Ronald 121n16
The Great Acceleration 64n24
The Great Derangement: Climate Change and the Unthinkable (Ghosh): climate and fiction 23n12, 71–77, 79, 88–89, 92, 102, 111, 112, 120n6; empire and imperialism 30–31, 74; future knowledge 135n9; on the Paris Agreement 34, 48, 64n19, 112, 132–33
Green Earth (Robinson) 72, 77, 80–81, 82, 84–85n17; critical praise for 80–81, 84n17; geoengineering 81–82, 84n16; neoliberal boosterism 81
Green New Deal 8n4, 62n4
Greif, Mark 34
Gwinner, Donovan 96, 102

Hall, Stuart 63n11
Halliday, M. A. K. 122n17
Hamilton, Clive 5, 8n6, 20, 35; *Requiem for a Species* 55–57
Hansen, James 19–20, 24n14, 27, 36n4, 130
Haraway, Donna 4, 5, 36n7
Hartman, Geoffrey H. 120n5
Heartland Institute Conference 40
Heede, Richard 8n4, 37n8
Heffernan, Virginia 103
Heise, Ursula 23n8, 49, 73, 80, 85n17, 103
Hickman, Caroline 64n29
Hirsch, Marianne 19
Hoban, Russell *see Riddley Walker* (Hoban)
Hoberek, Andrew 73, 82n4, 102
Hoggett, Paul 22n6, 47–48, 61n2, 63n16, 63n17

Holocaust 19–20, 23n13, 88–89, 91, 119n2, 120n6, 121n16, 127
Holocene 3, 28, 36n7, 75, 76, 83n10
Horn, Steve 62n5
Hulme, Mike 2–3, 43–48, 54, 63n10–11, 63n16
Hussein, Saddam 46
hydrofracking 62n5
Hyperobjects (Morton) 3, 23n8, 71

IBM 36n6
Ikea 51
Immelt, Jeffrey 49
An Inconvenient Truth (Gore) 48–51
incrementalism 4–5, 59, 65n33
industrial capitalism 6, 16, 29, 30–33, 35, 36n7, 49
Industrial Revolution 31, 36n7, 37n10, 121n13; water power vs. steam power 31–32
Institute for Public Policy Research 45
Intergenerational violence 16, 104, 110, 117, 119, 133
Intergovernmental Panel on Climate Change (IPCC) 7–8n2, 36n1, 41, 51, 62n6, 64n20, 136n14

James, Clair 121n15
Jameson, Fredric 73
Jasanoff, Sheila 71
Jensen, Liz *see The Rapture* (Jensen)
Johns-Putra, Adeline 71–73, 80, 82n5, 95, 102–3, 125

Kacandes, Irene 19
Kaplan, E. Ann *see Climate Trauma* (Kaplan)
Kelley, Colin 9n7
Keystone pipeline 15, 24n14
Kilgore 81, 84–85n17
Kingsolver, Barbara *see Flight Behavior* (Kingsolver)
Klein, Melanie 15, 17, 92
Klein, Naomi 8n4, 20, 35n1, 36n3, 40, 42, 62–63n8, 65n32, 83n12; *This Changes Everything: Capitalism vs. The Climate* 9n9, 30, 37n14, 84n16
Klump, Edward 62n6
Knapp, Kathy 83n12
Kristeva, Julia 120n5

Lacan, Jacques 15, 120n4n5, 134n4; on the dream of the burning child 127–29
LaCapra, Dominick 77
Latour, Bruno 13, 22n2, 75, 82–83n7
Laub, Dori 89, 91–92
Laudato Si' (Pope Francis) 33, 34, 40, 64n19
Le Guin, Ursula K., "The Carrier-Bag Theory of Fiction" 70, 72, 75–76, 77, 81, 92
Leiserowitz, Anthony 53–54; *see also* Yale Program on Climate Communication
Leys, Ruth 21n1
Lincoln, Kenneth 121n7
Linden, Eugene 1–2, 27, 43
literary realism 72, 73, 78, 82n4, 88
Living in Denial: Climate Change, Emotions, and Everyday Life (Norgaard) 57–59, 62n2
Lovelock, James 47
Luckhurst, Roger 19, 23n13, 89, 94, 119n3

Malm, Andreas 8n3–4, 19, 22n2, 82–83n7; *Fossil Capital: The Rise of Steam Power and the Roots of Global Warming* 9n9, 31–33
Malthus, Thomas 31
Markley, Robert 80–81, 85n17
Marsh, James 82n3
Marshall, George 63n13
Marx, Karl 31
Matthews, Susan 9n8, 62n3
Maus (Spiegelman) 19–20, 88, 96, 104, 111, 112, 119n1; Beckett 89–90, 104; containment 91–93, 94; media 90–91; representational impasse 89–91
McCarthy, Cormac *see The Road* (McCarthy)
McKenna, Phil 36n3
McKibben, Bill 3, 27–28, 34, 64n22, 81, 125, 130
Mean, Edward P. 121n13
media 9n8, 18, 23n11, 43, 63n9, 64–65n39, 90–91, 106; mass media 18, 23n11, 43, 63n9, 78, 90; mediasphere 5, 19, 37n9, 51, 112; social media 78, 79; sound bites 91
Media Matters 23n11
Merrill, James 133
Meyer, Robinson 62n8

Monbiot, George 95
Moore, Jason 7n2, 29, 36n7, 83n9
Moretti, Franco 74–75
Morton, Timothy 1, 3–4, 82–83n7; *Hyperobjects* 3, 23n8, 71

nameless dread (Bion) 12, 92, 96, 97
neoliberalism 4, 37n8, 63n11, 83n12
New York Times 15, 41–43, 46, 51, 53, 62n8
Nixon, Rob 23n8–10, 37n8, 53; *Slow Violence and the Environmentalism of the Poor* 18–19
Norgaard, Kari *see Living in Denial: Climate Change, Emotions, and Everyday Life* (Norgaard)
normalized denial *see* denial
nuclear war 1, 50, 63n17, 94–95, 100, 103, 108, 110, 133; nuclear winter 63n17; *Riddley Walker* 103, 110; *The Road* 94, 95

Obama, Barack 14–15, 41–42, 51, 62n3, 63n5–6, 65n33
Oberhaus, Daniel 22n4
O'Hagan, Andrew 95
Orange, Donna, *Climate Crisis, Psychoanalysis, and Radical Ethics* 15–16, 20, 23n7, 100, 112, 113, 119
Oreskes, Naomi 61n1, 131
Oskin, Becky 63n15
Otto, Eric C. 79

paedophagia *see* cannibalism
Parenti, Christian 9n7
Paris Agreement 19, 34, 36n1, 37n13, 48, 62n5, 64n19, 65n30, 74, 81, 112, 132–33
Paris Climate Change Conference 18–19, 34, 48; *see also* Paris Agreement
Pearce, Fred 7n2
Perry, William J. 63n17, 95
Phillips, Dana 95, 102
Plummer, Brad 27, 36n1
Porter, Jeffrey 111, 121n15, 122n17
potential space (Winnicott) 93, 94, 98, 99, 100, 101
psychoanalysis 6, 15, 47, 61–62n2, 94, 128

Queally, Jon 8n2

142 Index

The Rapture (Jensen) 72, 77, 78–80, 82, 88
representational impasse 88–89, 92, 96–97, 104, 108, 111–12, 118, 125
Revkin, Andrew 35–36n1, 51, 52, 53, 57
Ricardo, David 31
Rice, Christopher 84n16
Rich, Nathaniel 62n8
Riddley Walker (Hoban) 70, 82n6, 88, 102, 103–11, 112, 117, 118, 119, 125; child-eating 103–4, 108–9; defamiliarizing language 111, 122n17; disrupting traumatic history 106–8, 121–22n16; forms of knowing/reading 105–6, 108–11, 121n14, 135n10; mute dialogue 104–5, 107; representational impasse 104; symbolic action 107–9; torture 109, 110, 121–22n16
Rigby, Kate 70, 82n1
Risbey, James 2, 45–46, 47, 53, 55, 63n16
The Road (McCarthy) 82n6, 88, 95–103; containment 97–99; ethic of care 96–97, 102; nuclear winter 94–95; representational impasse 96–97; seeing 100–1
Robinson, Kim Stanley *see Green Earth* (Robinson)
Ropeik, David 51–52
Rothenberg, Michael 89

Sagan, Claire 134–35n8
Said, Edward 18
San Francisco Employees Retirement System 21
Schell, Jonathan 1, 5
Schwenger, Peter 105–6, 112
Science in the Capital see Green Earth (Robinson)
science fiction 20, 72–73
Sedgwick, Eve 5, 61
Segal, Hanna 99
Semprun, Jorge 19
Sheldon, Rebekah 121n8, 134n8
Shell Oil 42, 61n1, 65n35
Shelley, Mary (*Frankenstein*) 129–30
Shengold, Leonard 128–29, 134n1
slavery 15, 50, 100, 112, 114–16, 122n20
slow violence 16, 18–19, 23n9, 53
Slow Violence and the Environmentalism of the Poor (Nixon) 18–19
Solnit, Rebecca 21, 41

Spiegelman, Art *see Maus* (Spiegelman)
Spratt, David 7–8n2, 8–9n6
Stark, Hannah 95, 100, 102, 121n10
State of Fear (film) 84n16
Steffen, Will 7n2, 64n24
Stephens, Brett 15
Stephenson, Wen 40–41
Sze, Julie 48–49, 64n20

Taylor, Jesse Oak 73, 80
Thatcherism 44, 63n11
This Changes Everything: Capitalism vs. The Climate (Klein) 9n9, 30, 37n14, 84n16
Thunberg, Greta 135–36n14
tipping point 1–4, 7–8n2, 8–9n6, 27, 35–36n1, 46, 55, 62n5, 135–36n14
torture: in *George Anderson: Notes for a Love Song in Imperial Time* 112, 113, 114, 119, 122n18; in *Riddley Walker* 109, 110, 121–22n16; slavery (American) 122n21
trauma 6, 12–15, 20, 49, 61, 64n22, 88, 91, 94, 110, 116, 118, 121n16, 127–28; containment 92–93; cultural trauma 19; disavowal of 83n12, 84n17, 110, 119; pre-trauma 14, 22n4; representational challenge of 19–20, 72, 76, 88–90, 120n6; trauma studies 13, 19, 21n1, 22n5, 23n13, 94, 120n4, 120n5
Trexler, Adam 72–74, 77–78, 80, 82–83n7
triumphalism 16, 50, 81, 83n12, 84n17, 114, 118, 131
Trump, Donald 34, 41, 62n3
Tsing, Anna (*The Mushroom at the End of the World: On the Possibility of Life in Capitalist Ruins*) 70, 83n11
Tyndall Centre for Climate Change Research 2, 21, 44

Unclaimed Experience (Caruth) 6, 12–14, 19, 23n13, 61, 88, 94, 119, 119–20n3, 127–29, 134n1

Waldman, Scott 7–8n2
Wallace-Wells, David 8–9n6, 9n8
Wal-Mart 51
Weintrobe, Sally 15, 16–18, 22n6, 61–62n2
Werner, Brad 2

Whitman, Walt 76
Willer, Robb 52–53
Winnicott, D. W. 12, 13, 15, 93–94, 98, 99–100, 118, 120n4–5, 128, 134n3–4; potential space 93–94, 98–101
witnessing 89, 91–93, 97, 121n10, 127
Wood, David 22n2, 36n2, 65n35, 134n5
Wood, Ellen Meiksins 9n10, 29, 30, 33
Wordsworth, William 93, 104

Yale Program on Climate Change Communication 53–55
Yanarella, Ernest J. 84n16
Yuen, Eddie 64n25, 73

Zimmerman, Lee 36n4, 134n6
Ziser, Michael 48
Žižek, Slavoj 23n9

For Product Safety Concerns and Information please contact our EU representative GPSR@taylorandfrancis.com
Taylor & Francis Verlag GmbH, Kaufingerstraße 24, 80331 München, Germany

www.ingramcontent.com/pod-product-compliance
Lightning Source LLC
Chambersburg PA
CBHW052129300426
44116CB00010B/1832